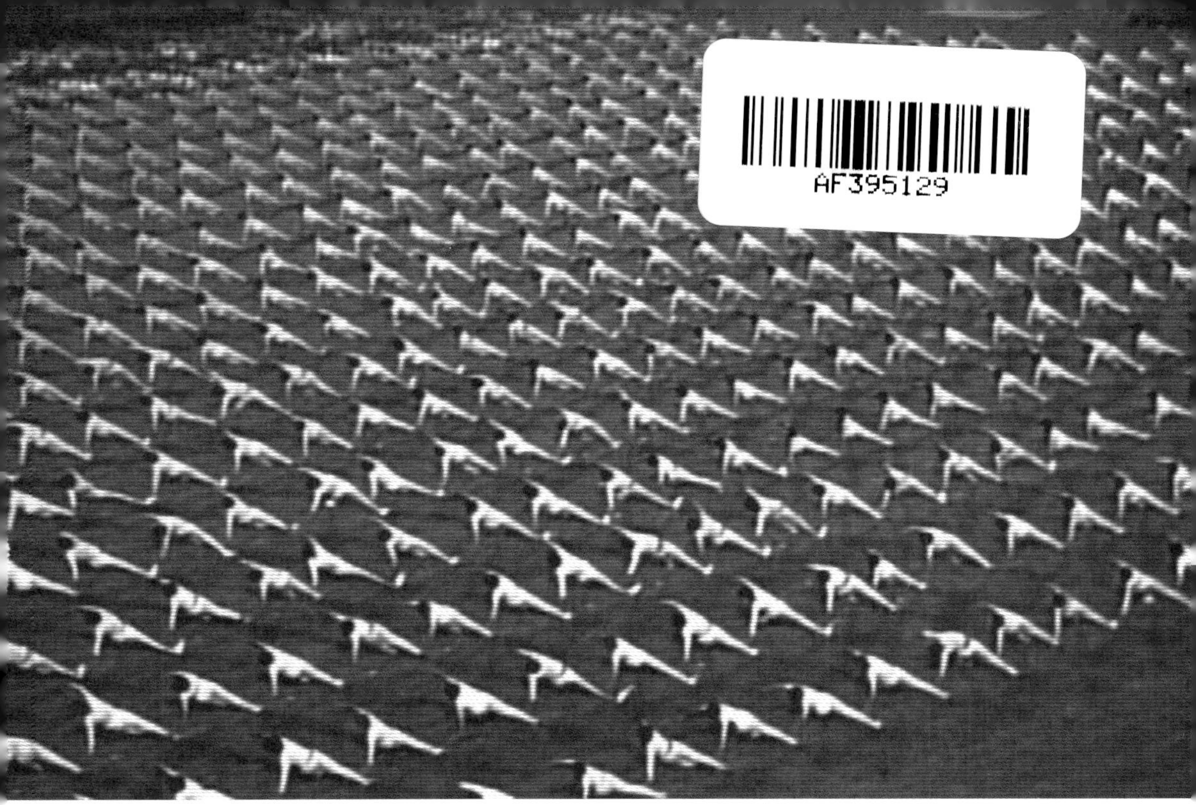

Bojana Cvejić and Ana Vujanović

Public Sphere by Performance

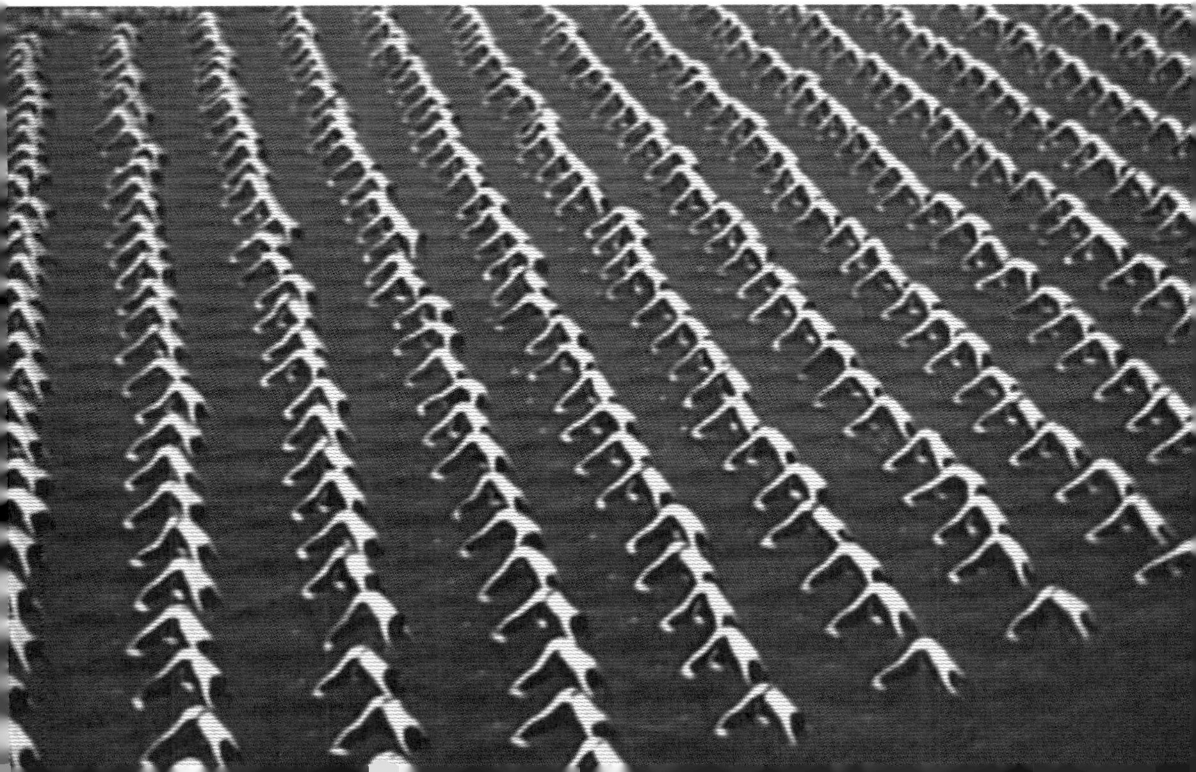

This book focuses on the problem of the public sphere, whose articulation unfolds along a double conceptual axis, determined, on the one side, by the question of the *public sphere* as a social and political concept and, on the other, by the parallel problem of the *performance* of the public sphere as the object and site of its own performance. While the former calls for a social scientific approach—political theory, sociology, anthropology, and so on—the latter engages performance studies and the theory of performance in social, cultural, and artistic terms. This double articulation doesn't make for an interdisciplinary study, which would imply a mobilization of expertise from two independent, equally pronounced disciplines intersecting through a common problem. We opted for another method here. Our expertise lies in the domain of performance and remains rooted therein, forgoing any ambition to extend and accompany itself with social scientific methods. At best, this book explores the advantages (and shortcomings) of transdisciplinarity by staying in the one field of study and pointing to other fields that it feels affiliated with. The affiliation is, however, motivated politically. It comes from a challenge we set for ourselves: what can we do as citizens? Rather than seeking action *aside from* our theoretical work, a course which may be suggested by the above question, we force the following question: what can we as citizens do with what we know and have "in our hands," or in our case, with theoretical and practical expertise in the field of performance?

Our position bears an affinity with two quite remote voices, both of whom, however, reflect on their own capacity and methodology for thinking critically and acting politically according to their theoretical and artistic professional competencies: theater director and performer from New York who reported on her participation in Occupy Wall Street, Annie Dorsen; and sociologist and philosopher from the Frankfurt School of critical theory, Max Horkheimer:

> The scholarly specialist "as" scientist regards social reality and its products as extrinsic to him, and "as" citizen exercises his interest in them through political articles, membership in political parties or social service organizations, and participation in elections. But he does not unify these two activities, and his other activities as well, except, at best, by psychological interpretation. Critical thinking, on the contrary, is motivated today by the effort really to transcend the tension and to abolish the opposition between the individual's purposefulness, spontaneity, and rationality, and those work-process relationships on which society is built.[1]

Dorsen describes one of the assemblies at OWS:

> A paper was being passed around, and we were asked to provide email addresses, a list of our skills and of the equipment we owned that we could put into service. Of the 35 or so people at the meeting, I informally counted twelve filmmakers, six or seven editors, three video artists, a couple of sound engineers and a director of commercials. Probably everyone there had been writing, shooting, recording, editing and uploading his own work since grade school. The average age was around thirty, and the debate about software, platforms and compatibility was fierce. I dutifully wrote down "theater director" and listed as skills ... um ... good communicator? knowledgeable about space? strong familiarity with the plays and essays of Brecht?[2]

To ask what we can do with our "familiarity with the plays and essays of Brecht" is to probe citizenship practices of our time, investing the concept of performance in this exploration, aided with related inquiries from the social sciences and political theory. Hence we liken our position to the Brechtian "radical dilettante": the one who observes the problem from an external position, a position ignorant of the ruling paradigm that defines the problem and its solutions. This book has been written, moreover, as an attempt to solve the problem Walter Lippmann identified in stating that "democracy has never developed an education for the public." Lippmann lucidly remarks that the public is lost as soon as it delegates the solving of this problem to holders of specialist knowledge, because in doing so, it accepts its ignorance regarding matters that concern all citizens. No one else can make and be the public but us citizens. Exactly for this reason, this study ventures beyond the regions of the discipline of performance studies, but without assuming that we shall arrive on another stable shore. Herein lies the transdisciplinarity.

The book is composed of three parts divided into several chapters. Part one, "The Public Sphere and Its Discontents," introduces the problem of the public and its related categories and terms as has been studied in social science, political theory, and philosophy, bringing us to our main thesis: the public sphere is constituted performatively through the concepts of action and performative act. We test our thesis in four parables, each of which

1 | Max Horkheimer, *Critical Theory: Selected Essays* (New York: Continuum, 2002), 209–10.
2 | Annie Dorsen, "In Zuccotti Park," *LRB Blog*, October 12, 2008, http://www.lrb.co.uk/blog/2011/10/12/annie-dorsen/in-zuccotti-park/.

discusses a form of hacking the public through one of the constitutive principles thereof, namely, the freedom of speech. We locate and analyze said principle in four figures that mark four significant contexts of this study: Athenian democracy in the fifth and fourth centuries BC, the transition from *ancien régime* to bourgeois society in the mid eighteenth century, (liberal or soft) socialism in postwar Yugoslavia, and democracy and neoliberalism in contemporary control society. Part two, "Ideology and Mass Performances," derives two complementary methods from performance studies and social science which we further as a hybrid framework for an analysis of the public sphere today: social choreography and social drama. These two methods focus on mass performances of the state, of people, or of special groups, and on the political unconscious and the conscious performances of ideology, especially as regards individualism and collectivism. In part three, "The Self and the Public," the focus shifts to the performance of the self within a range of concepts (habitus, social role, man as actor, technologies of the self, and performing identity). Two distinct problems associated with the self and individualism as the reigning ideology in contemporary society are tackled through their intensive expression in art: authorship in relation to the personal and its public performance, and solo dance performance as a technique of the self.

Another characteristic of this study stems, once again, from our political motivations. Our preoccupation with the public is contextual through and through. The first person plural "we" refers to the joint authorship of this book, shared by Ana Vujanović and Bojana Cvejić, members of the Belgrade editorial collective *Teorija koja Hoda* (*Walking Theory*). Both of us were born in Belgrade, the capital city of former socialist Yugoslavia, and we both currently live in the European Union and are working on the international performance scene as theorists and practitioners. Our experience of several crucial historical moments that radically reissued the question of the role and position of the public could be broken down like so: In Yugoslavia we witnessed how the socialist social order with its communist ideology exhausted itself in the late 80s and ended in radical rupture. The disruption of socialism led to a multiparty political system, but only through civil wars, the collapse of the country, and a new nationalistic ideology. We experienced the regime of Slobodan Milošević in Serbia in the 1990s, which mixed traces of an overbureaucratized socialism with nationalism, rendering Serbia a society isolated from the international community and at war with other former Yugoslav republics. The regime was continuously followed by mass dissatisfaction on the part of impoverished and humiliated citizens who sought democracy, an end to the wars, and, more simply, a "normal life." We experienced the overturn of that regime on October 5, 2000, whereupon a demand for democracy was formulated. We also experienced how this democracy has been instilled only as a lateral side of neoliberal capitalism and how it has operated hand in hand with corruption; political assassinations; criminal privatization of state and social ownership, public factories and companies; and an overall "feudalization of the public sphere." Finally, we have seen many Serbian citizens from our generation, who having previously decided to stay and help build a new democratic society after the regime change in 2000, recently leave Serbia. The drain of highly qualified and politically disillusioned young people continues. Their sense of political dispossession is by no means dissipated by the current crises in Europe, where principles of solidarity are sacrificed for economic security.

We cannot but ask: What has the role of the public been in all these historical and current moments? Even if the public has not been passive and invisible in all of them, what has its position and its power been? Did it effectuate changes? Moreover, even if it has had political and social effects, we are inclined to repeat John Dewey's question: was this public aware of the consequences of its actions? Did the citizens who euphorically hailed Milošević in Gazimestan in 1989 want civil wars? Did the citizens of Belgrade and Serbia on October 5, 2000, know, when they thought they were choosing democracy, that they were also asking for capitalism? What did we ask for when we as a public arose in protest? And how does this correspond to what we got in return, supporting or opposing the one or the other political actor on the public scene? Some of these questions are answered through the cases we study and visually document in this book. Our goal is not to resolve political dilemmas related to the murky circumstances of Yugoslav history, but to offer conceptual analyses as well as tools to those who feel similarly unqualified or politically disabled and stultified, tools they may implement to critically envisage civil action in their own respective contexts.

***

The book before you results from a two-year research project during our residency at Les Laboratoires d'Aubervilliers near Paris (2011–2012), which was conducted together with film- and video-maker Marta Popivoda, also a member of the TkH editorial collective. Her part of this research gave rise to the documentary film *Yugoslavia: How Ideology Moved Our Collective Body*, based on television and film archives from Serbia during Yugoslavia's socialist period (1945–2000). As a practical laboratory on "performative technologies of the group," Bojana Cvejić and Marta Popivoda conducted a workshop which tested two technologies in two simulated situations: team-building for business workers, and a gathering of performers for an ad-hoc collaboration. The workshop was held in collaboration with the performance artists Siegmar Zacharias and Christine De Smedt. In addition, Ana Vujanović and Siniša Ilić researched visual representations and rhetoric in current protests against austerity measures throughout neoliberal capitalist societies, which resulted in the theoretical comic *Dull Smart Mobs*, also published in this book. Besides the theoretical study of diverse materials, our research also included three open days of presentations where we shared our questions, claims, and materials with a group of invited theorists, activists, and artists before an audience in hetveem theater, Amsterdam, July 1, 2011; in Les Laboratoires d'Aubervilliers in Paris, January 7, 2012; and in Tanzfabrik, Uferstudios, Berlin, January 24, 2012.

We would like to thank everyone who gave their support and collaboration to this research: Dragana Jovović, Jelena Knežević, Siniša Ilić, Bojan Đorđev, and Katarina Popović from TkH collective; Alice Chauchat, Virginie Bobin, Nataša Petrešin-Bachelez, and Claire Harsany from Les Laboratoires d'Aubervilliers; Heinz Emigholz, Michèle Soulignac, Abraham Cohen, Mileta Kečina, Nataša Damnjanović, Jelena Vesić, Julie Heintz, Vanessa Theodoropolou, Frank Leibovici, Bojana Mladenović, Bojana Kunst, Igor Dobričić, Sigrid Merx, Joe Kelleher, Liesbeth Groot-Nibbelink, Chiel Kattenbelt, Ludger Orlok, Isabell Lorey, Siegmar Zacharias, Christine De Smedt, Antonia Baehr, Nicolas Siepen, and Ligna. A special thanks goes to William Wheeler for excellent copyediting and Katarina Popović for her design of this book.

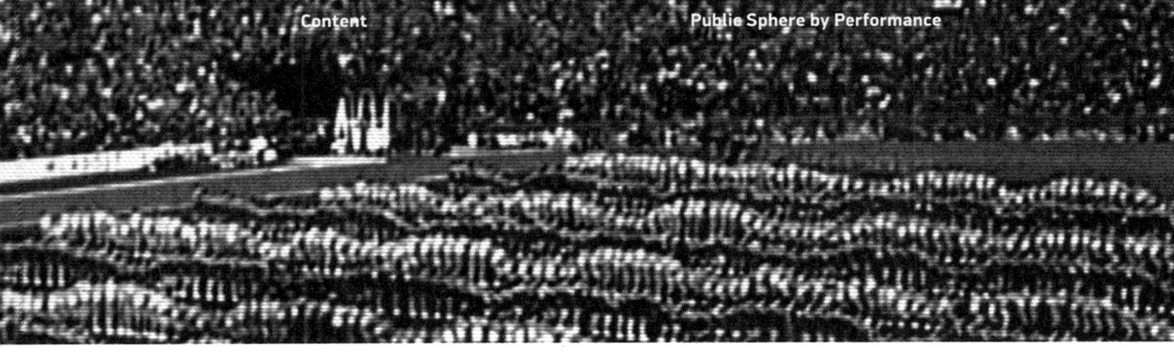

Part I
The Public Sphere and its Discontents

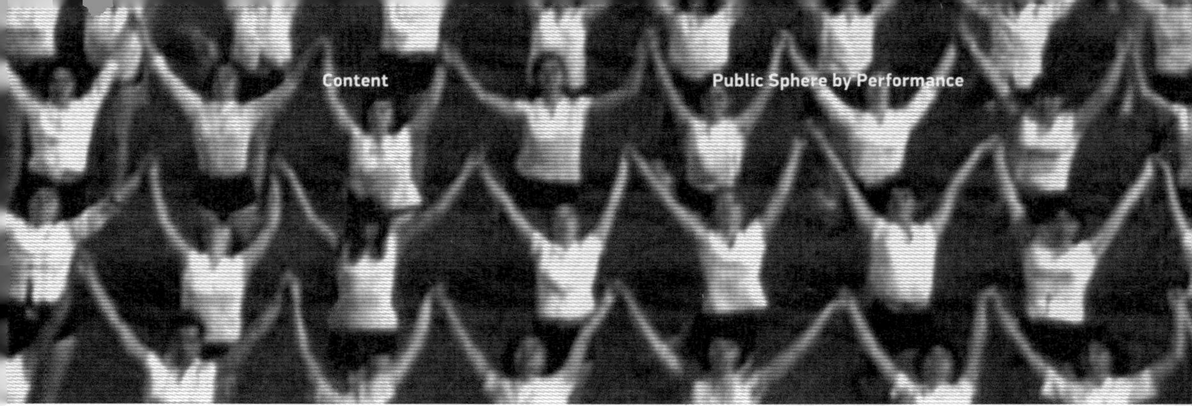

Part II
Ideology and Mass Performances

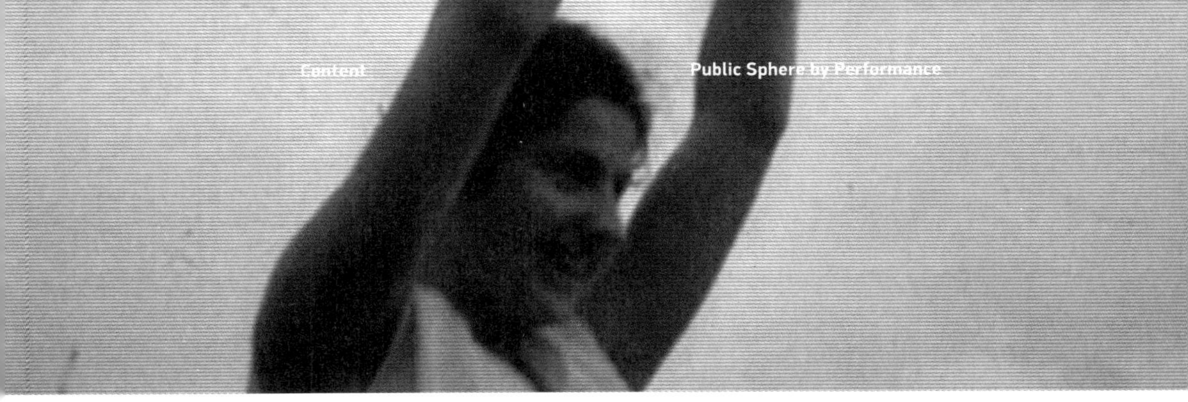

Part III
The Self and the Public

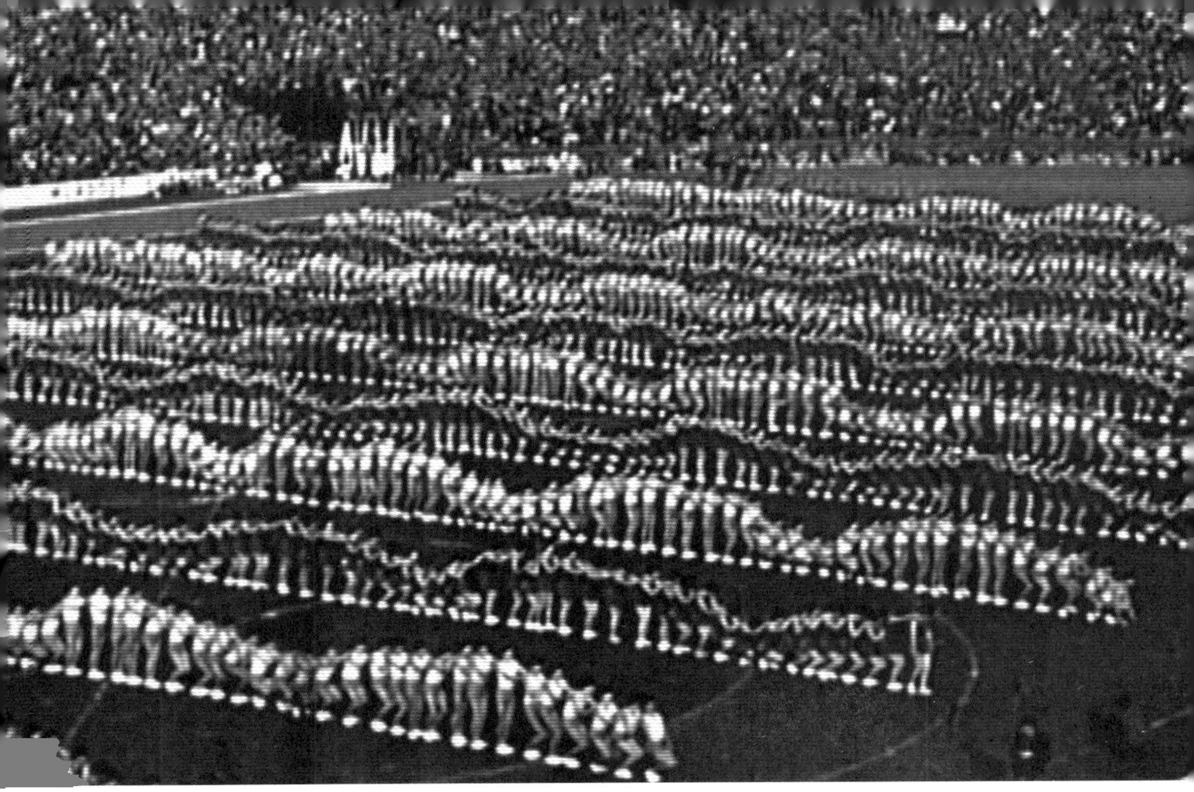

Part I   The Public Sphere and its Discontents

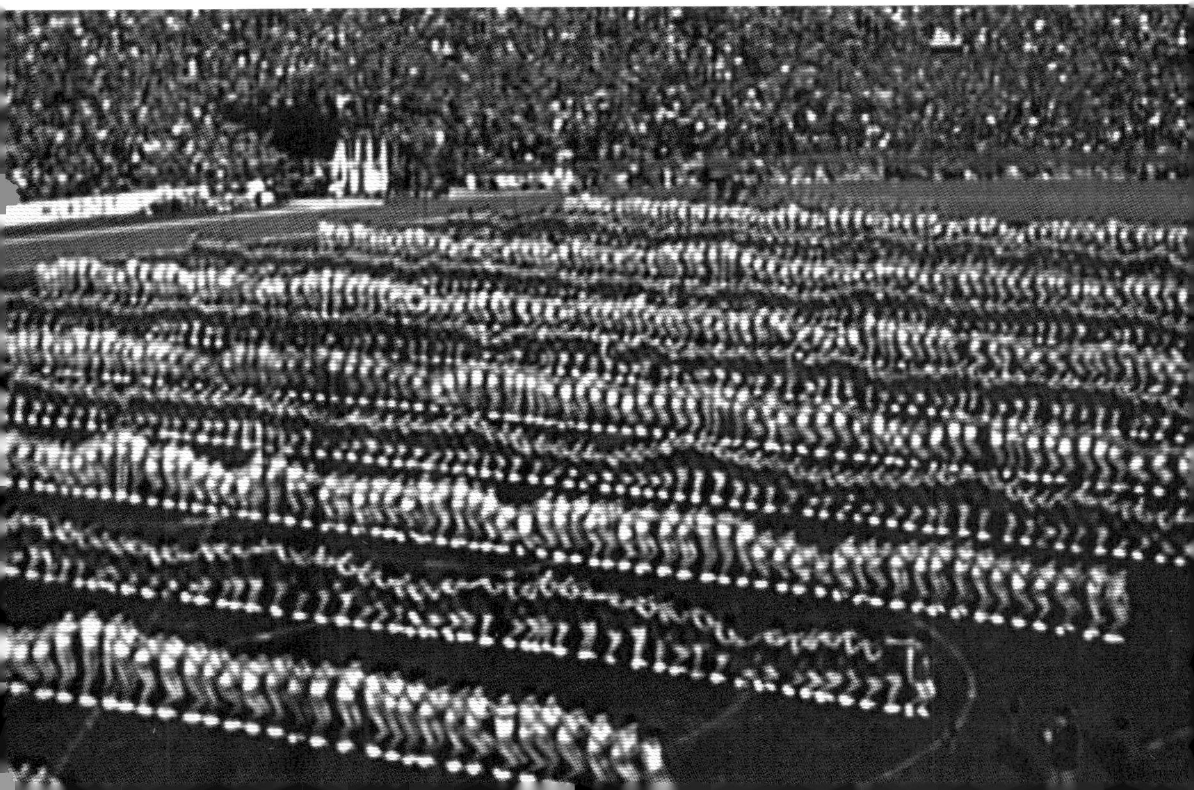

We conceive of the public as a discursive sphere of society which consists of citizens' speech, actions, and movements, the "words and deeds," as Hannah Arendt would have it, that can be considered articulations and expressions of ideology. In order to operate politically, the public sphere needs, and hence seeks, public space. Our main reason for engaging in research on the public sphere is our concern with its crisis, which is not only associated with an ongoing privatization of public space in neoliberal capitalism, but is also, more broadly, seen as a crisis of representation in representative democracy.

Since the 1920s, the public has presented a recurrent problem, and questions similar to those we begin with here were already posed a century ago: Is the public in crisis? Does it exist at all? Has it changed? What is it? In *Public Opinion* (1922)[3] and the especially influential book *The Phantom Public* (1925),[4] Walter Lippmann, an American journalist who observed the manipulation of public opinion after World War I, expresses his lack of faith in the democratic system in its reliance on a mistaken conception of the public. He argues that the public as conceived by democratic theory—as a social agency made up of well-informed, continuously interested, "sovereign, and omnipotent citizens"—exists

3 | Walter Lippmann, *Public Opinion* (New York: Macmillan, 1922).
4 | Lippmann, *The Phantom Public* (New Brunswick, NJ: Transaction, 1930).

merely as an illusion, myth, abstraction, and, inevitably, a phantom. Turning from theory to social reality, he regards the citizen of his time as a private person generally neither educated, nor interested in taking part in public affairs, which are managed and governed "at distant centers, from behind the scenes, by unnamed powers."[5] Developing this thesis, he infers that when speaking about the public sphere, one should differentiate between actors (insiders, leaders, or officials vested with the power to take decisive and executive action in the public realm) and bystanders (outsiders concerned with their private affairs and the pursuit of individual interests, who function as detached observers of the action or as "deaf spectators in the back row"). In his attempt at unmasking the public as an abstraction which modern democracies continuously count on, Lippmann, playing with theatrical vocabulary, identified "spectators," or "*publicum*," as the subjects who really constitute the public in 1920s (American) democratic society. The reasoning behind assigning such a role to the public boils down to the belief that citizens cannot but remain passive, delegating their civil activities to experts, since they are incapable of grasping all details operative on the public scene, either because they have no time or because the details are not transparently available or shared, and since they are ill equipped, lacking in the knowledge and skills required for acting in public:[6]

> The random collections of bystanders who constitute the public could not, even if they had a mind to, intervene in all the problems of the day … Normally they leave their proxies to a kind of professional public consisting of more or less eminent persons. Most issues are never carried beyond this ruling group; the lay publics catch only echoes of the debate.[7]

In Lippmann's view, citizens mobilize only occasionally, in moments of crisis. However, even in those moments, they do not act directly, but rather appear as a mere majority in support of, or opposition to, the actors, who govern; therefore, according to Lippmann, "when men take a position in respect to the purposes of others, they are acting as a public."[8] Faced with the predicament of how a public who is badly informed about the substance of a problem, and thus unable to judge the actors on their intrinsic merits, should then decide to support or oppose the actors, Lippmann is even more pessimistic: the public is accustomed to making decisions according to "rough external evidences" and the leanings of political representatives. For that reason, throughout his book he takes a perspective on democracy which will later be characterized as elitist, insisting on the need for a new mode of education of the public, one completely different from preexisting modes of training in fields of specialist knowledge.

Following up on Lippmann's debate on the crisis of the public, John Dewey tried to mitigate Lippmann's harsh diagnosis with a more optimistic view of how the public should "recognize and articulate itself." In order to grasp what is distinctive and still topical about Dewey's analysis of the public's crisis in his book *The Public and its Problems* (1927),[9] we must first look at his pragmatist conception of the public sphere, from which his arguments of its renewal ensue. In Dewey's definition of the public sphere, the relation between the private and the public is contrary to the common view:

5 | Lippmann, *The Phantom Public*, 3.
6 | "Democracy, therefore, has never developed an education for the public … The result is a bewildered public and a mass of insufficiently trained officials." Ibid., 138–9.
7 | Ibid., 115.
8 | Ibid., 188.
9 | John Dewey, *The Public and its Problems* (Athens, OH: Ohio University Press, 1927).

> When A and B carry on a conversation together the action is a trans-action: both are concerned in it; its results pass, as it were, across from one to the other. One or other or both may be helped or harmed thereby. But, presumably, the consequences of advantage and injury do not extend beyond A and B; the activity lies between them; it is private. Yet if it is found that the consequences of conversation extend beyond the two directly concerned, that they affect the welfare of many others, the act acquires a public capacity.[10]

We can thus conclude that the public arises from what Dewey calls "indirect consequences of action," which aren't regulated by an existing procedure or limited to and absorbed by the interests of private individuals who are the only ones concerned by the given action. On the one hand, this view is libertarian, because it disentangles the public from the state which Dewey identifies as the "public agency" in recession, and on the other hand, it accounts for the public as a democratic, socially organized community.

According to Dewey, the public isn't a phantom; it is in eclipse, "lost," "bewildered," "uncertain and obscure," and "remote from government." Its main characteristic is "indifference":

> Indifference is the evidence of current apathy, and apathy is testimony to the fact that the public is so bewildered that it cannot find itself … What is the public? If there is a public, what are the obstacles in the way of its recognizing and articulating itself? Is the public a myth? Or does it come into being only in periods of marked social transition when crucial alternative issues stand out, such as that between throwing one's lot in with the conservation of established institutions or with forwarding new tendencies? In a reaction against dynastic rule which has come to be felt as despotically oppressive? In a transfer of social power from agrarian classes to industrial? Is not the problem at the present time that of securing experts to manage administrative matters, other than the framing of policies?[11]

The apathy he pinpoints here has several root causes, and consequently harbors several ways to counteract these causes and make the public rise up again. The first set of causes, similar to those in Lippmann, involves the administrative system found in the democracy of Dewey's time (and still existent today in an even more advanced and extreme form) where the specialization of competencies isolates ordinary people from public concerns. Citizens in democracy, or "people," as he prefers to call them, have no say in the choosing of experts to whom they entrust all social matters. These experts are "legislators," "executives," judges, doctors, educators, traders, and, most importantly, as he repeats throughout the text, managers and politicians, revealing economism as an early tendency in capitalist democracy: "Persons have their own business to attend to, and 'business' has its own precise and specialized meaning. Politics thus tends to become just another 'business': the especial concern of bosses and the managers of the machine."[12] He goes as far as claiming that experts form a special class whose task is to keep social matters private and prevent them from becoming public.[13]

---

10 | Ibid., 13.
11 | Ibid., 122–3.
12 | Ibid., 138.
13 | "A class of experts is inevitably so removed from common interests as to become a class with private interests and private knowledge, which in social matters is not knowledge at all." Ibid., 207.

The public fails to recognize itself, to articulate and identify itself with definite issues, because it is bereft of understanding, of insight into how the state and the total social field in their diverse domains of work, leisure, and politics function. Dewey's view poignantly echoes the bewildering sense of the public's ignorance and incompetence in the face of the recent economic crisis and the accompanying "austerity measures":

> Men feel that they are caught in the sweep of forces too vast to understand or master. Thought is brought to a standstill and action paralyzed. Even the specialist finds it difficult to trace the chain of "cause and effect"; and even he operates only after the event, looking backward, while meantime social activities have moved on to effect a new state of affairs.[14]

However, unlike Lippmann, Dewey doesn't lose faith in democracy altogether, but tries to rescue it in the literal sense of the word through the empowerment of the people in the public, conceived as the "Great Community." Thus he proposes to reconsider the model of local community that rests on the bonds of family, neighborhood, and locality, by which early American settlers organized work and social life. These local communities in America were based on the social idea of democracy, which Dewey distinguishes from the political system of democracy. The main ideological obstacle to communitarianism in democracy is "individualism," which he regards as the ideology of the system of administration he was living in. There are differences that manifest themselves in diverse attachments that an individual entertains, but Dewey advocates the belief that these differences can be integrated by means of common interests and goals, which are social and beyond individual or private interests:

> From the standpoint of the individual, [the public] consists in having responsible share according to capacity in forming and directing the activities of the groups to which one belongs and in participating according to need in the values which the groups sustain. From the standpoint of the groups, it demands liberation of the potentialities of members of a group in harmony with the interests and goods which are common. Since every individual is a member of many groups, this specification cannot be fulfilled except when different groups interact flexibly and fully in connection with other groups.

For a public to rise as a "Great Community," individuals and groups must gather by means of various and often disparate matters that concern them. Dewey offers four mechanisms by which this can be done: attachment to the matters of the community's concern; communication that entails in-depth inquiry into these matters, and dissemination of that knowledge, which makes the matters of concern public; engagement that implies rational consideration of the consequences of communal activity; and "face-to-face" participation in the public dialogue. While attachment is different from affection and implies a readiness to act upon principle, the other three mechanisms centralize social knowledge, "a kind of knowledge and insight which does not yet exist," which is not abstract, but rather based, pragmatically, on the importance of considering consequences in all proceedings in social matters; because "there is no public without full publicity in respect to all consequences which concern it. Whatever obstructs and restricts publicity, limits and distorts public opinion and checks and distorts thinking on social affairs."[15] Dewey proposes that systematic continuous inquiry "in the sense of being connected as well as persistent"

14 | Dewey, 135.
15 | Ibid., 167.

be substituted for the passive formation of public opinion as a "habit." Lastly, the main problem of the public, he concludes, is a lack of methods and conditions for debate, discussion, and persuasion, whose improvement would be a prerequisite for democratic participation:

> Systematic and continuous inquiry into all the conditions which affect association and their dissemination in print is a precondition of the creation of a true public. But it and its results are but tools after all. Their final actuality is accomplished in face-to-face relationships by means of direct give and take. Logic in its fulfillment recurs to the primitive sense of the word: dialogue.[16]

Dewey's position has recently been renewed by the sociologist Bruno Latour, who, in confrontation with current trends of managerial administration, reinforces the view of the gathering of various actors—a kind of *Dingpolitik* instead of *Realpolitik*, based on the etymology of the Scandinavian and Germanic word *Ding*, or assembly, as opposed to the so-called real facts and interests dominating political rhetoric since the time of Bismarck.[17] Latour advocates the invention of new prostheses for a politically handicapped public sphere, which in his view should include an assembly of scientists, politicians, artists, and all others who might be concerned with various attachments that also separate them.

In Latour's insistence on disagreement in the matters of concern that assemble various actors hides an implicit critique of a prominent early conception of the public sphere by the German sociologist and philosopher from the second generation of the Frankfurt School of critical theory, Jürgen Habermas. In *The Structural Transformation of the Public Sphere* (1962),[18] Habermas examines the rise of the bourgeois public sphere in eighteenth-century Europe as a third instance that mediates between society and state. Since being excluded from decision-making in the absolutist and monarchist states of that time, private individuals started to develop the practice of "public use of one's reason" in Britain's coffeehouses, France's salons, and Germany's *Tischgesellschaften*—first in the domain of literary matters and later on in regard to political affairs as well—from which the liberal public sphere gradually arose. This public sphere, which supposedly achieves consensus on the grounds of (better) argument, is a modern social institution whose function is to guarantee society as a sphere of private autonomy and uphold the restriction of public (feudal, state) authority to only a few functions. What is specifically different about Habermas's conception in comparison with Dewey's, or even more so, Latour's, is that Habermas envisages the liberal public sphere as a public body that transmits the needs of bourgeois society to the state. Its main mechanism, the principle of monitoring and supervision, demands from the state that political proceedings be made public, and "publicity" (*Publizität*) is the degree of public effect generated by the public act. At the core of this mechanism lies public opinion, based on the reasoning, critical judgment, argument, and rational debate of the public body:

16 | Ibid., 218.
17 | Cf. Bruno Latour, "From Realpolitik to Dingpolitik or How to Make Things Public," In *Making Things Public: Atmospheres of Democracy*, ed. Bruno Latour and Peter Weibel (Cambridge, MA: MIT Press, 2005), 4–32; Latour, "Why Has Critique Run out of Steam? From Matters of Fact to Matters of Concern," *Critical Inquiry* 30, no. 2 (2004): 225–48; Latour, "The Year in Climate Controversy," *Artforum* 49, no. 4 (2010): 1–3; Bojana Cvejić, Ana Vujanović, and Marta Popivoda, "Interview with Bruno Latour," in "Art and the Public," special issue, *TkH*, no. 20 (2012): 72–81.
18 | Jürgen Habermas, *The Structural Transformation of the Public Sphere: An Inquiry Into a Category of Bourgeois Society* (Cambridge, MA: MIT Press, 1991).

> The expression of "public opinion" refers to the tasks of criticism and control which a public body of citizens informally—and, in periodic elections, formally as well—practices *vis-à-vis* the ruling structure organized in the form of a state.[19]

The crisis of the political public sphere, for Habermas, begins with the withering of the critical function of the press. The permanent legalization of a "politically functioning public sphere" in the second half of nineteenth century meant that the intellectual press that flourished between 1789 and 1848 in struggle for political freedom and public opinion was relieved of the pressure of its political mission. However, since the establishment of the bourgeois constitutional state, the press has abandoned its polemical position in favor of a more commercial undertaking. Thereby, the principles of free circulation of news, commodities, and matters of common concern were reduced to the principle of a free market of interests, which resulted in the capitalist-driven, consumerist mass media of the twentieth century. According to Habermas, the epoch of the liberal bourgeois public sphere went into decline in the nineteenth century because the public body expanded beyond the bourgeoisie and the public scene was penetrated by various social groups with "competing interests" and demands for protection from the state:[20]

> Once the public sphere of civil society had developed, however, thoughtful contemporaries could not help but notice how this veil was rent. The public was expanded, informally at first, by the proliferation of press and propaganda; along with its social exclusiveness it also lost the coherence afforded by the institutions of sociability and a relatively high level of education. Conflicts hitherto pushed aside into the private sphere now emerged in public. Group needs that could not expect to be satisfied by a self-regulating market tended to favor regulation by the state. The public sphere, which now had to deal with these demands, became an arena of competing interests fought out in the coarser forms of violent conflict.[21]

This line of thought, its reasoning, and concerns can be traced back to Hannah Arendt, the postwar German-American political theorist and public intellectual, in whose writing the public sphere figures prominently.[22] She identifies it with political life in shared public space, which is predicated on public interests, seen as a stake in the "common world." For Arendt too, the public sphere is in eclipse, because the public interest in modern capitalist society is predominantly seen as a sum of individual interests wherein the idea of the common world disappears from the horizon. According to Arendt—whose thought reverberates throughout Habermas' elaborations—, starting with the French Revolution politics took an increasing interest in "social issues," thereby legitimating the penetration of private interests and distribution of goods into the public sphere. For Arendt, politics is, as *vita activa*, the discursive practice (words and deeds) of free citizens interested in the organization and running of the *polis*, performed on the public stage of society. It

---

19 | Jürgen Habermas, "The Public Sphere: An Encyclopedia Article," *New German Critique*, no. 3 (1974): 49.

20 | However, what Habermas didn't elaborate in clear political terms is that one of the first "social groups" that penetrated the bourgeois public sphere was the Chartist movement, the first working-class movement in Britain. In a wider perspective, a number of feminist theorists later brought this problem into sharper focus; and an important critical contribution came from Jacques Rancière as well, who introduced the distinction between the concepts of police and politics, whereby politics begins precisely when the plebs penetrate the public scene.

21 | Habermas, *The Structural Transformation of the Public Sphere*, 131–2.

22 | Hannah Arendt, *The Human Condition* (Chicago: University of Chicago Press, 1998); Arendt, *On Revolution* (New York: Viking, 1963).

concerns current "appearances on that stage" as well as the appearances of those stages themselves. And as such it is concerned neither with constituting eternal truths, which belong to the domain of *vita contemplativa*, nor with issues pertaining to the *oikos*, or private life, personal interests, material goods.

In Arendt, the socialization of politics and its approximation to economics led to its demise. In her key writings she mostly refers to the Athenian model of democracy, where politics was a form of human activity called practice. Practice (*praxis*) is not geared to fulfilling the citizens' existential needs and reproducing life (as is everyday *labor*), and, unlike production and creation (*poiesis*), it does not produce material objects as investments into civilization (as do arts and crafts). Instead, it is realized and exhausted within itself, affecting current social relations. Political practice is therefore a public activity performed by free citizens, driven not by their existential needs or interest in material goods, but by the will and desire of human beings as political beings to organize relations between humans. From that perspective, the entrance of social issues—private issues that have become publicly relevant, such as the distribution of goods—on the public stage leads to the instrumentalization and therefore also demise of politics in the classically democratic sense. The other path through which Arendt indentifies an eclipse of the public sphere from the viewpoint of the reconfiguation of the private and the public is connected to the artificial and performance-related dimensions of public political activity. This is where Habermas will completely depart from her framework, insisting on reasoning and rational debate in lieu of performance. For Arendt, "others" are vital to public activity, even if not empirically present; and even rational reasoning involves an internalized presence of others, rendering it a public performance. In *On Revolution* (1963) she focuses on the context of the French revolution as the arena where changes in the public/private relation occurred in regard to the artificial/performative and the natural/authentic activity and actor. Discussing appearances, masks, and persona and considering artificiality in positive terms, as "man-made," she infers that after role-playing acquired its negative connotation of hypocrisy in the *ancien régime*, we were furnished with a cult of the natural, authentic, or original man and the attendant replacement of solidarity with compassion and, consequently, of politics with intimacy. Habermas, however, reduces public activity as performance to the "manipulative theatricality" or "show" in mass (media) society, where his rationalist opposition of argument and debate to performance and theater again evokes the argument of hypocrisy. On the other hand, those theses will later be elaborated in detail by sociologist Richard Sennett, whose concept of "the fall of public man" will largely correspond to Arendt's concerns without referencing them explicitly.[23]

In his study of public life in Western Europe, *The Fall of the Public Man* (1976),[24] Sennett offers a historical perspective on what he calls the end of public culture. He locates it in the shift from *ancien régime* in the eighteenth century, where public experience was connected to the formation of social order, to the formation of a new capitalist urban culture in the nineteenth century, where public behavior and personality became confused. The decline

23 | The issue of authenticity and role-playing will be furthered in Chapter 7 of this book. For more about Arendt's "theatrical" approach to the public sphere and differences between Arendt, Sennett, and Habermas in this matter, see also Dana R. Villa, "Theatricality and the Public Realm," in *Politics, Philosophy, Terror: Essays on the Thought of Hannah Arendt* (Princeton, NJ: Princeton University Press, 1999).

24 | Richard Sennet, *The Fall of Public Man* (New York: W. W. Norton, 1976).

of public life is measured against the constitution of the public sphere in the eighteenth century as a domain of impersonal action and of social roles under the artificiality of masks and coded "theatrical" expression, a domain which sharply distinguishes between the public and the private. The public life of the eighteenth century is often described through the cliché *theatrum mundi*, where Sennett contends that all men were artists because they could act. In the nineteenth century the belief in the expressive powers of individuals who together build a common social order is lost; that is, expression is delegated to the professional artist who embodies a radical subjectivism that elevates her expression as a special ability above ordinary citizens. The impersonality and artificiality of public actions based on a transcendent code from the eighteenth century is replaced by emotional representation, where expression is contingent on immanent and authentic feeling:

> Western societies are moving from something like an other-directed condition to an inner-directed condition—except that in the midst of self-absorption no one can say what is inside. As a result, confusion has arisen between public and intimate life; people are working out in terms of personal feelings public matters which properly can be dealt with only through codes of impersonal meaning.[25]

The private domain, which was characterized by the authenticity of the human being and was, in the eighteenth century, segregated from the public domain, now enters that domain. The objective character of action is deflated, while the importance of actors' subjective states of feeling is inflated, culminating, as Sennett states, in an obsession with the idea of intimacy: "Now what matters is not what you have done, but how you feel about it." This is reflected in the political realm, where the leader becomes the one whose personality is strongly declared, a political personage who offers his intentions, his sentiments, rather than his acts, for the consumption of citizens—while the citizen remains a passive spectator. Two forms of the degradation of political life in the intimate society are singled out in Sennett. From the figure of Napoleon to this day, the cult of personality associates political leadership with a charisma that depends on the ability of the leader to dramatize his own motivation, allowing the media to divert the attention of citizens from any evaluation of political acts by appealing to their empathy for his personal, private persona. In addition to charismatic leadership, Sennett criticizes communitarianism, which fragments, specializes, and privatizes the public sphere according to the principles of identity and shared interest. The notion of community is based on a fantasy of a shared collective personality. Contrary to Dewey, who takes local communities as a model for the rise of a new public, communitarianism for Sennett implies "fraternicide," because it narrows fraternity down to the common that excludes outsiders. Drawing a parallel to the darkening of the theater auditorium as sharply contrasted with the illuminated stage, Sennett describes the paradox of an alienating anonymity coupled with an intimacy that has compensated for alienation in public life since the nineteenth century:

> There grew up the notion that strangers had no right to speak to each other, that each man possessed as a public right an invisible shield, a right to be left alone. Public behavior was a matter of observation, of passive participation, of a certain kind of voyeurism. The "gastronomy of the eye" (Balzac); defense through withdrawal and silence . . . Intimacy is an attempt to solve the public problem by denying that the public exists.[26]

25 | Sennett, *The Fall of Public Man*, 5.
26 | Sennett, 27.

Sennett's last point sheds light on the widespread standpoint of equating the private with the public, a view which has been furthered lately by social media.[27]

When we bring the discussion onto the terrain of contemporary society, the crisis of the public, in our view, can be outlined in the following four points:

The changed configuration between the state and the private in neoliberal capitalism – The neoliberal state uses its public authority to promote private capital, i.e. the agenda of corporations, since it appropriated its instrumental economic mode of operation, whereby reality is equated with political economy. The new alliance between the state and the private, that is, corporate capital, has been confirmed by the recent transformation of the global financial crisis into the global fiscal crisis, caused by governments who used public money to bail out banks and are consequently now introducing austerity measures. Here, the question of ownership of public space arises, since public space is becoming less and less a public and common good and more and more privatized. That which constituted the public as common good in welfare states and former real socialist states—healthcare, education, arts, and independent cultural production provided by the state—is now the target of austerity measures, reducing, or even altogether dispensing with, the public sector and its services.

The "depoliticization" of civil society, whose citizens are politically dispossessed and handicapped – The political life of citizens is mostly reduced to voting, and so mechanisms for allying oneself to particular concerns and for assembling in public spaces are lacking. Political representation's discontents call our attention to a growing dilemma. In addition, transnational capitalism and nomadism as predominant forms of life that result from the migrations of living labor complicate, blur, and hinder many citizens' sense of belonging, responsibility, entitlement to political action, and participation in political life. The process of depoliticization was also already fueled in the 1990s by the establishment of non-governmental organizations who took over the public services of the state.

The paradox of freedom of speech – In the information age, the wide accessibility of information and the right to freedom of speech do not necessarily presuppose political concern and action. There exists a cynicism asserting that anything can be said because it won't have any consequences, so we can say that public speech is harmless in fiscalized societies.

A special concern with the role and place of art in society – Can we defend art as a public good on a par with the political life of citizens? Or does art offer, as some sociologists argue, a playground where the current form of capitalism can test its mechanisms of privatization, precarization, and political disempowerment? Or should art no longer be taken as an exceptional activity from which a political revolution is to be expected and instead be regarded as just one more indicator of the crisis of the public sphere?[28]

---

27 | See Igor Dobričić and Sigrid Merx, "Sharp Thoughts, Igor Dobričić vs. Sigrid Merx: The 'Public/Private' and Private-Public: Reactivating the Distinction (response to Dobričić)," in "Art and the Public Good," special issue, *TkH*, no. 20 (2012): 64–71.
28 | See "Art and the Public Good," special issue, *TkH*, no. 20 (2012).

MAPPING THE PUBLIC SPHERE IN THE SOCIAL FIELD

We would like to distinguish what constitutes the public sphere in regard to society by addressing the present situation in European neoliberal societies, and at the same time by drawing upon the decisive historical and theoretical paradigms that brought about new conceptions of the public sphere—Athenian democracy of the fifth and fourth centuries BC, the emergence of the bourgeois public sphere in the eighteenth century, and the real socialist countries in the second half of the twentieth century.

The point of departure for this mapping is the social field as an encompassing category. It addresses the institutionalized, administratively constituted community, the community of people who share something, but are also divided by and because of something. Our reason for beginning with society as an association of people is that it comprises what the notion "community" with its references to commune, common, commonality, and communism neglects, namely, the conflicts, disputes, and disagreements, as opposed to the sharing, solidarity, consensus, and so on. In our view, opting for society rather than community is preferable, because the only thing that the members of society have in common is the world, not the common world in Arendt's sense, but the world in which they all *have to* live. In sum, society, unlike community, doesn't specify in advance any other qualities of the association upon which it is based.[29]

Society bifurcates into two big categories: the private and the public domains. It seems there is a clear distinction and division between them: the private involves the personal, familiar, domestic matters and interests; while the public involves the concerns, issues, and goods that relate to society as a whole or to all the members of society.[30] For some thinkers, like Arendt, what belongs to the private should stay there and only there, as any penetration of private interests into the public leads to the instrumentalization of politics, which consequently means the end of any politics. Today, in neoliberal capitalism, predicated as it is on the collusion between the protection of individual rights, globalization, and corporate capital, this far-reaching critique is manifested on an unprecedented scale. Still, we now need a more careful consideration of the relationship between the economic and the political, that is, the private and the public, which are today completely entangled; and it should be the starting point of the analysis of how their relation determines the public sphere. According to Italian post-Operaist and bio-political theorists who attempt to explain the prevalence of post-industrial and post-Fordist production in today's society, the borders are blurred from the outset, since production has already integrated elements of political practice. Paolo Virno, for instance, explains:

> I believe that in today's forms of life one has a direct perception of the fact that the coupling of the terms public-private, as well as the coupling of the terms collective-individual, can no longer stand up on their own, that they are gasping for air, burning themselves out. This is just like what is happening in the world of contemporary production, provided that production—

29 | For further discussion on the community and communitas, see Chapter 5 in this book.
30 | Accordingly, public space, for instance, is defined as space that is free, accessible, and open to all.

loaded as it is with ethos, culture, linguistic interaction—not give itself over to econometric analysis, but rather be understood as a broad-based experience of the world.[31]

On the other hand, from a broader perspective, it is important to understand that the private and public categories are not naturally given, but always socially constructed, as Nancy Fraser articulated in her reaction to Habermas' thinking of the public and the private.[32] For instance, sexual orientation could be both a private and a public issue, depending exactly on the historical and social contexts and their divisions between public and private realms. In the same manner we can observe how the national question—that is, nationalism—in the USSR and other real socialist countries, which belonged to the private, domestic realm for so long thereafter became a public issue all of a sudden, even the dominant issue during perestroika and glasnost in the late 80s.[33] Therefore, we don't want to propose maintaining an impenetrability of boundaries between public and private; nor do we wish to advocate their unproblematic mixture. Our proposal is that we look for the mechanisms by which private issues are made public, the specific procedures and protocols.

At this point we need to consider the third crucial component for orienting the public within the social field: the state. This concept belongs to modern societies and theories of society (Locke and later Habermas). Lockean liberal orientation separated the people and the government as their agent, while Habermas emphasized the mediating role of the public sphere between society and the oppressive state. This separation didn't exist in democratic Athens, where the people were the state—due to direct democracy—and where the concept of government didn't exist; thus we speak about Athenian "democracy" rather than "demarchy."[34] This modern break of the public/private binary helps resolve the confusing notion that everything outside the private and domestic belongs to the public sphere. Such a break may equip us with a tool for making a preliminary differentiation between the public sphere and the public sector in neoliberal societies, a tool needed increasingly in the time of austerity measures, Occupy, and similar protest movements from the US to Spain, Greece, and elsewhere, where we can see the division at work in the collapse of the public sector and the uprising of the public sphere. The related question is, for example, should we fight for art as a public good by asking the state to protect it from the market, which would lead to a reaffirmation of state cultural policy and the state's role as both guarantor of public good and regulator of the cultural scene? Or is art as a public good located precisely between these two categories, in a projected public sphere?

31 | Paolo Virno, *A Grammar of the Multitude* (Los Angeles: Semiotext(e), 2004), 26.

32 | Nancy Fraser, "Rethinking the Public Sphere: A Contribution to the Critique of Actually Existing Democracy," *Social Text*, no. 25–26 (1990): 56–80; Fraser, "Sex, Lies, and the Public Sphere: Some Reflections on the Confirmation of Clarence Thomas," *Critical Inquiry* 18, no. 3 (1992): 595–612.

33 | "At first, most nationalist mobilization centered around calls for freedom of movement, increased autonomy, and linguistic and cultural expression, following closely the liberalizing and reformist spirit underlying *glasnost*. But as institutional constraints diminished, and as events took on a momentum of their own, demands began to be framed with increasing boldness, focusing in a number of republics on outright secession." Mark R. Beissinger, "How the Impossible Becomes Inevitable: The Public Sphere and the Collapse of Soviet Communism," in "20th Anniversary of the Fall of the Wall," special issue in "Public Sphere Formation," also a special issue of the online journal *Transformations of the Public Sphere*, the website of the Social Science Research Council, November 2, 2009, http://publicsphere.ssrc.org/beissinger-the-public-sphere-and-the-collapse-of-soviet-communism/.

34 | Etymologically, democracy is about the power (*kratos*) of the people (*demos*) rather than the governing (*arkhein*) by the *demos*.

The question of the role of the state is, on the other hand, crucial for understanding the construction of the public sphere in real-socialist societies—where the state is the people, or, even better, the surrogate for the people. As a result, the state in fact dismissed the public sphere as a democratic space, converting it into the space for state monologues instead of dialogues among citizens, as we will consider later.[35] Neoliberal societies bring about a completely new set of problems in this regard, since the state and its public sector become the agent of the private (capital) and no longer play the role of oppressing the private; what is oppressed in neoliberalism, due to the alliance between the state and private capital, is the public itself.[36]

Now we must distinguish the various categories that pertain to the notion of public. Continuing where we left off with our brief demonstration above of why the public sector is a category belonging to the notion of the state rather than to the public, we recognize, in our definition of the public, two close yet divergent categories: the public space and the public sphere. Quite similar notions, they are usually used as variants or synonyms with different emphases. Most often, public space is understood as a physical, spatial category, while public sphere is a discursive one (including speech and action). However, in keeping with this functional distinction, we would propose not to mix these concepts, because their implications are not symmetrical: although the public sphere needs public space, which Arendt, for instance, deems a precondition for the former, public space is not necessarily the space of the public sphere (the social sphere of the political or of citizenship activities), but can also be a space of tourism, entertainment, leisure time, labor, and production, or state monologues (which belong to the state, to production, or to the private domain of the life of citizens where they take part as private individuals or persons). This differentiation could be a challenging insight into our current situation, where "public space" becomes the buzzword in the same breath that we experience an eclipse of the public sphere.[37]

An important issue in and around the public is its degree of inclusivity, since its very publicness can be thereby measured. Athenian democracy was characterized by the participatory public sphere, which, programmatically, included all citizens—regardless of their economic status, nobility, eloquence, reputation, or prominence. Therefore, on the one hand, in Athens all were equal and everyone's voice had the same weight. For instance, Arlene Saxonhouse, who researched free speech in Athens, emphasizes the following:

> As Ober nicely describes the democratic scene: "Now the vote of 'nobody, son of nobody' had precisely the same weight in deciding the outcome of a debate as that of the noblest scion of the noblest house. Moreover 'nobody, son of nobody' might actually choose to raise his voice in public—if not as a formal speaker in the citizen Assembly, then in concert with his fellow nobodies attending that Assembly as voting members, hooting and jeering at the distinguished men who dared to speak."[38]

35 | See also Marta Popivoda's documentary film *Yugoslavia: How Ideology Moved Our Collective Body*, 2012.
36 | In her polemical article "The Only Good Public is a Moving Public," Nina Power looks at the London riots of July 2011 to consider the political and legal processes that divide the public sphere in public space into the "good" public, which merely defends its own property and thus agrees with the state's protection of private capital, and the "bad" public or "rabble," which rises against social injustice and a democracy that is smothering the public. *TkH*, no. 20 (2012): 10–15.
37 | This especially addresses the domain of art; see, for instance, "Performing Publics," special issue, *Performance Research* 16, no. 2 (2011).
38 | Arlene W. Saxonhouse, *Free Speech and Democracy in Ancient Athens*

However, at the same time, the right to participate in politics was rather exclusive in democratic Athens, which was nonetheless referred to as a participative democracy. It was a prerogative extended only to free citizens, barring, in fact, the majority of Athenians from the public stage: the women, the children, the slaves, the foreigners, the freed slaves, and those who had lost their citizens' rights. Inclusivity is, according to Habermas, one of the three main "institutional criteria" that the eighteenth-century public sphere upheld (the other two are disregard of social status and the creation of the domain of common concern). Criticizing Habermas' attribution of inclusivity to the bourgeois public sphere, Nancy Fraser claims that the latter discriminated against women and society's lower social strata:

> This network of clubs and associations—philanthropic, civic, professional, and cultural—was anything but accessible to everyone. On the contrary, it was the arena, the training ground and eventually the power base of a stratum of bourgeois men who were coming to see themselves as a "universal class" and preparing to assert their fitness to govern.[39]

And, from another perspective, she remarks:

> In fact, the historiography of Ryan and others demonstrates that the bourgeois public was never the public. On the contrary, virtually contemporaneous with the bourgeois public there arose a host of competing counterpublics, including nationalist publics, popular peasant publics, elite women's publics, and working class publics. Thus, there were competing publics from the start, not just from the late nineteenth and twentieth centuries, as Habermas implies.[40]

The last level of our mapping of the public sphere focuses on its epistemic background. In theory, there are basically two approaches: one maintains that the public sphere is based on reasoning and rational debate that supposedly leads to a consensus, and the other emphasizes the role of ideology, which includes affects, passions, and also beliefs, and could also result in the sharpening of conflicts, struggles, and antagonisms. Our concern is ideology rather than rational debate: first of all, we hold that rational debate often hides its irrational ground, thanks to hegemony; also, we find ideology the most powerful fuel for constructing public spheres in modern and current societies as we know them. We identify two predominant ideological discourses: individualism and collectivism, which we will give more attention to later.

Our hypothesis regarding the public's position in society returns to the relationship between the public and the private. The public as a political sphere has to be constructed along a clear divide between private interests and public concern, and a delimited space for political debate should admit the intrusion of the private only on the terms of public concerns. These concerns are defined ideologically. The public's function as political sphere is based on protocols and conventions whose publicness depends on their transparency. As histories of public life as well as theories of the public demonstrate, these conventions and protocols are constantly negotiated and liable to transformation. Hence, they reveal the dimension of the performance of the public, which opens questions about mechanisms of acting in public and about the possibility of constructing new apparatuses which can effectuate change.

(Cambridge: Cambridge University Press, 2008), 2n2.
39 | Fraser, "Rethinking the Public Sphere," 60.
40 | Ibid., 61.

Our main thesis addresses the relationship between the public sphere and performance by way of the following questions: Is the public sphere the domain of performance? Or, can it only be performed? Why, and in which sense "performance," and why "only": is performance too little, or just enough?

Performance has figured in various historical tropes of the public sphere as determined by political activity, the two prominent paradigms being the theater in Athenian democracy and the eighteenth-century idea of *theatrum mundi* ("All the world's a stage"). Yet it has also served as a model for interpretation and analysis of the social in both private and public spheres. Several concepts rooted in performance surged as formal and functional analytical models in sociology, anthropology, and performance studies, such as social drama and dramaturgy, social choreography, man as actor, social roles, performance of the self, and so forth. The relationship between these two axes of articulating the social and the public, i.e. the methodological and descriptive usages of performance, hasn't been examined explicitly. Our objective is to test the conjunction of performance and the public sphere with the aim of accounting for activities of citizenship in neoliberal capitalist and representative-democratic society.

The recurrence of the metaphor that frames politics and the public as theater/performance—appearing from Ancient Greece to the present by way of the Christian Middle Ages, the Elisabethan era, the Baroque period, and eighteenth-century bourgeois society—echoes with different connotations of the condensed cliché *theatrum mundi*. It ranges from humans merely performing a play for the gods to bourgeois codes of behavior in public, to us performing our social roles in the never-ending reality-TV show of the contemporary society of the spectacle. Still, what is common to all these conceptions is an awareness that the human being is never alone and that she is always exposed to the gaze and presence of others. It is a commonly held view today that the moment we step into the public—if not even prior to that, since we are social beings from the start—we turn into performers performing our selves for and before others.

The legacy of both theater and democracy in Western civilization can be traced to ancient Greece, where theater and politics were some of the many forms of performance practiced by the citizens of the polis. A similar continuum could be observed in the public sphere of eighteenth-century bourgeois society between the coffeehouses, salons, and theaters of cosmopolitan London and Paris. Furthermore, there is a wealth of historical evidence documenting the impact of theater, especially comedy and satire, on the formation of public opinion and political positions in Athens, which would happen again in the eighteenth century when artist-performers gained special social standing as "public figures." Notwithstanding the differences in their respective statuses, functions, and disciplinary specificities, theater and politics belonged to the same order of activities: the public performance of citizenship, predicated on conventions, procedures, and skills and exposed to the gaze, opinions, assessments, and critiques of others. The same applies to the early bourgeois public sphere; although there the primary association was between theater, on the one hand, and public conduct and debate, on the other. During these two historical periods, theater performance served as a public forum for debating political issues. Theater performances and theatricality in general constituted an important social practice, not only because theater sometimes thematized current political issues, but also because it fulfilled the structural role of providing models for social behavior conceived as acting in public and testing hypothetical subject positions, forms of subjectivity and social relations. The boundaries between theater performances and public and political activities were porous, and they could therefore shape one another mutually. This points to a significant and distinct feature of public behavior in these two remote historical periods—Athens in the fifth and fourth century BC and France, Germany, and Britain in the eighteenth century—as compared to the tradition of the nineteenth and twentieth centuries. Public behavior and political practices were anything but spontaneous, direct, and natural; rather, they were performative—artificial, codified, and institutionalized within the discourses that framed and constituted citizenship. Our point here is that the association between theater/performance and public sphere/political practice isn't a matter of ahistorical conceptual synchrony, or a trope based on structural resemblance. As Arendt and Sennett show, the conjunction between theater and public qua political sphere is specifically historical, situated in these two periods. Bearing in mind the historicity of the relationship between performance and public, our challenge is to examine the conjunction in the current social context, characterized by neoliberal capitalism, representative democracy, and a total mediation and mediatization of social life.

PERFORMANCE AND ACTION

At the outset of this inquiry, two terms require distinction if they are to describe the range of activities of citizenship in the public: performance and action.

The initial question is to locate the line that separates our acts and actions from our performances, regardless of whether we speak about art, the public sphere, or our private lives. If we rely on common sense for a moment, there arises a binary opposition between act/action as a real and authentic activity and performance as an artificial, theatrical, fictional one. However, the relation between these two terms is far more complicated, since it is almost impossible, in current social systems of representation and mediatization, to break the chain of representation and actual condition to the extent that we would be certain of the degree to which something is "real" or "represented." Richard Schechner tried to map out the demarcation line between action and performance and gave an important contribution to the subject by distinguishing between the concepts of *doing*, which refers to all human actions, including ordinary life behavior; and *showing doing*, which refers to performance, both in art and beyond. According to him, showing doing does not mean that the performed act is fictional, insincere, or fake, but (only) that the performing subject is aware that she is performing; so she points to it, emphasizes, and stresses it for those observing her.[41] Still, even if we are equipped with this theoretical tool, it will be difficult to draw the line in social reality, precisely because human beings are always already social and as such constituted among, with, and before other humans—even if those others, as some thinkers would say, may not always be empirically present.

We will try to take this distinction further than Schechner's proposition. Schechner's differentiation can help us understand that act/action and performance do not stand in binary opposition since they cannot be separated by a line marking a difference between the real or authentic and the unreal, fictional, or representational. In a word, we cannot say that an act is real while a performance is not. This is also due to the issue of an act's intervention into and effect on a social context, where the collapse of the demarcation line prevents us from hasty divisions between the action, and performance as something other than such an act (because performance reiterates the protocols and conventions it rests upon, even when it breaks them). Moreover, even if it is completely fictional and representational (like traditional dramatic theater), a performance is a social practice, and the reality of its represented fiction may have real social effects, outcomes, and consequences. It can affect our thinking, it can provide us with a model of behavior, it can bring us to the street, or it can even construct and "rehearse" a real social situation of the community of spectators, which belongs to the reality of its fictional order. Thus, what Schechner's differentiation implies instead is that performance is a type of act/action, or in other words that an act/action and a performance operate in different degrees of publicity and different registers of the discursive order of society. So we can understand them as a literal act and an artificial act, or as a spontaneous, unpredicted/unpredictable and codified/ritualized act, or, even better, as an act/action that may be both physical and discursive and that is always symbolic or signifying in another way (like a speech act).[42]

41 | Richard Schechner, *Performance Studies: An Introduction* (London: Routledge, 2006), 22.
42 | Here we refer to a root of the term in the notion of the performative by John Austin; see J. L. Austin, *How to Do Things with Words* (Cambridge, MA: Harvard University Press, 1975). He himself never considered the performative as opposite

The notion of act/action derives initially from production and creation (the Greek *poiesis*) and is later identified with products and effects (the Latin *agere*), but in the course of Western epistemic history from the eighteenth century onward it became a synonym for a new and broad concept of practice signifying doing driven by the human will and oriented to its purpose in the effect, the result, the change that it effectuates.[43] Performance,[44] from the perspective of performance studies, signifies showing doing to others. In speech act theory, it refers to a speech, discursive, or signifying action, an action that, if understood and communicated correctly, produces a meaning which creates a certain social situation. From both viewpoints, performance is an act that deeply depends on a social context, as it depends on social and cultural conditions and rules known to all involved in the situation. These conditions and rules have to be fulfilled in order for a performance to be happy or felicitous, to create a meaningful social situation within a dialogical process. Since politics and other kinds of citizens' public activity as we know them throughout Western history are codified social practices based on rules and conventions—this also applies to direct democracy—we could conclude that the public can indeed only be performed. However, when we claim this, we refer to those activities that take place in the configuration of the public sphere as it is; or, as Arendt would say, we limit these performances to "the appearances on the public scene." Staying within that frame, a performance based on the principles of the performative is an act/action that, although it can be effective and create new social situations, cannot effectuate the change of the context itself, since it depends on the conditions, conventions, protocols, and procedures that are already established and operative in a certain social context. If this is not fulfilled, that is, if a performance does not recognize and adhere to its conditions, then we can speak of failure or, in strict theoretical terms, the "unhappy performative." However, it may be politically ambitious to claim that a public activity that breaks the rules and conventions in its spontaneity and unpredictability does not necessarily remain an unhappy performative, becoming instead a self-proclaimed performative. And in such a case, we can speak of activity as action in a narrower sense. Thus, a political action may be regarded as an activity that forces the conditions needed to make it performative—through the scale of the mass and the collective, or the support of other bodies, through the physical occupation of public space, through its temporality and duration, and so on. It is about the other aspect of the public, to which Arendt referred as "the appearances of the public scene itself." Citizens in political action, therefore, do not act according to the rules and conventions of political practice as established in a public scene, but breach old in favor of new conventions that they don't have a right to, aren't entitled to, though they nevertheless express the power to install them. This may be a politically crucial distinction between performance and action, and we would propose understanding action as an un-prescribed and non-predeterminate social

to action, but rather as an action done by and with language or speech, which he later broadens to signify practice: "The [performative] is derived, of course, from 'perform,' the usual verb with the noun 'action': it indicates that the issuing of the utterance is the performing of an action—it is not normally thought of as just saying something" (ibid., 6–7).

43 | See Chapter 8 in this book, as well as Giorgio Agamben, "Poiesis and Praxis," in *The Man Without Content* (Palo Alto, CA: Stanford University Press, 1999).

44 | The word "to perform" was established in Middle English in the fourteenth century (*performen, perfournen*). It originates from the Anglo-Norman French *parfourmer*, a conjunction of *par* ("through, during") and *fournir* ("to furnish, provide") as an alteration of the Old French *parfornir, parfurnir*, which signified "to do, carry out, finish, accomplish." The same notion in French develops in parallel to English through the verb *parfaire*, whose first meaning in the twelfth century is "to complete, round off," and whose second meaning in the fifteenth century is "to perfect." The theatrical and musical denotation of performance in English as "live show or concert" dates from the early seventeenth century.

activity that constitutes itself and imposes its performative power in the public. From this we should not deduce a need to reinstate the initial dichotomy and again conceive of performance and action in binary opposition, since in fact many public activities start as actions and end as performatives or start as performatives and become actions in the course of a social process. The crucial point to be observed in this dynamics is that oscillations between action, unsuccessful performance, and successful performance outline the borders of a public sphere with its political practices and revolutions that go beyond politics and bring about a new configuration of the public sphere.

HACKERS OF THE PUBLIC:
FOUR PARABLES

The four theoretical fictions that follow examine four historical models of public sphere as well as the limitations they impose on citizens' activity: the story of Socrates, the first known "civil disobedient" in the context of democratic Athens; the story of John Wilkes, "the scandalous father of civil liberty" in the time of the emerging bourgeois public sphere in eighteenth-century Europe; the story of Vladimir Dapčević, a Yugoslav political dissident who from the position of radical Marxist-Leninist communism criticized socialism in Yugoslavia as "soft"; and an analysis of how WikiLeaks hacks the borders of freedom of speech/press in today's neoliberal democratic society.

#1 PARRHESIAST
SOCRATES, THE
FIRST KNOWN CIVIL
DISOBEDIENT

Athenian democracy of the fifth and fourth centuries BC (ca. 508–322) is the first known democratic social system in Western history and provides our story's social context. Succeeding a period of tyranny and later adopted by the other Greek city-states, this political system is based on participatory and direct democracy—but the social order in Athens amounts to a slave society. The public sphere plays a crucial role here; the private sphere also exists, but is clearly separated from the public sphere and has only marginal significance for the life of the society. Government as a concept does not exist and is replaced with self-ruled democracy, where demos itself is in power. Accordingly, the state is not considered an enemy of the public or of the people, because the people are the state, due to direct democracy. This participatory public sphere includes all citizens who don't elect representatives to vote on their behalf, but instead cast their own votes in assembly, council, and court. Be that as it may, the right to participate in politics is quite exclusive in Athens, extended only to free citizens and exclusive of women, children, slaves, foreigners, freed slaves, and people no longer in possession of citizens' rights.

Parrhesia (*parrhêsia*) is the foundation and most highly valued category of the Athenian public sphere. As free speech that allows everyone, that is, every citizen to speak truth in public, parrhesia is based on two main principles: shamelessness and historical amnesia.

Shamelessness signifies responsibility to the truth and freedom from respect for those of higher social standing, which provides equality among citizens; while historical amnesia refers to the breach with and freedom from the legacy of the old hierarchical social order from the tyrannical period, which is ruptured radically by a democracy that establishes itself within a historical discontinuity.[45]

This is the public scene on which Socrates, the first known civil disobedient,[46] appears. He is a classical philosopher, one of the founders of Western philosophy, known for the "Socratic method" of skeptical inquiry, a debate based on serial questioning. In the public sphere, in which he partakes prominently—as a member of the council, for instance—he is a well-known democrat who speaks freely using his philosophical method to question common sense in highly valued public categories such as politics, ethics, or religion. He thereby practices radically shameless free speech and criticizes the Athenian democratic system, especially its self-ruling principle, while promoting the idea that philosophers and other competent citizens should lead society. In doing this he in fact challenges the core of parrhesia, by testing its limits or, even better, its supposed "unlimitedness."

However, the limits are not as far away as they seem. In 399 BC, as we know from Plato's *Apology*, Socrates is accused of corruption of the youth and of "impiety" (contempt for the city's Gods), as these two formal charges explain:

> Socrates is an evildoer, and a curious person, who searches into things under the earth and in heaven, and he makes the worse appear the better cause; and he teaches the aforesaid doctrines to others.[47]
> Socrates is a doer of evil, who corrupts the youth; and who does not believe in the gods of the State, but has other divinities of his own.[48]

At his notorious trial he attempts not to defend himself, but to bring the jury face-to-face with the incorrectness of their ways of thinking. His quarrel is thus not with Athenian law, but with the jurors. Finally, the five-hundred-and-one-man jury sentences him to death, and instead of escaping by going into exile, he accepts the decision and dies by drinking hemlock poison. This gesture, with which he demonstrates to Athenians that their democratic system must be improved lest it kill a citizen precisely for his practicing democracy, is highly ambivalent. With it, Socrates in fact demonstrates his respect to democratic laws (since political parrhesia, according to Foucault, involves logos, truth, courage, and nomos) and follows his principle of ethical parrhesia (which means accordance between logos, truth, courage, and bios) till the end.[49]

45 | See Saxonhouse, *Free Speech and Democracy in Ancient Athens*; Michel Foucault, *Discourse and Truth: the Problematization of Parrhesia*, at *foucault. info.* (online archive), http://foucault.info/documents/parrhesia/; also published in Michel Foucault, *Fearless Speech*, ed. Joseph Pearson (Los Angeles: Semiotext(e), 2001).
46 | See Hannah Arendt, "Civil Disobedience," in *Crises of the Republic* (New York: Harcourt Brace, 1972).
47 | Plato, *Apology*, 19b (Speech 1, Defense, The Old Accusers), http://socrates. clarke.edu/aplg0101.htm.
48 | Plato, *Apology*, 24c (Speech 1, Defense, Corruption of Youth), http://socrates. clarke.edu/aplg0103.htm.
49 | For more about the relations between civil disobedience and the law, especially compatibility and obedience or acceptance of the punishment for lawbreaking, see Arendt, "Civil Disobedience," and Foucault, "The Practice of Parrhesia," under "Socratic Parrhesia," in *Discourse and Truth*, http://foucault.info/ documents/parrhesia/foucault.DT4.praticeParrhesia.en.html.

The trial of Socrates and his death raise several questions. First of all, the story shows that the democratic public sphere based on free speech intrinsically bears its own abuse. Indeed, it can punish "excessively democratic" actions and speech, namely, any free speech and shamelessness that irritates and angers the majority, by purely democratic tools—here, the public voting by jurors chosen by the drawing of lots by citizens—where the voice of the majority has decisive power. At the same time, by this process the democratic public sphere contests its own basic principle: free speech.

This leads us to a paradox of parrhesia in a democratic public sphere. Parrhesia means speaking the truth freely, directly, and openly, saying what one thinks to others. And Socrates, the greatest Athenian parrhesiast, is punished exactly for practicing parrhesia, this fetishized foundation of Greek democracy itself, synonymous with the equality and freedom of its citizens. "The *parrhesiastes* spoke the truth precisely because he was a good citizen, was well-born, had a respectful relation to the city, to the law, and to truth."[50] However, parrhesia is the most dangerous speech activity and its danger is inherent. Foucault explains that "the commitment involved in parrhesia is linked to a certain social situation, to a difference of status between the speaker and his audience, to the fact that the *parrhesiastes* says something which is dangerous to himself and thus involves a risk."[51] On the other hand, since "in *parrhesia* the danger always comes from the fact that the said truth is capable of hurting or angering the interlocutor,"[52] both the speaker and the interlocutor take a risk. The case of Socrates demonstrates that parrhesia might be practiced at the risk of one's life; and at the same time, it raises the question of whether parrhesia in its pure form is at all possible or socially acceptable. In democratic Athens it was obviously possible, but not acceptable, and Athens thereby delimited the realm of its democratic public sphere and dismissed its ideal. But if we continue with this issue, projecting the future of the democratic public, we could ask, can the non-democratic respect for those of higher social standing be replaced by a "democratic shame and respect," a respect for that which has been democratically decided (which Gods to praise, for instance) or for the perspectives, lives, and feelings of other citizens? As elaborated in Alrene Saxonhouse, shameless speech may also in fact be asocial just because it is free, whereas shame indicates a sensitivity to the social community since its cause lies in an awareness and attentiveness to others' perception of us and our doing, and how we and our doing affect them. "And I argue," she writes, "that Socrates' failure to blush—to care what others think of him, to be ashamed were he to stand open with his vulnerabilities revealed—lies behind the decision of the Athenians to execute him."[53]

This problematic opens the question of the right to freedom of speech and the prohibition of hate speech that addresses contemporary society. While in Athens free speech was its citizens' expression of freedom, their freedom from tyranny and from the old, hierarchical regime, in liberal democracy free speech is a right guaranteed to an individual—she possesses it and this possession is guaranteed by constitutions and laws.[54] From this

50 | Michel Foucault, "Parrhesia in the Tragedies of Euripides," in *Discourse and Truth*,http://foucault.info/documents/parrhesia/foucault.DT2.parrhesiaEuripides.en.html.

51 | Michel Foucault, "The Meaning and Evolution of the Word 'Parrhesia,'" in *Discourse and Truth*, http://foucault.info/documents/parrhesia/foucault.DT1.wordParrhesia.en.html.

52 | Ibid.

53 | Saxonhouse, *Free Speech and Democracy in Ancient Athens*, 5.

54 | The first and most famous example is the First Amendment to the United States Constitution (1791) which reads: "Congress shall make no law respecting an establishment of religion, or prohibiting the free exercise thereof; or abridging

Saxonhouse concludes that the Athenian citizen is not equal or similar, but rather radically different from the modern liberal individual.[55] To understand the difference better, we would like to propose thinking this issue in three categories: free speech, the right to freedom of speech, and the prohibition of hate speech. Firstly, we would say that the right to freedom of speech and the prohibition of hate speech seem mutually exclusive. A common interpretation of the freedom of speech calls it the freedom to speak freely, that is, without censorship. However, many modern constitutions and laws that guarantee freedom of speech limit it simultaneously, considering hate speech incompatible with free speech while prohibiting and punishing it. It seems contradictory but it isn't. In fact both categories belong to liberal and neoliberal democracy, which protects individuals with laws, assigning them freedom of speech or prohibiting any speech with which they might insult, offend, threaten, or harm other individuals. Therefore, it is not a paradox of liberalism but its intrinsic and probably inevitable self-limitation, since it is a social order, even if centered on the notion of the individual. The second point that we would like to clarify here is that free speech is something quite different than both the right to freedom of speech and the prohibition of hate speech. In the Athenian model of democracy it was a practice engaged in by free citizens whereby they publicly exercised their freedom and their social position as "free people who governed themselves."[56] Saxonhouse explains that "freedom of speech in Athens is the opportunity for those who are considered equals to say openly whatever they may think in a world of equal citizens."[57] The individual or the private person was not considered a category, nor was he one who "possessed the freedom of speech." The aim of public discussions among citizens was to achieve the truth so the best possible decisions for the city could be made. Therefore, in Athens, free speech—which, as noted before, was no celebration of diversity—included insults and hate speech; any restriction, prohibition, or punishment was judged as a corruption and violation of the democratic principle. That is why it collapsed de facto with the trial of Socrates.

The story of Socrates is far from black and white, yet it still points precisely to an ambivalence of a self-ruled public which will subsequently become a concern for both the theory and the practice of democracy. On the one hand, self-rule is important for any understanding of democracy's core ideals, since the principle allows citizens to decide about their society autonomously, i.e. without pressure from individual or private interests and without domination by the few (as in oligarchy). On the other hand, it gives power to each and every citizen, even the "worst" ones. And, as Foucault remarked, "Because *parrhesia* is given even to the worst citizens, the overwhelming influence of bad, immoral, or ignorant speakers may lead the citizenry into tyranny, or may otherwise endanger the city. Hence *parrhesia* may be dangerous for democracy itself."[58] This fatal consequence has occurred more than once in Western history: for instance, in the Weimar Republic democratic elections passed rulership to the Nazi Party, who proceeded to abolish democracy promptly by legal measures of "coordination"; or in the period of newly introduced democracy in Yugoslavia at the beginning of the 1990s, which immediately sparked nationalism as the political discourse, leading the country into civil wars and

the freedom of speech, or of the press; or the right of the people peaceably to assemble, and to petition the Government for a redress of grievances," U.S. Const. amend. I.

55 | Saxonhouse, 24, 208.

56 | Saxonhouse, 28.

57 | Ibid., 29.

58 | Foucault, "Parrhesia and the Crisis of Democratic Institutions," in *Discourse and Truth*, http://foucault.info/documents/parrhesia/foucault.DT3.democracy.en. html.

the multinational socialist state's dissolution. Even if we neglect this last instance, the principle of self-ruling "normally" leads to a "tyranny of majority," as the thought of Alexis De Tocqueville and John Stuart-Mills explains. We could conclude from the story of Socrates, with its bothersome Foucauldian conclusion, that real and critical *parrhesia* cannot exist where real, self-ruled democracy exists. Herein lies the crucial ambivalence of the democratic public sphere, an ambivalence that we inherited from the history of democracy and that remains for the most part unresolved within the democratic system.[59]

#2 JOHN WILKES, OR THE VICISSITUDES OF THE PUBLIC AND PERSONAL LIMITS TO FREEDOM OF SPEECH

The story of John Wilkes, "the scandalous father of liberty,"[60] begins around 1760, during the period of the English parliamentary monarchy. Wilkes' story is connected with the birth of liberalism, the ideology which will motivate the American and French Revolutions to put an end to the arbitrary rule of the sovereign monarch in the name of inalienable "human rights." What interests us here are the mechanisms Wilkes used to promote the future postulates of liberal democracy: freedom of the press, wider political representation, the right to privacy, and religious tolerance. In a transition from the public qua social order of *ancien régime* to the rise of the bourgeois public sphere, Wilkes' "performance" changes the *modus operandi* of the eighteenth century "man as actor." As we will see, it explicitly uses insult and libel against public persons in office, as well as the manipulation of public opinion, to transgress limitations on the freedom of public speech that are instituted monarchically. This gesture turns him into a public figure whose acts have political impact, and whose personality beyond these acts begins to blaze an exemplary trail toward political liberty. A liberal and a libertine, Wilkes was one of the first to cross the dividing line between public politics and private character (Wilke's own character being that of a rake). The new configuration between the public act and private personality will change the principle of performing in the public sphere towards the end of the eighteenth century.

In Wilkes' time, the political public sphere developed through the wars of rhetoric between newspapers that practiced public insult. The mechanism of public insult could be described as follows: a person was attacked personally on the grounds of his public association with a policy or political faction, or his capacity in conducting policy, but the author of the verbal delict was anonymous. In parodic contrast to the voice of British government, the newspaper *Briton*, Wilkes founded *The North Briton*. The use of "north" in the title dis-

---

59 | One of the most well-known answers to this question, offered by Socrates and Plato and much later by Lippmann and Dewey, is that only those who are wise and competent should rule—the philosophers, the experts, and the like. Dewey argued that "the obvious alternative is rule by those intellectually qualified, by expert intellectuals." (205). However, this answer already transcends the borders of democracy without reframing the problem as a problem of democracy.

60 | Arthur Cash, *John Wilkes: The Scandalous Father of Liberty* (New Haven, CT: Yale University Press, 2007).

closed an implicit accusation against Jacobites, supporters of the deposed James II who were supported by the Catholic clans in Scotland, the northernmost part of Britain. Wilkes was virtuosic in his insulting witticisms, and the down-and-dirty tone of his scandalous rumours and insults against King George III's administration garnered his paper a rate of circulation four times that of the official *Briton*.[61] When *The North Briton* sold 2000 copies a week, the reach these rumours had into society seemed dangerous, capable of turning public opinion against the authority of the king. To illustrate the tone of *The North Briton*, we will quote a few insults. Lord Egremont was "a weak, passionate, and insolent secretary of state," and Secretary of the Treasury Samuel Martin was "the most treacherous, base, selfish, mean, abject, low-lived and dirty fellow, that ever *wriggled* himself into a secretaryship."[62] Wilkes himself explained the nature of such speech by means of a difference between "liberty" and "license." Liberty is "when some perfectly respectable person gets up and says something everybody agrees to," while "license is when some infernal scoundrel, who ought to be hanged anyway, gets up and says something that is true." The word license adequately describes Wilkes' act: he licensed, or gave himself permission to insult others in the name of truth, which wasn't noble. This gave way to a simple equation between the symbolic assassination of public character and the defense of liberty.

When in the famous issue 45 of *The North Briton* he indirectly yet unmistakably insulted the King, Wilkes crossed a line, breaking the strict rule that placed the king above reproach while only his ministers could be criticized. Insulting the sovereign was considered treason to the Crown. Wilkes implicitly accused King George III of lying in his speech in celebration of the end of the Seven Year's War, an act which was then declared "seditious libel." The King's ministers drew a general warrant for the arrest of the publishers and seizure of the newspapers, but mentioned no names of the persons charged with the crime. As the article in issue 45 was anonymous, forty-nine persons were arrested and the prosecution made procedural blunders that Wilkes took advantage of for his defense. He used his trials in the Court of Common Pleas before a large audience to state his principles in fiery speech. He said that his case would "teach ministers of arbitrary principles, that the liberty of an English subject is not to be sported away with impunity, in this cruel and despotic manner." His trial would "determine at once whether English liberty be a reality or a shadow."[63] This action led to the nullification of "general warrant," the unpopular instrument of *ancien régime*, which was unpopular because it represented arbitrary power and was considered dubious because it authorized the king's officers to arrest anyone they suspected without evidence. General warrants were particularly disliked by American colonists, who saw in Wilkes' case an example for rebellion in favor of liberty against monarchy.

For Wilkes, a series of arrests followed, as did reelections to British Parliament as the representative of Middlesex, and ousting attempts in the House of Commons, which, had they been successful, would have annuled his immunization against lawsuits. All this was mainly linked with Wilkes' efforts to enact radical political reforms. Wilkes fought for a wider popular representation where Parliament wouldn't be composed of only landowners, noblemen, judges, and clergy, as his speech on March 23, 1775, evinces:

61 | Daniel McCarthy, "In Praise of John Wilkes: How a filthy, philandering deadbeat helped secure British and American liberty," *Reason* 38, no. 3 (2006), http://reason.com/archives/2006/07/01/in-praise-of-john-wilkes/1.
62 | Jack Lynch, "Wilkes, Liberty, and Number 45," *CW Journal* (Summer 2003), http://www.history.org/foundation/journal/summer03/wilkes.cfm.
63 | Lynch, "Wilkes, Liberty, and Number 45," http://www.history.org/foundation/journal/summer03/wilkes.cfm.

> That every free agent in this kingdom should, in my wish, be represented in Parliament. That the metropolis, which contains in itself a ninth part of the people, and the counties of Middlesex, York, and others, which so greatly abound with inhabitants, should receive an increase in their representation.[64]

This marshalled him great support among the middle and working classes in England, but also among the rebellious colonists in America who were seeking independence from the British crown and struggling for the right to be represented by someone they would elect as opposed to someone appointed to represent them. Wilkes also advocated a bill against the ministry's excise tax, not because he was against government taxes, but because collecting it would legitimate forced entry and search of private property while providing politicians with information for use against their adversaries. In addition to promoting the right of privacy, he argued for religious tolerance:

> I wish to see rising in the neighborhood of a Christian cathedral, near its Gothic towers, the minaret of a Turkish mosque, a Chinese pagoda, and a Jewish synagogue, with a temple of the sun, if any Persians could be found to inhabit this island and worship in this gloomy climate the God of their idolatry.[65]

What shook Wilkes' reputation and handed his opponents a strong case against him, based on charges of—this time—not seditious but obscene blasphemous libel, was his *Essay on Woman* (1755), a pornographic satire of Alexander Pope's *Essay on Man*, considered a highly esteemed document of humanist Enlightenment ethics. In his *Essay on Woman*, co-written with his friend Thomas Potter, Wilkes presents his libertarian lifestyle of a rake, and recommends it with many other licentious expressions, such as "life can little more supply than just a few good fucks, and then we die,"[66] mixed with obscene mockery of his political opponents. This work disclosed the identity of the man who had been behind many other insulting articles in the past, articles he had anonymously authored, and it also earned him a temporary exile in France.

Why was Wilkes recognized as a hero of the underdogs while he himself won the privileges of nobility as a libertine? As he fashioned himself as someone who stood for less privileged members of society, the lower classes sought to redeem his immoral character, the middle classes denied his immoral conduct, and the working classes converted it into a sign of rebellion against the established order on the grounds of making public the hypocrisy of the upper classes. Wilkes' case is paradigmatic for the shift that his public performance caused: "Every action of the person Wilkes had of necessity a symbolic or public character." The very life of John Wilkes, the person, turned into a symbol of what liberty itself meant: "the man and the principle became one,"[67] as Sennett writes. The moment Wilkes appeared on the historical political scene, in Sennett's view, his supporters lacked a clear idea of liberty and felt misrepresented and confused by the style of an upperclass language of government based on a fixed set of ideas, on an established, known, but passing order. They may not have been cognizant of the full meaning of liberty that Wilkes was proposing, but they were drawn into the dramatic turn of events through which Wilkes overcame the

64 | *The Parliamentary History of England from the Earliest Period to the Year 1803*, ed. T.C. Hansard (London, 1813), 18:1295.
65 | Wilkes quoted in Cash, 360.
66 | John Wilkes, *Essay on Woman in Three Epistles*, (London, ca. 1755), 2:1–8.
67 | Sennet, *The Fall of Public Man*, 103.

assaults against him and unfailingly achieved the reinstatement of his power. The same supporters felt betrayed when twenty years later Wilkes turned more conservative, using his office to suppress the anti-catholic Gordon Riots (1780) and disapproving of the French Revolution. His earlier, radical actions made him a hero of populist democracy. As populism doesn't guarantee the articulation of an ideological program, but is instead the result of general discontent as a social affect, it needs and seeks a personality who will *embody* this affect, which can be assessed in the recent cases of Pim Fortuyn[68] or Silvio Berlusconi.

Four points in the controversy surrounding the conjoining of liberty and representation, on the one hand, with political power and the personal, on the other, could be inferred here. In the first place, hacking the idea of freedom of speech by hurling it beyond the borders between the domains of private and public implies shamelessness and the suspension of any public order. The idea of liberty introduced into ordinary social life implied that the demand and desire for liberty become joined to a belief in individual character as a social principle. So, in the second place, libertarian and liberal uprisings against a sovereign power gave rise to the understanding of freedom as a matter of the individual. The motto written at the entrance of the gentlemen's club to which Wilkes belonged (the quite notorious Hellfire Club, which engaged in a secret society, called the Knights of St. Francis of Wycombe, that parodied Roman Catholic rituals in drunken orgies often involving prostitutes dressed as nuns)—*Fais ce que tu voudras* (Do what thou wilt)—is the libertine equivalent of *laissez-faire*, the libertarian restriction of the power of the state, the ultimate instance of which is anarchy. Thus Wilkes' formula of libertarianism-cum-libertinage reveals a paradox wherein the right of political representation of every man and the idea of liberty as individual freedom become incompatible, because they mutually diminish one another. In the third place, the idea of liberty in the image of the person as the symbol of liberty brings the performing identity of the private person into politics, and hence blurs the political meaning of the act through the ethical understanding of the affect that accompanies its performance. And fourthly, the reinforcement of the individual as the social principle in political leadership instigates a process of taming and moralizing the personality, establishing performative standards for judging the political figure as a morally "credible" and respectable person. After Wilkes's time, the mechanism of personal insult as tool for the symbolic assassination of a public figure will continue to be implemented, which many a case of moral scandals hounding politicians and other politically powerful figures testifies to.[69]

68 | Pim Fortuyn was a politician, civil servant, author, and professor as well as founder of an extreme right-wing party in the Netherlands in 2002 called "Pim Fortuyn List" (LPF). He had a dandyish gay performance that distinguished his personality and yet attracted the populist working class in Rotterdam to a racist politics against immigrants, multiculturalism, and especially Islam in Holland. He was murdered by a leftist activist nine days before general elections in 2002. Cf. Herman Asselberghs and Dieter Lesage, "Homo politicus. Pim Fortuyn: A Case Study," *nettime.org, nettime-l* (mailing list), 2002, http://amsterdam.nettime.org/Lists-Archives/nettime-l-0207/msg00102.html.

69 | We are reminded of the cases of Bill Clinton, Dominique Strauss-Kahn, and Julian Assange, all instances when public opinion on moral issues is reinforced by legal prosecutions.

#3 COMRADE VLADO DAPČEVIĆ: IDEOLOGICAL OVERIDENTIFICATION AND ITS UNHAPPY POLITICAL PERFORMATIVE

The social context in which the story of Vladimir "Vlado" Dapčević (1917–2001) takes place is the turbulent geopolitical category of Yugoslavia, and the story stretches throughout Yugoslavia's different historical moments, the first being the Kingdom of Yugoslavia, a capitalist parliamentary monarchy in the 1930s; the next, the "second," socialist Yugoslavia, including the period of the 1940s–50s; then 1975–1988; and finally, the 1990s. Over this time span, the state indicatively changed its name a few times. First, in the period from before until the beginning of World War II it was called the Kingdom of Yugoslavia—during which the antifascist liberation war was led against the occupying Axis powers, coupled with an internal social revolution led by the Communist Party of Yugoslavia (KPJ / CPY). During WWII it changed its name to Democratic Federal Yugoslavia (in 1943), which then became the Federal People's Republic of Yugoslavia in 1946, finally becoming the Socialist Federal Republic of Yugoslavia (SFRJ / SFRY) in 1963 and remaining so until 1992. In this final phase, Yugoslavia is a real socialist society, but develops "Yugoslavia's third way"—a CPY-led, socialist one-party political system that accommodates some elements of capitalism, like the free market; and its economy is predicated on associated labor and workers' self-management. Politically, the SFRY positions itself between East and West, refusing to be a member of the Eastern Bloc and thereby become inflicted with the Cold War, hence it initiates the Non-Aligned Movement.[70] In the late 1980s and early 90s the Yugoslav third way ended in democratization and the establishment of a multiparty political system, as well as civil wars, the dissolution of the state, and a transition toward neoliberal democracy and capitalism. Dapčević's story takes place not only in Yugoslavia, but also in the USSR during the 60s—(1958–66), the era of Kruschev, the Cold War, and world domination by opposing superpowers (the US and the USSR)—as well as in Belgium, France, Switzerland, and the Netherlands (1966–75), all capitalist democratic welfare societies. This complex historical positioning of the story is an integral part thereof, but we will focus here only on the segments occurring in socialist Yugoslavia in the 1940s–50s and from 1975 to 1988.

From the perspective of the public sphere in this context, it is a commonly held belief that the public sphere in real socialist countries doesn't exist. However, even if this is true, there is an intriguing conceptual trajectory that led to this state of affairs. Basically we can say

70 | See the following transcription of a videotaped interview between Todor Kuljić and Oliver Ressler as part of Ressler's installation project *alternative economics, alternative societies*: "Yugoslavia's Workers Self-Management," in "alternative economics, alternative societies," special issue of the online journal *transversal* (August 2005), http://eipcp.net/transversal/0805/kuljic/en; Kuljić, *Tito* (Zrenjanin: Gradska biblioteka, 2005); Kuljić, *Sociologija generacije* (Belgrade: Čigoja, 2009); Kuljić, "Memory of Titoism: Hegemony Frameworks," *Filozofija i društvo* no. 2 (2010), http://www.doiserbia.nb.rs/img/doi/0353-5738/2010/0353-57381002225K.pdf; Kuljić, "Titoizam: tri perspektive," http://www.kczr.org/download/tekstovi/todor_kuljic_titoizam_tri_perspektive.pdf; and also Gal Kirn, "Jugoslavija: od partizanske politike do postfordističke tendencije," *Up&Underground* no. 17–18 (2010), http://www.up-underground.com/wp-content/uploads/2011/04/1718_gal_kirn.pdf; Kirn, "Elementi za analizu jugoslavenskog samoupravljanja: između socijalizma i kapitalizma—interview with Catherine Samary," *Novosti*, no. 669 (2012), http://www.novossti.com/2012/10/elementi-za-analizu-jugoslavenskog-samoupravljanja-izmedu-socijalizma-i-kapitalizma/.

that in socialist countries governments accepted Aristotle's definitions of democracy as rule by the poor versus oligarchy as rule by the rich. In the socialist version this principle was called, following Marx, "the dictatorship of the proletariat," which was supposed to lead to a classless society. Within this configuration of society and its public sphere, every voice that problematized, questioned, or contested the dictatorship of the proletariat was dubbed a counterrevolutionary class enemy. As an effect of such a system, real-socialist countries practically cancelled the public sphere as the realm of society where citizens talk, negotiate, argue, and confront each other about the public good and interest of the society they live in. The SFRY with Tito's regime of "soft-totalitarianism," however, has its specificities, as this instance of socialism goes hand in hand with a certain decentralization and gradual liberalization from the 1960s onward. Yet the public sphere as we know it from the history of democracy appeared more or less only three times: in and after 1948, around 1968, and in the late 80s.

This is the "stage" Vlado Dapčević acts on.[71] The most prominent Yugoslav political dissident, a Marxist-Leninist revolutionary who identifies with the principles of Marxism-Leninism that the Yugoslav state itself is also identified with, Dapčević is a fighter for freedom, equality, democracy and republic, workers' solidarity, national brotherhood and internationalism; and against the creeping of fascism, Nazism, royalism, capitalism, imperialism, nationalism, and "bourgeoisation" into socialism. Not only did he "overidentify" with the ideology of communism; his ideology was overdetermined too: he was a freedom-fighter. Already as a student in the 1930s he had been a communist activist, a member of the Alliance of Communist Youth of Yugoslavia, then of the CPY. He spread leaflets, took part in the struggle for the autonomy of the university in Belgrade, and signed up to fight for the republic in the Spanish Civil War—and he was arrested three times because of his communist activities. During WWII he was involved in the Yugoslav resistance, and in spite of clashes within the CPY he was promoted to commander and took part in all important historical battles in the region, gaining a high position in the new postwar government.

Soon thereafter, his "communist criticism of communism" takes shape. The crucial moment is the Fifth Congress of the CPY in 1948, where the resolution of the Informbureau (Cominform),[72] which declares that the CPY is revisionist and anti-Marxist, is discussed.[73]

71 | The information given about Dapčević's life and work is taken from the following sources: the website of the Partija Rada (Party of Labour), http://www.partijarada.org/; *Vlado Dapčević—Govorio je* [Memoirs of Vlado Dapčević] (Belgrade: Partija rada, 2001), http://www.partijarada.org/; and http://www.mltranslations.org/serbcroat/dapcevic.htm; Slavko Ćuruvija, *IBEOVAC. Ja, Vlado Dapčević* (Belgrade: Filip Višnjić, 1990); Information Department of Partija Rada, "Vlado Dapčević," *Espresso Stalinist* (blog), blog entry by ES, October 5, 2011, http://espressostalinist.wordpress.com/2011/10/05/vlado-dapcevic/; "Vlado Dapčević na robiji," vimeo video, 41:16, interview with Vlado Dapčević in Zabela prison for TV Belgrade, April 1987, posted by "Vlado Dapčević," 2011, http://vimeo.com/22480850; "Vlado Dapčević u emisili Klub 91 na TVSA," vimeo video, 1:33:06, interview with Vlado Dapčević for the TV show *Klub 91*, TV Sarajevo, 1991, posted by "Vlado Dapčević," 2011, http://vimeo.com/22802882.

72 | Informbureau or Cominform refers to the Information Bureau of the Communist and Workers' Parties, which was an international organization of Communist parties, established in 1947, with the aim of coordinating the activities of the communist parties of the Soviet-dominated Eastern Bloc countries.

73 | See Vojin Majstorović, "The Rise and Fall of the Yugoslav-Soviet Alliance, 1945–1948," *Past Imperfect*, no. 16 (2010); Leonid Gibianskii, "The Soviet-Yugoslav Split and the Cominform," in *The Establishment of Communist Regimes in Eastern Europe, 1944–1949*, eds. Norman Naimark and Leonid Gibianskii (Boulder, CO: Westwood Press, 1997).

The party rejects the resolution, saying a historical and categorical "no" to Stalin, whereas Dapčević openly accepts it. He does so because in a broader sense he is critical of the CPY, which is in favor of the liberalization of socialism, independence from Soviet Stalinism, and collaboration with Western capitalist countries.[74]

And what is the outcome of his overidentification with Marxism-Leninism, which the Yugoslav state—at least officially—embraces? He spends 22 years in various jails and in the communist camp Goli otok, he is expelled from the country and lives in exile, he escapes from an assassination organized by the UDBA,[75] and he is even sentenced to death.[76] The paradox, which is the crux of our story, is that all this is caused by Dapčević's open critique of Yugoslav socialism for being too "soft" and liberal, while the too-liberal SFRY, which renounces the critique of the Informbureau and thus rejects the path of Stalinist totalitarianism, wishing to develop its "socialism with a human face," handles Dapčević by exercising the most classical Stalinist method of force—"purge." This is why his critical free speech as political practice could be considered an "unhappy performative" which misunderstands the conventions and protocols of public speech in socialism and fails to achieve the establishment of new ones. As we said, a political practice may effectuate change either when it is a successful performative that recognizes, follows, and fulfils preexisting procedures and conventions, or when it establishes new ones. But, for establishing a new one, a political practice should be an action that expresses and imposes power to be accepted as performative, thus introducing new rules, procedures, protocols, and conventions. It seems this would require a certain critical mass or force, or a historical need that itself forces the circumstances to change. Dapčević, however, proposed a new political practice—the free public critique of state communism from the perspective of communism—which remained unsuccessful, prohibited, and punished.

Dapčević's misunderstanding and overidentification are by no means evidence of naivety; they form a political practice that, however unsuccessful its performative is, provokes the object of criticism to reveal its own cynicism. He criticized the CPY for not accepting Stalinist critique, and it punished him with the Stalinist method of purge; he accused Yugoslav socialism for being too liberal, and it showed its totalitarian face. Later on, in the 1980s, overidentification will be articulated as a critical cultural-artistic tactic in socialist Yugoslavia, as practiced by the Slovenian music group Laibach (within the movement Neue Slowenische Kunst, or NSK). According to Slavoj Žižek,[77] overidentification may be a powerful tool which uncovers otherwise invisible social problems—or, in this particular case, the invisible or hidden underside of Yugoslavian soft-totalitarian socialism—though its potential to bring about change remains questionable. In contrast to the critical art of

74 | Later on, during his time in the USSR, Dapčević will be critical of the CPSU, which will be in favor of the coexistence of capitalism and socialism, which could prevail in one part of the world, whereas Dapčević will adopt the Chinese line of permanent struggle between them in order to achieve global communism. During his stay in Western Europe, he will enact a communist criticism of Western imperialism, organizing and volunteering for the Viet Cong and for Cuba during the Cuban Missile Crisis, and he will participate in workers' movements. During the last period, the civil war in Yugoslavia, Dapčević will work on empowering democracy and preservation of "brotherhood and unity," acting for the most part against the nationalist regime of Slobodan Milošević, and he will establish the Party of Labour.
75 | UDBA, or the State Security Administration, was the secret police organization of Yugoslavia.
76 | The punishment is later changed to twenty years of hard labor.
77 | See Slavoj Žižek, "Why are the NSK and Laibach Not Fascists?" *M'ARS*, no. 3–4 (1993).

the 1980s, Dapčević's overidentification is not cynical in itself, but provokes—far more radically—uncovers the cynicism of the state and its liberal socialist discourse. And it may be only a distant historical-political interpretation that Dapčević's practice practically did what Žižek finds most powerful in overidentification as a tactic, namely, that Dapčević did not produce an affirmation of something or someone with which, or whom, one can overidentify—which in this case would be Stalinist developments in Marxism-Leninism— but that he instead produced a a radical critique of it. Ironically, this is the outcome of the whole story when the state abandons its soft-totalitarian public discourse and reacts in a thoroughly Stalinist way, punishing its critic by demonstrating, at the same time, how totalitarian socialism actually operates.

This problematic raises the following question: is free speech possible in socialist-communist countries, even the most liberal ones? The story of Dapčević tells us that it probably isn't, due to the complex role of the socialist-communist state and its relation to the public. The classical division of society results in two realms, the public and the private; while in modern society the third category, the state, is introduced either as the agent of the people, where the public sphere is involved in chains of delegation within government and decision making (as civil society), or an oppressive apparatus that necessitates the public sphere as an instance of moderation between the state and the people. The question of the role of the state is specific in the case of real socialist societies—where the state is the surrogate for the people, therefore eliminating any need for a public sphere. Nancy Fraser gives a lucid account of the structure of such a public sphere:

> Take the longstanding failure in the dominant wing of the socialist and Marxist tradition to appreciate the distinction between the apparatuses of the state, on the one hand, and public arenas of citizen discourse and association, on the other. All too often it was assumed that to subject the economy to the control of the socialist state was to subject it to the control of the socialist citizenry. Of course that was not the case. But the conflation of the state with the public sphere provided ballast to processes whereby the socialist vision became institutionalized in an authoritarian statist form instead of in a participatory democratic form. The result has been to jeopardize the very idea of socialist democracy.[78]

In addition, the story of Vlado Dapčević reveals differences between the public space and the public sphere as well as the importance of their differentiation. The Fifth Congress of the CPY in 1948 and the ensuing discussion of Cominform's resolution were transparent and, we could also confidently say, quite public—2,400 delegates were present (Dapčević too), there was full radio streaming, detailed newspaper reports, and so forth. However, in fact, this was not indicative of a public sphere, but of an occupation of public space by a monologue—that of the party—which was accessible publicly, though in no way open to criticism and polemics. Herein lies the blind spot of Dapčević's gesture, which in the long run, as we said, reveals the cynicism of party and state discourse.

This brings us to the last question we wish to open, a question that in a long historical ellipse transports us right into the present—the question of the degree of inclusivity/exclusivity of the public sphere. In this particular case, the fence is obviously solid and high. In the critical moments of liberal socialist Yugoslavia, when the crucial decisions

78 | Nancy Fraser, "Rethinking the Public Sphere: A Contribution to the Critique of Actually Existing Democracy," *Social Text*, no. 25–26 (1990): 56.

about society had to be made, only CPY communists, and among them only "proper communists," took part in public discussion. They were the sole deciders of what public interest and public good could be. They were truly the only actors on the scene; all the other voices were excluded or purged—and we call this totalitarianism. But have we ever had a public sphere that is not exclusive, or is such a thing merely a theoretical fiction that we project onto the lost good old days of history, like the days of Athenian democracy, or of the early liberal public sphere? As we mentioned, in the public sphere of Athenian democracy, only citizens took part in this ideal of participatory and direct democracy; in the eighteenth century's liberal public sphere, only bourgeois men; while in twentieth-century democracy, only political representatives of the citizenry decide. And the central recurrent question is, on whose behalf do they vote? Moreover, do they really represent us citizens?

**#4 WIKILEAKS:
OVERLAYING THE
POLITICAL ONTO THE
PUBLIC**

The last parable concerns a most recent and familiar case, that of WikiLeaks, which interests us as an attempt to give rise to a political counterpublic of individuals against the state. We will therefore filter it through the central problem we analyzed in the three previous parables: the relationship between the public sphere and freedom of speech and freedom of press, which, since the Bill of Rights, are considered pillars of liberal democracy.

WikiLeaks, which has existed officially since the end of 2006, started as more than a whistleblowing site with a history in "ethical computer hacktivism" based on the political convictions of its founders: internet activists. Julian Assange, who has emerged as its central figure due to media exposure and legal prosecution, invokes the First Amendment in the Bill of Rights as the principle that justifies the enormous leaking of confidential information. He explains that the rights of the press should be exempt from law because they are superior to it, because "free speech is what regulates government and regulates law."[79] In that way, he takes the First Amendment "too literally," as a principle upon which humanity should be built and not a political and legal framework of operation. He equates the public sphere with unlimited access to information and freedom of press, which permits him to crack the public (state) and private (corporate) codes that limit access to information and to distribute the so-called classified, confidential—or as he calls it "suppressed" (censored)—information that is leaked from governmental and other institutions. He also reiterates the principle of monitoring and supervision which Habermas understood as a characteristic of the liberal public sphere.

Assange's understanding of information, if we are to take it as representative of Wiki-Leaks, reveals its status *vis-à-vis* publicness in today's control society, which is based

79 | "Exclusive – Julian Assange Extended Interview," 11:39, from an episode of *The Colbert Report*, aired April 12, 2010, http://www.colbertnation.com/the-colbert-report-videos/260785/april-12-2010/exclusives---julian-assange-unedited-interview.

on the information economy, where control lies in the alliance between global private corporate capital and the state. Information falls into three categories: knowledge that is economically supported; "historical record," which dissipates over time; and "suppressed information."[80] According to Assange, what is "faintly glowing" about signals of censorship is the amount of economic work needed to suppress it:

> And why is so much economic work being done to suppress that information? Probably—not definitely, but probably—because the organization predicts that it's going to reduce the power of the institution that contains it. It's going to produce a change in the world, and the organization doesn't like that vision. Therefore, the containing institution engages in constant economic work to prevent that change. So, if you search for that signal of suppression, then you can find all this information that you should mark as information that should be released.

Releasing information to which access was previously denied is equivalent to its "liberation," and Assange's optimism concerning the detection of censorship lies, as he sees it, in the possibility of political change that the institution containing the information fears and needs to prevent. But he also admits that there are societies in which censorship doesn't exist in an obvious way, because publishing any information wouldn't affect ownership or control. Such societies have mastered control through the fiscalization of power relationships to the extent that their public sphere is thoroughly depoliticized.

With regard to the public sphere, WikiLeaks is an attempt to mobilize a counterpublic of individuals against the state through the monitoring of governments and other power structures. "Counterpublic" here deviates from Fraser's definition of the marginalized and historically excluded public and emphasizes a hacktivist sense of "counter" that discloses the domain of hidden activity underneath the hegemonic public sphere, turning something that would otherwise remain conspiracy into "transparency." What politically motivates this operation is a belief in ethical individualism, in individuals who recognize the power of the instrument of hacking by de-crypting and re-encrypting information in order to monitor or denounce the abuse of power:

> We saw that we could change the nature of the relationship between the individual and the state using cryptography. I wouldn't say that we came from a libertarian political tradition as much as from a libertarian temperament, with particular individuals who were capable of thinking in abstractions, but wanting to make them real. We had many who were comfortable with higher mathematics, cryptography, engineering or physics who were interested in politics and felt that the relationship between the individual and the state should be changed and that the abuse of power by states needed to be checked, in some manner, by individuals.

The power of the instrument of cryptography was overestimated by a technological fantasy:

> So if you and I agree on a particular encryption code, and it is mathematically strong, then the forces of every superpower brought to bear on that code still cannot crack it. So a state can

80 | If not otherwise indicated, all subsequent quotes of Assange are taken from the following interview: Hans Ulrich Obrist, "In Conversation with Julian Assange," Pts. 1 and 2. *e-flux*, no. 25 (2011), http://www.e-flux.com/journal/in-conversation-with-julian-assange-part-i/; no. 26 (2011), http://www.e-flux.com/journal/in-conversation-with-julian-assange-part-ii/.

desire to do something to an individual, yet it is simply not possible for the state to do it—and in this sense, mathematics and individuals are stronger than superpowers.

What WikiLeaks didn't count on was that the state would find other legal means to arrest its activity, targeting the individual, Assange, rather than the whole organization with its other members and numerous volunteers on moral grounds through staging a sexual crime for a court case. This is reminiscent of the control mechanisms—a kind of moral police—installed after Wilkes, which are based on the individual as the social principle: the public sphere seeks a face that will be held accountable and that will bear public opinion regarding the judgment of his private life. The public male figure morally misperformed in his private life. The question remains as to how responsible Assange himself is for the failure of WikiLeaks to present itself as a force of a multitude. But before WikiLeaks was suppressed, what did the repossession of knowledge, the stealing of information as governmental or corporate property, achieve in the public sphere? We will answer this by observing the operation of WikiLeaks in its successive steps.

The operation begins by obtaining suppressed information through leaks, where an advisory board chooses the interest and target where they will search for suppressed information and then finds whistleblowers. The obtained documents are then verified for their authenticity. In the third step, media are sought out to edit and publish information. The last step of publication proves to be the most difficult, firstly due to errors in re-encryption of the released documents, which are damaging to individuals responsible for leaking information. Secondly, and perhaps more importantly, the masses of information remain unprocessed. For instance, 400,000 documents were released about Iraq, the redaction of which was unachievable by the workforce of the mainstream or commercial media. Assange explains that he was looking for volunteer labor, for non-professional writers, i.e. bloggers, who would recognize the political potential of this enterprise for change and assess documents, analyze them, contextualize them, and insert them back into local communities. WikiLeaks hasn't spurred the investigative journalism that Assange hoped for, which recalls Dewey's in-depth inquiry into and evaluation of consequences. In Assange's conclusion, bloggers are prepared neither for intellectual debate, nor to proactively search for what is "newsworthy"; instead, they react cynically to the stories of the mainstream media in their own search for popular readership. In a word, a counterpublic hasn't been mobilized on the grand scale that WikiLeaks expected.

What political, ideological, and conceptual effects has WikiLeaks had on our understanding of the relations between the state, the public, and private capital? According to some commentators like Saroj Giri or Žižek,[81] WikiLeaks has a more radical political charge than many mass mobilizations and social movements, just because they challenge representative democracy by attacking the procedures and protocols that supposedly guarantee the transparency of governance. According to Žižek, WikiLeaks acts against

81 | Saroj Giri writes, "And here we must hand it to WikiLeaks that their subversiveness came precisely from the fact that even though they tend to espouse liberal ideas of free flow of information or, in semi-anarchist mode, think of power as merely conspiratorial their attack really came from outside the normal channels professing free flow of information and citizens right to know: they challenged power by challenging the normal channels of challenging power and revealing the truth, even though they are perhaps getting suckered now into the hands of corporate houses and other suspicious players." Saroj Giri, "WikiLeaks Beyond WikiLeaks," *Metamute.org*, the website of *Mute* magazine, http://www. metamute.org/en/articles/WikiLeaks_beyond_WikiLeaks.

shameless cynicism where citizens cannot pretend to not know what everyone knows that they know: "even if everyone knows an unpleasant fact, saying it in public changes everything."[82] The shame is not on those in power, but on citizens who tolerate such power. Nevertheless, critical voices who would rather applaud WikiLeaks from the left side question the operation's political legitimacy. For instance, a typical opinion claims that politics is a more complicated game that citizens are ignorant of. Therefore, understanding the freedom of speech and press literally leads to inaccuracies and tactical errors, and unlimited transparency is dangerous. Citizens therefore still prefer representation, however problematic it has become, because they are happier to delegate the filtering of information to the experts, which echoes Lippmann's and Dewey's views on the problem of the public. But what are the problems and questions that operations of WikiLeaks raise?

In conclusion, WikiLeaks attempts to repoliticize the public sphere by overlaying the political onto the public sphere. They do so by breaking the protocol of the performance of the public in media and devising a new performative in journalism (the release of suppressed information). Will this performative fail if it doesn't evolve to establish a new procedure for journalism? Until now it has failed by virtue of a paradox: the ultimate openness of public space meets the indifference of the public. There is no unilateral determination of cause and effect between the exposure of censored information and political mobilization. WikiLeaks points to the limits of the public sphere, not in the boundaries political power sets to keep information private, as Dewey would have it, but in the lack of response. We can discern two misfires in WikiLeaks' operation: on the one side, the liberalist promise of freedom by unlimited access, transparency, and openness; and, on the other, ethical individualism as a "default setting" of democracy, i.e., the assumption that private individuals identify with freedom of speech as a natural right they are driven to exercise. The operation didn't prove sufficient in creating the rise of a new conception of the public sphere; yet it not only pointed to, but also exploded the limits of representative democracy. Hence, we might ask, for WikiLeaks to fulfill a new happy performative, is it crucial that they train real journalist-terrorists to hijack the public sphere—the mainstream media itself?

82 | Slavoj Žižek, "Good Manners in the Age of WikiLeaks," *London Review of Books* 33, no. 2 (2011), http://www.lrb.co.uk/v33/n02/slavoj-zizek/good-manners-in-the-age-of-wikileaks.

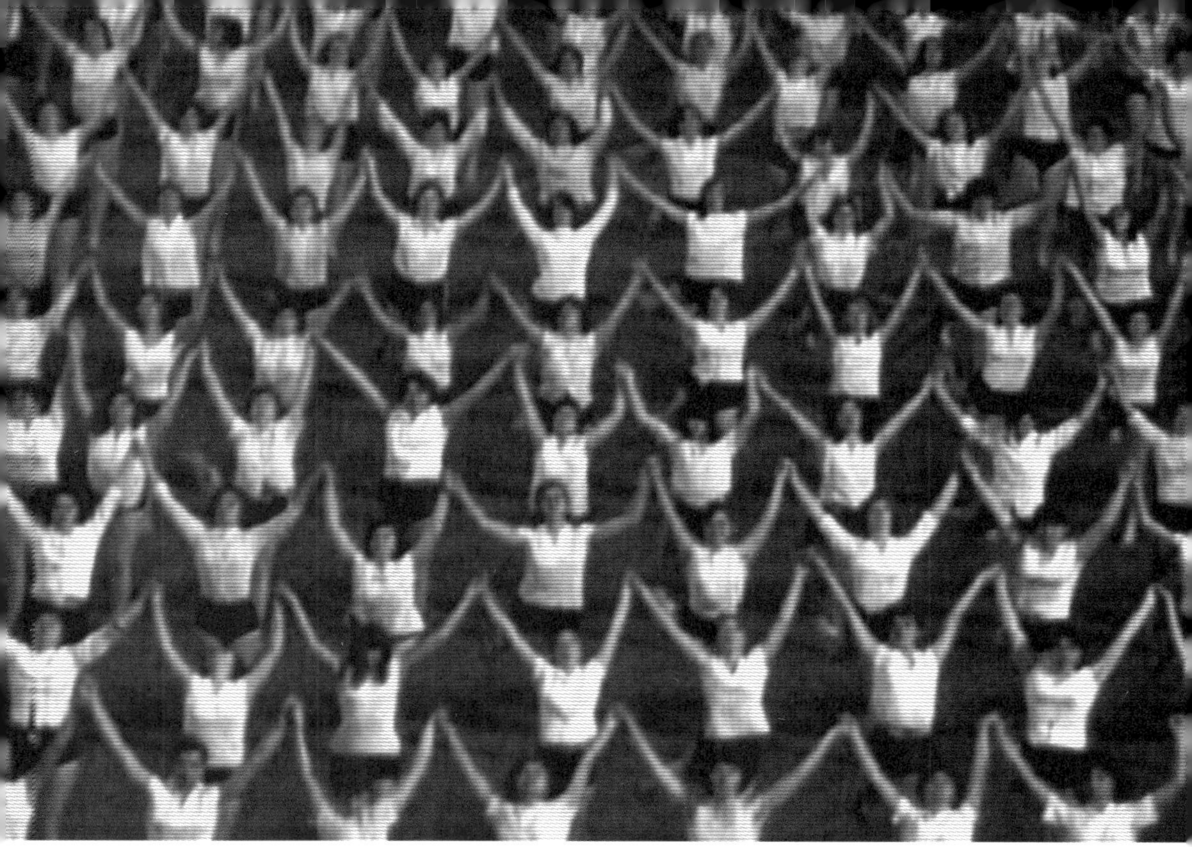

Part II   Ideology and Mass Performances

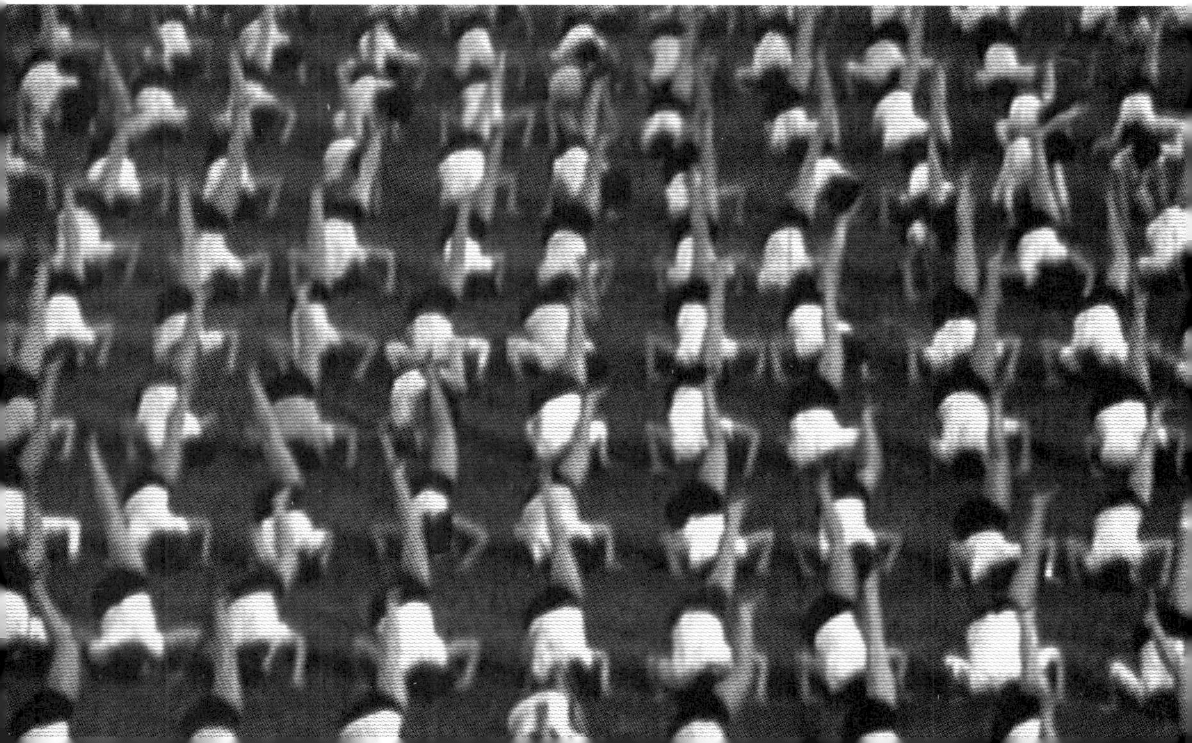

The conclusions of part one conveyed a broad, comprehensive view which holds that the public sphere as a political sphere can only be performed on the basis of (political) ideology. In chapter one we identified that one of the determinants of the crisis of the public sphere today is the ideological antagonism between collectivism and individualism. The two ideologies will be invoked, respectively, throughout part two, which focuses on massive and state public performances, and in part three, which critically examines performances, actions, and technologies of the self qua individual in everyday life and the performing arts. This chapter will elucidate our conception of ideology, which will be integrated into two models: social choreography and social drama.

Ideology in a conventional sense designates a set or system of ideas about how to configure society. Despite its broad and neutral thrust as a comprehensive worldview, or *Weltanschauung*, ideology is a rather unpopular term. It owes its renunciation in everyday speech to its pejorative connotation of totalitarianism, as associated with the twentieth century's extreme state ideologies of fascism and communism.[83] The political and, as we

83 | The negative connotation of ideology dates back to the Napoleonic era (specifically to 1796) when the word was coined by the French philosophers Destut de Tracy, Cabanis, and Constant to designate the study of ideas, their origins, and their laws. In accordance with the sensualist empiricism of Locke and Congillac, these philosophers claimed that all ideas derived from physical sense-

will argue here, ideological reasons for the commonsensical negative understanding of ideology are multifold. They can be critically traced back to the definitions of ideology in Marx and Engels as well as in Lenin. Marx's various writings on ideology are predicated on his materialist view of capitalist society as divided into a base and a superstructure and characterized by class antagonism and the division of labor. In Marx and Engels' classical work, *The German Ideology*, ideology belongs to the social superstructure: it is a production of ideas, of conceptions, of consciousness firmly tied to and conditioned by the modes of material production in a certain society, or by the base.[84] Since the superstructure holds a subordinate position as an expression or reflection of the distribution of forces among the classes and of real existing relations of production ruled by the bourgeoisie, ideology too cannot but be ruled by the bourgeoisie, thus presenting the thinking of the ruling class as the ruling thinking of an epoch. A famous paragraph from "Ruling Class and Ruling Ideas" explains it:

> The ruling ideas are nothing more than the ideal expression of the dominant material relationships, the dominant material relationships grasped as ideas; hence of the relationships which make the one class the ruling one, therefore, the ideas of its dominance. The individuals composing the ruling class possess among other things consciousness, and therefore think. Insofar, therefore, as they rule as a class and determine the extent and compass of an epoch, it is self-evident that they do this in its whole range, hence among other things rule also as thinkers, as producers of ideas, and regulate the production and distribution of the ideas of their age: thus their ideas are the ruling ideas of the epoch.[85]

Therefore, ideology in capitalist society functions as what Engels called the "false consciousness" of dominant social relations, which the ruling class imposes upon all social classes, thereby misleading them. Apart from Marx and Engels' own consideration of ideology as a negative term, the predominant pejorative connotation that ideology bears today could be connected with Lenin's usage of the notion as well, although he himself conceives it as a positive notion. As a revolutionary, Lenin referred to ideology in terms of political practice and proletarian struggle, trying to resolve the Marxist problem that the existence of revolutionary ideas presupposes the existence of a revolutionary class. Therefore, in *What Is to Be Done?* he promotes and encourages the possibility of the socialist ideology as opposite to that of the bourgeoisie, a possibility which can transform the proletarian class consciousness into the political class consciousness by means of "a comprehensive political exposure." For Lenin ideological work is of prime importance for social revolution, since the working masses can constitute a revolutionary class neither spontaneously nor only by political agitation on the level of the economic base. Ideology therefore acquires a positive connotation in his writing. In a word, ideology is for Lenin a tool for the revolutionization of the proletarian class, and it now has a negative connotation for this very reason.

perceptions. When Tracy and his companion *idéologues* refused to become servile members of the Napoleonic nobility, Napoleon began to use the word as a term of abuse. See Jack Hayward, *After the French Revolution: Six Critics of Democracy and Nationalism* (Hemel Hempstead, UK: Harvester Wheatsheaf, 1991) and Laurent Clauzade, *L'idéologie ou la révolution de l'analyse* (Paris: Gallimard, 1998).

84 | Karl Marx, Friedrich Engels, *The German Ideology* (Moscow: Progress Publishers, 1968).

85 | "Ruling Class and Ruling Ideas," in Karl Marx, Friedrich Engels, *The German Ideology*, http://www.marxists.org/archive/marx/works/download/Marx_The_German_Ideology.pdf.

The Marxist elaborations of ideology that were subsequently articulated by Marx and Engels and Lenin, and by many others, derive from their generally critical perspective on preexisting capitalist society. This perspective advocates a battleground of social classes where an end to antagonisms can be achieved only through the dictatorship of the proletariat, leading to a classless society where the ownership of the means of production is held in common. This thought has always annoyed capitalist society, whose ideology of (neo)liberalism and concomitant immanence of the principles of individualism and personal property rights is not seen as an ideology at all. In this way, capitalism manages to naturalize production and social relations as inherent to humans. What supposedly determines our times as "postideological" and "posthistorical" is, on the one hand, the global predominance of capitalist neoliberal democracy since the early 1990s, and, on the other, the pluralism on social microscales, never seen in terms of a fundamental social antagonism that encompasses both production and ideology as the ground of politics, legislation, education, culture, etc.[86] A tendency to evade the concept of ideology in critical theory in a wide sense can be identified in recent decades. Already in his conception of biopolitics, Foucault avoids the term in favor of micropower and a direct capture of bodies by disciplinary apparatuses and mechanisms of the society of control. Foucault's orientation toward micropolitics and biopolitics is furthered by the theorists of post-Operaia, who place the organization and management of the social, of the body, and of life itself above a political practice in an ideologically framed public sphere set by the ruling class.

But the commonsense opinion about the end of ideology has grown most prominently out of the neoliberal celebration of the end of the Cold War and the "victory of capitalism," where ideology is to be unmasked as false consciousness. The vision of the end of ideology in "posthistorical" time is rooted in Francis Fukuyama's influential article "The End of History" from 1989. Turning away from Marx's and toward Hegel's conception of history as progress, whose end no longer lies in communism's replacing capitalism, but in the establishment of a universal and homogeneous state based in democracy, he proclaims the following:

> What we may be witnessing is not just the end of the Cold War, or the passing of a particular period of postwar history, but the end of history as such: that is, the end point of mankind's ideological evolution and the universalization of Western liberal democracy as the final form of human government.[87]

86 | The pluralism that is defended by political theorists such as John Rawls and Isaiah Berlin is defined as a permanent feature of liberal, i.e. non-repressive, societies. For instance, in *Political Liberalism* Rawls argues that pluralism is "reasonable" and that philosophy can play a role in characterizing its public justification as well as the legitimate, democratic use of collective coercive power while accepting the same pluralism. See John Rawls, *Political Liberalism* (New York: Columbia University Press, 2005); Isaiah Berlin, "The Pursuit of the Ideal," in *The Crooked Timber of Humanity*, ed. H. Hardy (Princeton, NJ: Princeton University Press, 1998). Political pluralism should be distinguished from "methodological pluralism," which prevails in social sciences today. Methodological pluralism, as opposed to naturalism or methodological individualism, promotes the epistemological coexistence of discourses. However, rather than implying equivalence and the substitutability of views, opinions, and interests, or a value-free relativism, it implies social constructionism.

87 | Francis Fukuyama, "The End of History?," *The National Interest*, no. 16 (1989): 3–18, http://www.wesjones.com/eoh.htm. Later on, the following elaboration is added to the thesis: "That is, while earlier forms of government were characterized by grave defects and irrationalities that led to their eventual collapse, liberal democracy was arguably free from such fundamental internal contradictions." Francis Fukuyama, *The End of History and the Last Man* (New York: The Free Press, 1992), xi.

Having put forward this radical thesis right after the fall of the Berlin Wall, Fukuyama develops it further in *The End of History and the Last Man* (1992), emboldened to take a prophetic tone by the collapse of socialist regimes:

> What is emerging victorious, in other words, is not so much liberal practice, as the liberal idea. That is to say, for a very large part of the world, there is now no ideology with pretensions to universality that is in a position to challenge liberal democracy, and no universal principle of legitimacy other than the sovereignty of the people.[88]

We can observe here how ideology as a contextually constructed system of ideas accompanied by a historical-materialist perspective regarding their practice is dismissed and replaced by a universal idea based on a transcendent rationality. The universalist view on liberal democracy will prevail as reason based on common and good sense, equally driving both the transition processes undergone by former real-socialist societies and the expansion of the free-market economy on a global scale. From this viewpoint, all the difficulties and resistance that the implementation of neoliberal policies meets are regarded as signs of irrationality—that is, remnants of ideology—while being identified as totalitarian or just repressive in general. All means to eradicate these "ideological" obstacles are therefore appropriate and just: they are considered emancipatory tools for the rationalization of those who are themselves irrational enough to reject neoliberal capitalism.[89]

Today, it seems that it takes the occurrence of a financial crisis with "austerity measures" for the awareness of neoliberalism as ideology to arise. This recalls the stance of late Marxist ideological critique—made by Jameson, Žižek, Balibar, Laclau, Mouffe, and others who in recent decades didn't abandon the notion of ideology—according to which there is no privileged place for ideological critique. No place is exempt from ideology in order to critique ideology. Only ideology can fight ideology. When we say that only ideology can fight ideology, we don't claim that it is impossible to step out of ideology and proceed with an Althusserian debate on this question; rather, we want to emphasize that the public sphere is predicated on the ideology of the ruling class not only when it clearly appears in the form of totalitarian decrees from the state (as was the case in real-socialist societies), but also when it is vague, volatile, hegemonic, or universalized (as it is in neoliberal capitalist societies). That is exactly why we are focusing away from the "liberal idea," that is, from freedom as a universal and abstract idea which is opposed to totalitarianism, which is always identified as a socialist type of particularism, and toward the more material ideological categories of individualism and collectivism. In our view, individualism and collectivism, respectively, shaped the public spheres of capitalist and socialist societies into those societies' epistemic and aesthetic foundations, which were in turn conditioned by the specific production relations (already) found in each society. The antagonism between these two ideologies is emerging once again in currently widespread

---

88 | Fukuyama, *The End of History and the Last Man*, 45.
89 | Cementing the doxa about capitalism as both the only possible and the best system of production recalls Walter Benjamin's premonition from 1921 that the only religion will be capitalism, "a religious cult without dogma" where utilitarianism holds a special place. If capitalism has taken the vacant place of religion in Western secular societies, then the idea of freedom as free trade is its global currency, explaining why individualism, Protestant work ethics, and human rights aren't viewed as ideological matters.

anticapitalist protests—in the speech of protesters as well as in the way they compose their bodies within public space.[90]

In addition, the claim that only ideology can fight ideology allows us to reexamine the dubious conclusion about the end of ideology, beyond the rather obvious fact that it is an outcome of the recent global expansion and hegemony of one—neoliberal—ideology. Moving on to the domain of performance, we could say that what appears to be an end to ideology might be a mere shift in its performative, ritualistic mechanism. The naturalization and internalization of requests, expectations, models, and patterns of thinking, speaking, behaving, and acting have always been important mechanisms in the functioning of ideology. Hence we might want to exchange the Althusserian notion of "interpellation" (whereby individuals are turned into subjects by being hailed in to ideology) for "embodiment" (where ideology functions via the control and action of bodies). The shift could also be viewed as a renegotiation between the linguistic-semiotic and the corporeal-affective-experiential, which has begun to stand for the real. Ideology's change in ritualistic mechanism has shifted interpretive focus from speech act to bodily movement. This shift of focus might imply only a change of degree that manifests itself in the material form of the functioning of ideology within the same matrix of cynically enlightened consciousness that the late Marxists established. The function of the act of hailing the individual into ideology, making her a subject, the act which was supported with words, belief, or cynical knowledge, is now overtaken by procedures and compositional arrangements of an ambivalent nature: these mechanisms can both capture their subjects and enable them to act. Thus the total ideological discursive grip of early Marxism is now relaxed, therefore permitting physical and bodily failures, affective ruptures, gaps to be navigated, where diverse ideological interests can be negotiated.[91]

Our point is that the disruptions of ideology don't occur mainly inside the private sphere of the individual. In critical theories of the 1990s that focus on identity politics, the rupture, if ideological at all, is issued by and for the individual, whose subjectivation is a form of self-realization in the open field of particularized, yet-to-be-represented differences. The problem with the principle "the personal is political" is that in practice it is easily reverted to the abstract transcendental idea of individual freedom. In self-determination the self is more determinant than the vision of the society that the sum of the selves could make. For instance, the nongovernmental organization (NGO)—a mechanism by which identity politics and other particular interest groups advocating special missions have been most efficiently instituted in the public sphere, and whose funding is often private and non-

90 | On the other hand, the liberal idea already contested its own universality in the course of the transition processes undergone by real-socialist societies, wherein it functioned—sparked by the general and ideologically vague social appeals for liberalization made in the late 80s—as the herald of neoliberal capitalism, and therefore as a particular but hegemonic concept.

91 | See Judith Butler, Ernesto Laclau, and Slavoj Žižek, *Contingency, Hegemony, Universality: Contemporary Dialogues on the Left* (New York: Verso, 2000); Slavoj Žižek, *The Sublime Object of Ideology* (London: Verso, 1989); Claude Lefort, *Democracy and Political Theory* (Cambridge: Polity, 1991); Judith Butler, *Gender Trouble: Feminism and the Subversion of Identity* (London: Routledge, 1990); Butler, *Bodies That Matter: On the Discursive Limits of "Sex"* (London: Routledge, 1993); Butler, *Precarious Life: The Powers of Mourning and Violence* (London: Verso, 2004); Mladen Dolar, "Beyond Interpellation", *Qui Parle* 6, no. 2 (1993); Dolar, *A Voice and Nothing More* (Cambridge, MA: MIT Press, 2006); Chantal Mouffe, *On the political* (London: Routledge, 2005); Andrew Hewitt, *Social Choreography: Ideology as Performance in Dance and Everyday Movement* (Durham, NC: Duke University Press, 2005).

transparent vis-à-vis its activists—fragments the public sphere into multiple publics who struggle for influence in the arena of particular political, economic, and other interests. Our interest lies in probing how the public sphere is constituted by collectivist visions of social order without falling back into totalitarian ideology.[92]

Two approaches to the analysis of movement, speech, and the composition of bodies in time and space in the public sphere are explored here: social choreography and social drama. These two models are, as we will see, complementary and form one method. The main viewpoint on social structure and processes outlined by this method is predicated on the assumption that conflicts and antagonisms characterize contemporary neoliberal capitalist societies, the ideology of which is hegemonic while not exercising a total grip. In such societies, social choreography happens continuously, in art, in everyday life, in the economic relations of production as well as in social reproduction, thus conflating the two levels (the economic base and ideological superstructure) into the same aesthetic mode of operation. Social choreography shows how social order is aesthetically produced, instilled, and rehearsed. As a material practice of aesthetic ideology, social choreography isn't obvious at the time of its operation, but becomes visible within historical perspectives, like when its collapse gives way to social drama. Social drama happens exceptionally. The notion designates those intensive moments in the social process when one or more latent conflicts escalate to such an extent that they cannot be managed any longer, leading to a collapse in the social order. Liminal, public mass events in which social drama manifests itself mark those moments when the (economic, productive) base and (social, reproductive) superstructure no longer correspond with one another. Liminality appears as a short passage, a limited area of anti- and proto-structure where society critically reflects on what it is and was, though it is still not sure about what it might become.

The shift from ideology's hailing through the speech act (the famous formula of the structuralist Marxist philosopher Louis Althusser, "hey you!") to embodiment, where the materiality of actions is always already socially endorsed, prompted Andrew Hewitt, a literary scholar from the provenance of critical theory, to redefine ideology's mode of operation as "aesthetic" and to privilege "social choreography" as its prominent form. Although the term "social choreography" has entertained a variety of vague meanings in numerous research projects of dancers and dance scholars lately,[93] we will focus on the theoretical model proffered by Hewitt in his book *Social Choreography: Ideology as Performance in Dance and Everyday Movement* (2005).[94]

[93] | Recent projects that proclaim themselves as practices of social choreography today involve the mobilization of activists. Their point of departure is the "body-movement paradigm" of dance, referring to William Forsythe's movement language, which they seek to transform into the "social body." See Steve Valk's *Smallclub: Goldcoast* (2001) and the conference Framemakers: Choreography as an Aesthetics of Change (2005) in which, apart from Valk, Michael Kliën, declaring himself a proponent of social choreography, took part. Alan Shapiro, "Social Choreography: Steve Valk and the Situationists," *choreograph. net*, ed. Jeffrey Gormly, http://choreograph.net/articles/lead-article-social-choreography-steve-valk-and-the-situationists.

[94] | Andrew Hewitt, *Social Choreography: Ideology as Performance in Dance and Everyday Movement* (Durham, NC: Duke University Press, 2005).

Hewitt's approach sides against both the phenomenological, romanticizing conceptions of the body's experience of metaphysical transcendence and the culturalist, identitarian determinations of the body in performance and dance studies (through race, gender, sexuality). Since his analysis features literary texts and other kinds of discourses that observe movement and dance as a trope on a par with critical and poetical writings about early modern dance, Hewitt's book has been dismissed by dance scholarship on account of its lack of historical expertise.[95] A consideration of the significance that choreography might have outside the disciplinary history of dance is what interests us here: what makes choreography "social" and hence makes it offer a theoretical model for *seeing past* art and into the production of social and political realities? In contrast to his critics' claims, Hewitt's study is thoroughly historical, centered on the late bourgeois era (ca. 1850–1933) and the development of industrial capitalism and modernity in the sociopolitical and aesthetic sense—the same period in which Marx and Engels formulated their notion of ideology. Our first task will be to find out if and how social choreography might be appropriate as a theoretical framework for an analysis of political ideology in the public sphere today, in the era of neoliberalism. We will then examine the place it should take in relation to "social drama" within the method we propose for theorizing the public sphere.

THE ORIGINS OF THE IDEA OF "SOCIAL CHOREOGRAPHY"

Hewitt takes his first cue from a famous passage from a letter Friedrich Schiller wrote in 1793 to Christian Körner, which we will quote here at length:

> I can think of no more fitting image for the ideal of social conduct than an English dance, composed of many complicated figures and perfectly executed. A spectator in the gallery sees innumerable movements intersecting in the most chaotic fashion, changing direction swiftly and without rhyme or reason, yet never colliding. Everything is so ordered that the one has already yielded his place when the other arises; it is all so skillfully, and yet so artlessly, integrated into a form, that each seems only to be following his own inclination, yet without ever getting in the way of anybody else. It is the most perfectly appropriate symbol of the assertion of one's won freedom and regard for the freedom of others.[96]

The image invokes not only "a tradition of thinking about social order that derives its ideal from the aesthetic realm"[97]—the area in which Hewitt situates his study—but also the recurrent concerns in contemporary dance with performing a harmonious relationship between the individual and the collective. The aesthetic qua social ideal of the English ballroom for Schiller is a harmonious play of movements between dancers, which we are to see as a model of citizens's social intercourse. Hewitt reads Schiller's account as one of

---

95 | Mark Franko, "Social Choreography: Ideology as Performance in Dance and Everyday Movement," *Dance Research Journal* 38, no. 1–2 (2006): 188–93. Franko writes, "A critical theory of choreography unable to grasp dance in its historical density is equally unable to reveal choreography's ideological performativity in the social sphere, no matter how many theoretical positions it seeks to debunk along the way." (ibid., 192).
96 | Hewitt, 2.
97 | Ibid., 3.

the missions of the project of modernity, which he defines as "social choreography" that seeks to aesthetically instill a social order directly at the level of the body.

Siegfrid Kracauer's essay "The Mass Ornament" (1927) is a more direct precursor of this thesis of social choreography.[98] Kracauer, a cultural critic with close ties to the Frankfurt School, invents the aesthetic figure of "mass ornament" to describe the appearance of mass dancing in stadiums and the mechanized movement of revue routines, like Tiller Girls, as distractions from revolutionary political activity. Kracauer's interest in mass culture is in its tendency to demonstrate, more overtly than high art, its material conditioning by capitalism. What links the two distinct types of dancing, mass dancing in the stadium and the chorus line, is the rationalization of capitalist production, as Kracauer writes:

> Only as parts of a mass, not as individuals who believe themselves to be formed from within, do people become fractions of a figure. The ornament is an end in itself.[99]

Furthermore, he sees mass ornament as a form of irrational, fetishistic mythologization:

> It is the *rational and empty form* of the cult, devoid of any explicit meaning, that appears in the mass ornament. As such, it proves to be a relapse into mythology of an order so great that one can hardly imagine its being exceeded, a relapse which, in turn, again betrays the degree to which capitalist *Ratio* is closed off from reason.[100]

Mass ornament implies both the alienation of the individual and of the community:

> Physical training expropriates people's energy, while the production and mindless consumption of the ornamental patterns divert them from the imperative to change the reigning order. Reason can gain entrance only with difficulty when the masses it ought to pervade yield to sensations afforded by the godless mythological cult. The latter's social meaning is equivalent to that of the Roman *circus games*, which were sponsored by those in power.[101]

For a transmutation of social choreography into an aesthetic ideology, Hewitt takes his cue from Kracauer, who was the first to read the capitalist production process in the empty form of mass ornament, the famous hands in the factory that correspond to the legs in the chorus line. Hewitt's theory then takes Kracauer's lucid observations a step further by claiming that ideology—in the form of social choreography—operates aesthetically and performatively at the *base* of the relations of production. Thus Hewitt seeks to invert the classical Marxist model of base-superstructure according to which ideology belongs to the superstructure, as do religion, law, education, culture, etc. To do this, he aligns his notion of social choreography with Fredric Jameson's "political unconscious," the third important source of his theory, which we will consider in the next section. In conclusion to this section, we will briefly delineate Hewitt's theoretical project. "Ideology has a history that is not merely the history of its successive forms, but of its functions and functioning," he writes.[102] The distinctive mode of functioning that he posits here could be considered within Slavoj Žižek's scheme run through Marx's famous phrase designating ideology

---

98 | Siegfried Kracauer, "The Mass Ornament," in *The Mass Ornament* (Cambridge, MA: Harvard University Press, 1995).
99 | Kracauer, 76.
100 | Ibid., 83.
101 | Ibid., 85.
102 | Hewitt, 211.

as false consciousness: "They do not know it, but they are doing it." Žižek explains that ideology today might be difficult to pin down as an imposed and organized doctrine of the state, or of the ruling class, because of its diversity and vagueness and, we would add, in critique of liberalism, because of the illusion of rational parliamentary debate. It is equally elusive as a spontaneous belief of the people. What is left then, Žižek argues, is ideology's sheer material existence in ritual or practice. Or, as in the declination of the Marxist formula, we have moved from the false consciousness ("they do not know it, but they are doing it") to the cynical, enlightened consciousness in Sloterdijk's account ("they know very well what they are doing, yet they are doing it"). As a performance of an embodied ritual that generates its own ideological foundation, Hewitt's conception of ideology as performance in dance and everyday movement, or in a word, "social choreography," deserves a third, pragmatic twist in the formula we propose here: *because they are doing it, they believe it.* [103] The following section will elaborate the key arguments of Hewitt's theoretical method.

THE AESTHETIC CONTINUUM OF EVERYDAY MOVEMENT AND DANCE

The main claim of Hewitt's social choreography rests on the assumption that there exists an aesthetic continuum in bodily articulation that spans from everyday movement to dance. This continuous aesthetic spectrum is framed on the one end by the conscious or unconscious sensory experience of daily movements, gestures, postures, and relations between bodies in time and space, and on the other by "'the aesthetic' in the more limited sense as a socially endorsed framing of the sensual,"[104] which includes conventions of dance and social intercourse. The aesthetic continuum is best articulated in the following:

> If the body I dance with and the body I work and walk with are one and the same, I must, when dancing, necessarily entertain the suspicion that all of the body's movements are, to a greater or lesser extent, choreographed. This may sound like the thesis that dance reveals the ideological functions of the body as mere text. But an aesthetic continuum such as this is not a simple chain of cause and effect—rather, it runs both ways. Dance also serves to demonstrate how the "textual" acquires significance as social choreography only when embodied. This complicates the operation of any critique of ideology.[105]

103 | Our formula is derived from Žižek's twist on Marx in which he explains how instrumental reason operates in the current form of liberal capitalism. It cynically disguises itself as truth, the same as when a Western intervention in a Third World country is motivated and legitimated by human rights infringement. The intervention might improve the human rights record in that country, yet its real motivations are elsewhere, in economic interests, for example. Therefore the truth conceals the relation of domination which is established *ideologically.* A step further in this logic of instrumentality results in the automatism of procedures whose instrumentality is no longer questioned. Žižek takes Blaise Pascal to explain the mechanism of self-referential causality through which the procedure, supposed to be an effect of belief, becomes the cause of belief. Thus he suggests that Pascal's "Kneel down and you will believe!" should be read as "Kneel down and you will believe that you knelt down because you believed!" Slavoj Žižek, "The Spectre of Ideology," in *Mapping Ideology,* ed. Slavoj Žižek (London: Verso, 1995), 6.
104 | Hewitt, 79.
105 | Ibid., 17.

The body neither performs a prescripted social text, nor is it capable of pre-linguistic, pre-ideological expression.[106] Hewitt argues for a double perspective that conflates the textual and performative aspects of bodily expression. He describes his method:

> To examine choreography is necessarily to follow two trajectories: one tracing the ways in which everyday experience might be aestheticized (dance aestheticizes the most fundamental and defining motor attributes of the human animal); and another tracing the ways in which "the aesthetic" is, in fact, sectioned off and delineated as a distinct realm of experience. This is what I mean by the aesthetic continuum of social choreography.[107]

Although a reference to Jacques Rancière's philosophical theory of the "politics of aesthetics" is notably missing here, Hewitt's understanding of the aesthetic is close to it.[108] According to Rancière, the aesthetic sphere has no definite boundaries, as its regime is dual: the autonomy of art is its heteronomy as well. Reading Hewitt's assumption of the aesthetic continuum along with Rancière's "distribution of the sensible," which designates the configuration of actions, movements, gestures, bodies, roles, and patterns of perception by an order that Rancière calls "police," we could say that dance is social choreography in the aesthetic regime of art inasmuch as its movements belong to a separate sphere delineated as "art." And it is also social choreography inasmuch as its movements bear no specific difference to the movements of the other spheres.

Walking as a gesture is Hewitt's case in point here. Throughout the analysis of Honoré de Balzac's "Théorie du démarche," Henri Bergson's "On Laughter," and Delsarte's system of gestures and expressions, together with Giorgio Agamben's "Notes on Gesture" and earlier eighteenth century German literature on walking, Hewitt examines the changing status of social gestures in the history of the bourgeoisie. Walking as an activity was discussed and rehearsed in Germany from 1780 onward as an attempt by a new bourgeois class to develop its own lifestyle. All the topoi of romanticism run through this gesture: walking to escape from corrupt society, to return to nature, to commune with the people. As a social gesture, walking demonstrates bourgeois self-consciousness, as can be read in the statement of an enthusiastic German walker of the early nineteenth century: "I consider walking to be the most noble and independent thing about a man and believe that things would work better if people walked more."[109] Hewitt shows how the collapse of a system of social gestures in the late bourgeois era (from 1850 onward, symptomatically in Tourettism) led to a systematic interest in the legibility of gesture (as in Delsartism), which indicates social choreography as a hegemonic and therefore ideological, rather than coercive, form. If we examine the same gesture—walking—a century later on the other end of the aesthetic continuum, i.e. in pedestrian movement in American Post-Modern Dance, then illuminating its historicity as the political unconscious becomes interesting. Steve Paxton's *Satisfying Lover* (1967), a choreography for a large number of all kinds of

---

106 | As an advocate of the politics of affect who is otherwise sympathetic to Hewitt's experiential grounding of ideology, Derek P. McCormack criticizes Hewitt's "suspicion of any attempt to 'ground' identity and/or community in a pre-discursive or pre-ideological context," as "it becomes impossible for Hewitt to affirm any political sense or sensibility that might operate prior to ideology, however immanent." Derek P. McCormack, "Politics and Moving Bodies," in *Political Theory* 35, no. 6 (2007): 819.
107 | Hewitt, 19.
108 | Rancière Jacques, *The Politics of Aesthetics*, trans. Gabriel Rockhill (London: Verso, 2004).
109 | Hewitt, 81.

bodies crossing the stage in simple walking steps and halts, was supposed to warn against aesthetic excess and mark a zero-degree of dance: walking as all that it is, a simple step. The quotidian or pedestrian movement in daily gestures like walking was hailed in the 1960s[110] as an emancipation of "democracy's body" while coinciding with the marches of the civil rights movements.

SOCIAL CHOREOGRAPHY
AND THE POLITICAL
UNCONSCIOUS

Although he never properly explains the relation between his notion of social choreography and Jameson's "political unconscious," Hewitt draws on it as an important forerunner of his own theory.[111] Jameson's theory of the political unconscious is a revision of Althusser's model of base-superstructure in Marxism. It lays the ground for Hewitt's claim about ideology operating at the (economic) base. We will now unpack the relations between Althusser's, Jameson's, and Hewitt's models.

It is well known that Althusser transposed Marx's edifice model of social system, comprised of the base and the superstructure(s), into the model of a structure where the economic base—in Althusser, the "mode of production," which includes forces of production, labor process, technical development, and relations of production—would become a less determining instance. Consequently, the superstructures, comprising culture, ideology, philosophy, religion, the legal system, and the state, gain relative autonomy, i.e. become semi-independent of the base. The model is illustrated by the following diagram in Jameson[112]:

Superstructures	CULTURE IDEOLOGY (philosophy, religion, etc.) THE LEGAL SYSTEM POLITICAL SUPERSTRUCTURES AND THE STATE

Base or *Infrastructures*	THE ECONOMIC, OR MODE OF PRODUCTION	RELATIONS OF PRODUCTION (classes) FORCES OF PRODUCTION (technology, ecology, population)

Jameson shows that Althusser's structuralist reading of the law of base-superstructure introduces the concept of the mode of production in order to expand the base beyond the more narrowly economic and toward the synchronic system of social relations as a whole, i.e. structure. What makes the mode of production a structure is its function of

110 | Sally Banes, *Democracy's Body: Judson Dance Theater 1962–1964* (Durham, NC: Duke University Press, 1995).

111 | Hewitt writes, "Whereas the mimetic ideology approximates a traditional model of ideology as false consciousness, the performative would be something more like a political unconscious" (Hewitt, 21). We will return to this fragment later on.

112 | Fredric Jameson, *The Political Unconscious: Narrative as a Socially Symbolic Act* (London: Routledge, 1981), 17.

an "absent cause," "not a part of the whole or one of the levels, but rather the entire system of relationships among those levels."[113] In his poststructuralist reconfiguration of Althusser's model, Jameson takes history to be the absent cause in lieu of structure:

> We would therefore propose the following revised formulation: that history is not a text, not a narrative, master or otherwise, but that, as an absent cause, it is inaccessible to us except in textual form, and that our approach to it and to the Real itself necessarily passes through its prior textualization, its narrativization in the political unconscious.[114]

The political unconscious in Jameson is the contradiction which is compensated, displaced, or repressed in a text, or the object of critical analysis, because the text doesn't manage to resolve it.[115] This is why Jameson proposes the historical contextual analysis where history is treated as the absent cause that needs to be produced into a narrative so that it can explain the relationships from which the political unconscious arises. The short version of the method is in his famous motto: "Always historicize!"

In addition, Jameson claims that the hierarchical two-level model that Althusser retains from Marx (albeit by weakening its economic determinism) should be spread out into a horizontal structure of mutual relationships in which the economic and technological mode of production is immediately related to culture, ideology, the juridical, the political, etc., as in the following diagram in Jameson[116]:

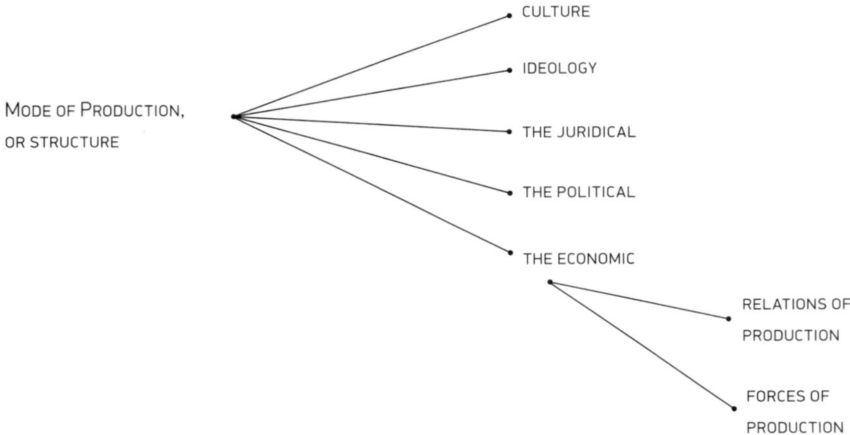

Jameson's web of mutual relationships, where no one thread is privileged as an ultimate cause, is Hewitt's point of departure. Hewitt claims that what makes an ideology aesthetic is that the aesthetic operates at the level of the base. Ideology doesn't serve only to reproduce social relations of production, or to reflect or represent the social order, it directly participates in its production. Thus Hewitt elaborates on Jameson's method by claiming that the mode of production itself is aesthetic. "Choreography is a medium for rehearsing social order. This means that the social order is both reflected in and shaped

---

113 | Ibid., 21.
114 | Ibid., 20.
115 | Jameson's primary interest is in literature, but the method of critical analysis of the political unconscious isn't confined to literary texts alone.
116 | Ibid., 21.

by aesthetic concerns."[117] Hewitt's model of reversible relations between production and reproduction of the social and aesthetic orders is represented in the following diagram:

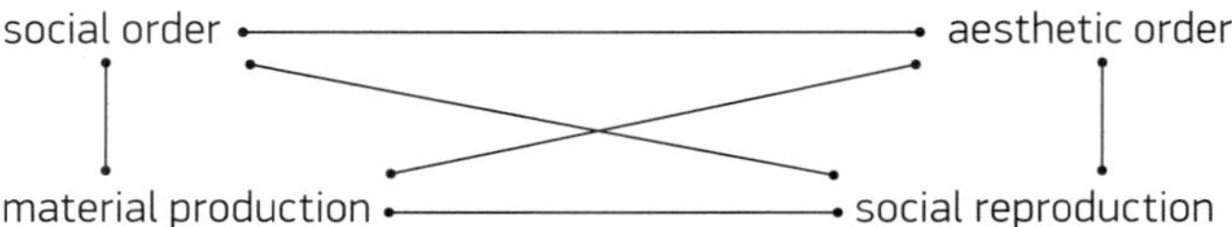

The two cases we will present next expound the model above by illuminating how ideas of labor and play were negotiated, displaced, masked, or repressed in various kinds of discourses and practices that invoked the aesthetic ideal of dance. The first concerns a cluster of texts from early anthropology and sociology of labor wherein dance came to signify a new automatic, antivoluntaristic, non-alienating, and yet pleasurable model of human labor power, a model based on a parallel drawn between physiology and mechanism:

> Dance served to explicate the notion of natural labor that might harness and regenerate labor power through energy and enthusiasm that went into the playful performance of dance rather than simply use it up. Dance in the "primitives" demonstrated in vitalistic fashion the existence of a human instinct toward activity; not a form of work, but an activity to which man in the state of nature dedicates himself with great gusto and diligence (...) dance [was regarded] as a spontaneous activity that produced a greater social energy than it consumed: it was potentially self-regenerative.[118]

To deploy Jameson's method of historicizing the political unconscious would mean to detect how anthropological and sociological discourses in the nineteenth century echoed vitalism or *Lebensphilosophie*, which placed physical immanence as central, celebrated energy in motion, and subsumed the subject not by her ideal humanity but by the vital, muscular energies and "vibrations" that pass through her body.[119] In the same period of early modernity, modern dance was born in denying work, suppressing its material conditions in play—as in the dances of Isadora Duncan, or Laban's experiments at Monte Verità. However, in the writings of the English sociologist Herbert Spencer, the proponent of social Darwinism, dance could provide the image of undifferentiated labor where, according to Arendt's definition, "labor is the activity which corresponds to the biological process of the human body"[120]:

> Labor is "unalienated" because the performance of labor does not yet demand a self-conscious human subject: but, by the same token, it is animalistic because the absence of an object

---

117 | Hewitt, 12.

118 | Ibid., 40, 43. The texts include Herbert Spencer, "Professional Institutions: III. Dancer and Musician," *Contemporary Review* 68 (1895): 114–26; M. G. Ferrero, "Les formes primitives du travail," *Revue scientifique* series 4, 5, no. 11 (1896): 331–4; Karl Bücher, *Arbeit und Rhythmus* (Leipzig: Raubner, 1902); Charles Féré, *Travail et Plaisir* (Paris: Félix Alcan, 1904); Anson Rabinbach, *The Human Motor: Energy, Fatigue, and the Origins of Modernity* (Berkeley, CA: University of California Press, 1992); and, most notably, Rudolf Laban and F. C. Lawrence, *Effort: Economy in Body Movement* (London: Macdonald and Evands, 1947).

119 | We refer here to the work of Hans A. E. Driesch, German biologist, a proponent of a neo-vitalist *Lebensphilosophie* in the end of the nineteenth century. Dreisch, *The Science & Philosophy of the Organism*, 2 vols. (Aberdeen: University of Aberdeen, 1908).

120 | Hannah Arendt, *The Human Condition*. (Chicago: University of Chicago Press, 1958), 7.

> denies man the possibility of becoming a subject in contradistinction to that object. By putting the entire body in motion, dance figures a movement beyond the manufactural and opens up the possibility of a totalizing—if not, indeed, totalitarian—model of social order.[121]

So, the political unconscious of both modern dance and its instrumentalization in the theories of labor (Laban's fascination with Taylorism is well-documented in his book, co-authored with Lawrence, *Effort: Economy in Body Movement*, 1947) lies in the affect of enthusiasm. The enthusiasm of a dancing body isn't just a universal form of magic, or a kinaesthesia where bodies talk to bodies. It is a social and political affect that still defines "the human condition" of labor in the various linkages made between dance and the contemporary form of capitalism.[122] The affect relies on the possibility of a physiological sublime as a mode of the self-perpetuating social choreography. Today, numerous body systems and practices, often close to techniques of contemporary dance, attest to the self-perpetuating social choreography as a technology of the self. They are still grounded on the truism of modern dance in Martha Graham's dictum that "the body doesn't lie." Vitalism is the ideology that still produces and reproduces capitalist production processes today. It doesn't take a wild act of the imagination to visualize millions of bodies working out right now in gyms or thousands of bodies de-stressing, or bodies stretching in yoga positions. All those apparatuses of vitalist desubjectivation feed into the industry of New Age products and services today.

The second demonstration of aesthetic ideology in Hewitt's study—where material production and ideological reproduction meet in a choreography—is the *Girlkultur*, a specimen of what Adorno and Horkheimer dubbed "cultural industry," of the "revue" type of entertainment in the Weimar period. Rapid, belated modernization in Germany absorbed the new American phenomenon of physical culture and then transformed it into the eugenic physical regeneration and drilling of the German race in the 1930s. The "girls" from the 1920s performed the "Taylorized" body of the American production line, which Kracauer identified in the famous chorus line of the Tiller Girls. Hewitt's contribution to this analysis lies in his underlining the transmutation of sexual play into work, which is covered up by purposes of entertainment. The mechanical movement of the same body part in a line, mostly a row of legs, is a dance to the rhythm of Fordist production. The overt sexual exposure of female body parts has a desexualizing effect here, marking a shift away from the figure of the woman, who reveals the hidden truth to the girl, who displays the sheer functioning of a mechanized ballet. In Hewitt's words, the girls "are not creatures, they are creators, emblems of the very principle of capitalist mass production." He elaborates their function in the following:

121 | Hewitt, 63.

122 | The post-Operaist sociologist Maurizio Lazzarato criticizes the current trend of instrumentalizing artistic activity as a model of neoliberal policies in sociology in Luc Boltanski and Eva Chiapiello, *Le nouvel esprit du Capitalisme* (Paris: Gallimard, 1999); Pierre-Michel Menger, *Portrait d'artiste en travailleur: Métamorphoses du capitalisme* (Paris: La République des Idées / Seuil, 2003); and Menger, *Les intermittents du spectacle: Sociologie d'une exception* (Paris: EHESS, 2005). He points out that many commentaries on artistic freelance labor or the system of "intermittent" labor fail to recognize its different and critical status from other forms of employment or independent self-employment, because they attempt to correct it as an "exception" or "anomaly" according to the so-called "normal" or "ordinary" forms of employment and unemployment in the free market of labor. Maurizio Lazzarato, "The Misfortunes of the "Artistic Critique" and of Cultural Employment," in "creativity hypes," special issue of the online journal *transversal* (February 2007), http://eipcp.net/transversal/0207/lazzarato/en.

> Just what do they create? As synchronized performers—whose rigor seemed to stand in opposition to an increasing and disturbing cultural syncopation—they are not individual objects of feminine display in the traditional sense. And yet there is no actual object or work to which we can point as the result of their cultural *Leistung* [achievement]. They are a puzzle: they produce, yet they produce no thing. They are not "femininely" self-centered and self-centering because their entire performance relies on a synchronization with others. Fulfillment (sexual and aesthetic) is deferred along the endless line of identical legs.[123]

In the chorus line that signifies the performance of production, Hewitt reads a shift in the function of ideology wherein the place of truth changes from truth with a referent, as something to be revealed, to truth as something dynamic, something to be performatively produced. The very fact of production, its automatic unstoppable nature, becomes the truth. When ideology loses its promise that it will unveil something unknown, something we have hitherto been unconscious of, we enter the realm of cynicism. Contrary to Sloterdijk and Žižek, Hewitt argues that this already happens in the early period of industrial capitalism and mass culture, in the marked shift from the principle of revelation to sheer functioning:

> In this new configuration, ideology is no longer a system of belief that holds at its core a (sexual) truth that can be laid bare. It has become a *function*, a system of deferral that keeps *disbelief* in motion. The shift from woman to girl . . . is a shift from ideology as a system of belief to ideology as a self-sustaining and self-legitimating social function, a shift from the promise of revelation to the reality of mere motion or function.[124]

The conclusion of this analysis has purchase on Hewitt's claim that social choreography is a *performative* rather than a *mimetic* mode of ideology. We will now examine it critically.

PERFORMATIVE VS. MIMETIC MODE OF AESTHETIC IDEOLOGY

While every social order in history has yielded its aesthetic representation, the most notable example being the invention of *ballet de cour* by, with, and for Louis XIV, most of these representations were constructed on the basis of the inclusion and exclusion of power. What distinguishes social choreography in the late bourgeois era, and what Schiller already anticipates in his letter from 1793, is a fantasy of totality: a possibility of an integrative or participatory ideological performance. Therefore Hewitt insists on coining social choreography as the "performative" or "integrative" aesthetic ideology, "one in which art does not simply misrepresent, in a palliative manner, an existing social order. Instead, the aesthetic now becomes the realm in which new social orders are produced (rather than represented) and in which the integration of all social members is possible."[125] The juxtaposition between the performative and the mimetic is necessary for Hewitt to renew the notion of ideology beyond the classical, pejorative sense of "false consciousness" and introduce the aesthetic component at the very base of material production. But how plausible is this?

123 | Hewitt, 190.
124 | Ibid., 191.
125 | Ibid., 21.

What Hewitt understands by the mimetic mode of ideology is a utopian projection of a social order that blinds its spectators by distorting the social realities they live. This is necessarily an ideology in a negative sense, for it "distracts us from the political praxis necessary to bring that utopian condition about in reality."[126] There are two problems with this thesis. First, mimesis can't be reduced to emulation, an improved copy that misrepresents life, since the meanings and modalities of mimesis are broader.[127] Second, the mimetic mode, as Hewitt fashions it, doesn't have to exclude performativity in the sense he deploys here—as production or rehearsal in which onlookers participate. Hewitt's main wager in substituting performative for representational ideology is that it allows for introducing, producing a new social order rather than reproducing or reflecting an existing one. His choice of choreography as opposed to, for instance, narrative, as in Jameson's case, resonates with the performative attribute. For Hewitt, choreography doesn't simply inscribe itself in time and space but rather transforms both time and space and brings into existence a "world," materializing it in a nontranscendent sense. If choreography can act as a blueprint of a new society, a vehicle for instilling and rehearsing a new social order, then the rich modernist tradition of mass dancing in Europe from the 1910s to the 1930s should be included therein. It is significantly missing from Hewitt's account of this period because, presumably, it belongs to mimetic ideology. Before we elaborate a counterexample, let's now consider what the method of social choreography, according to Hewitt, enables.

IS SOCIAL CHOREOGRAPHY A CRITICAL METHOD?

A brief answer would be, in most cases, no. This can be explained by using the Jamesonian method to historically "narrativize" the function that social choreography was born with in the late bourgeois era. In Hewitt's study, social choreography figures as a form of cultural hegemony particular to a rising bourgeoisie who foregrounded the aesthetic realm by way of the autonomy of art as a form of political liberty from the authority of the monarchy in the eighteenth century. Thus, art offered a place around 1800 in which one could reason freely, because the consensus was that art had no social consequence, as Hewitt infers here:

> The emerging class utilized this freedom to rehearse ideas that would only subsequently be set free into a truly political bourgeois public realm. The (aesthetic) form of expression allowed to the politically emergent bourgeois class cannot have been without effect on the content of the ideas that were developed under its protection. Thus, aesthetic concerns entered from the very beginning into bourgeois political calculations.[128]

What Hewitt's theory doesn't account for is the moment when the function of projecting, proposing, and exercising a new social order turns into a prescription of norms. These norms, codes, or conventions needn't be imposed from above mimetically, as Hewitt would have it, miming an ideal utopia in a totalitarian manner. They may also be inherently, immanently performed, internalized in a control regime in which the political unconscious

---

126 | Ibid.
127 | Cf. Philippe Lacoue-Labarthe and Peter Hallward, "Stagings of Mimesis: An interview," *Angelaki* 8, no. 2 (2003): 55–72.
128 | Hewitt, 16.

resides. As a social choreography, Delsartism was normative because it prescribed a taxonomy of behavioral gestures and signs that would regulate social self-presentation. Its political unconscious lay in the imperative of legibility of gestural signs, indicating a fear of the loss of the authentic style of a class.[129]

Social choreography is, on the one hand, an artifact with a distinctive form and a material practice, as we saw in *Girlkultur* or Delsartism, and on the other, an interpretive model whereby dance appears as the trope of the ideas of harmonious play or social labor, as in Schiller or early anthropology and sociology's interest in labor, dance, and "primitives." But as a model of interpreting ideology through the lens of movement, bodily expressions, and relations, can social choreography serve as a critique of ideology? Hewitt offers an explicit answer to this question:

> The predominance of performative, ritual, and choreographic modes of social cohesion in a given society does not necessarily lead to the emergence of a critical vocabulary for articulating or critiquing that society's choreography . . . Quite the contrary; it is only when a certain choreography breaks down, in periods of transition, that the operation of choreographic norms and conventions becomes explicit and a critique of social choreography becomes retroactively possible.[130]

Only when we are witness to a rupture—an aesthetic lapse, a slippage, or, as Hewitt remarks in reference to walking, a "stumbling"—of social choreography, whose mechanism otherwise functions seamlessly, and perhaps even invisibly, might we become aware of it as a normative, ideological regime. Thus, Hewitt assigns to social choreography the critical method only by exception, which aligns him with other thinkers like Jacques Rancière, Gilles Deleuze, or Bruno Latour, who conceive of politics, after the compelling concept of Carl Schmitt (1932),[131] as a matter of exception, or event.[132] We will first test the hypothesis about the exceptional breakdown of choreography with the case of mass dancing, which as a genre is altogether excluded from Hewitt's inquiry. Our second test case will focus on its opposite, normative function in a contemporary form of social choreography, which we will refer to here as "proceduralism."

129 | Delsartism was hugely popular in the US, where a manual like Anna Morgan's *An Hour with Delsarte* studied the attitudes of the head and those of all parts of the body, especially the various expressions of the eye, nose, and mouth, advising that they be carefully practiced before a mirror. "Most people consult their mirrors for the single purpose of seeing their attractiveness; we should study them for the purpose of seeing ourselves as others see us," Morgan advises. Anna Morgan, *An Hour with Delsarte: A Study of Expression* (Boston: Lee and Shepard, 1889), 11.

130 | Hewitt, 179.

131 | Carl Schmitt, *The Concept of the Political* (Chicago: University of Chicago Press, 1996) and *Political Theology: Four Chapters on the Concept of Sovereignty* (Chicago: University of Chicago Press, 2005).

132 | Peter Hallward, "The Politics of Prescription," *The South Atlantic Quarterly* 104, no. 4 (2005): 769–89.

MASS DANCING AND THE POLITICAL (UN)CONSCIOUS

The cases of mass dancing we will examine now—*Vom Tauwind und der Neuen Freude* as the last "choric consecration play," directed by Rudolf Laban (1936); and the second to last *Slet* from the SFRY, in Tito's postwar Yugoslavia (1987)—belong to genres that are often subsumed under the same aesthetic figures of totality.[133] In our view, the conflation of Nazi spectacles and communist parades into the same political ideology of totalitarianism points to an inaccurate, ahistorical perspective, which can be corrected by examining how the two ideologies—Nazism and communism—differ in their social choreographies. To do that, we will draw a parallel genealogy of mass dancing in the two cases.

The history of Laban's movement choirs (*Bewegungschöre*) is well-known: its formative period is during WWI, when Laban, together with many other artists, took refuge in the artistic commune near Ascona on Lago Maggiore in Monte Verità.[134] There he developed a form of community dance where he experimented with movement and with dancers and other artists often dancing nude in nature. The movement choirs, the famous example being the open air choral play *Sun Festival* (*Sonnenfest*, 1917), epitomize the aestheticization of life after a call for a restoration of the lost *Festkultur* of Ancient Greece.[135]

However, when Laban's disciples—Jenny Geertz, Otto Zimmermann, and Martin Gleisner—adopted the form of the movement choir to promote proletarian culture in the 1920s throughout Germany, Belgium, and the Netherlands, Laban reacted against its politicization, calling on the ideals of the transcendental, universal nature of movement, a kind of mystical premodern union with nature that withdraws from the city. These very arguments by which Laban refused the political instrumentalization of *Bewegungschöre* will allow him, paradoxically, to direct mass choreographies in Nazi spectacles but also to be ousted from his collaboration with the Nazis abruptly in 1936. His last major choric work, involving a thousand lay dancers from thirty German cities, was commissioned by Joseph Goebbels for the opening of the Olympic Games.

At the beginning of the performance, a quote from Nietzsche's *Also Sprach Zarathustra* was recited:

133 | Cf. Jeffrey T. Schnapp, "Fascist Mass Spectacle," *Representations* 43, no. 1 (1993): 89–125; and Henning Eichberg and Robert A. Jones, "The Nazi Thingspiel: Theater for the Masses in Fascism and Proletarian Culture," *New German Critique*, no. 11 (1977): 133–50.

134 | For an excellent detailed study of the complex relations between mass dancing, the culture of nudity (*Nacktkultur* and *Freikörperkultur*), early German expressionist dance (*Ausdruckstanz*), and fascism, see Karl Toepfer, *Empire of Ecstasy: Nudity and Movement in German Body Culture, 1910–1935* (Berkeley, CA: University of California Press, 1997), especially the chapter "Mass Dancing: Significant Theorists of Mass Movement; Totenmal; The Dance Congresses; Nazi Concepts of Mass Movement," http://publishing.cdlib.org/ucpressebooks/view?docId=ft167nb0sp&chunk.id=d0e7144&toc.depth=100&toc.id=d0e7144&brand=eschol.

135 | For a relevant discussion on the conversion of experimental movement choirs into Nazi mass dances, see Carole Kew, "From Weimar Movement Choir to Nazi Community Dance: The Rise and Fall of Rudolf Laban's 'Festkultur,'" *Dance Research* 17, no. 2 (1999): 73–96.

> If we can learn to have more pleasure, then we will unlearn best how to do others harm and to imagine how to strive. It is not where you come from that gives you honour but: where you are going with your will and your feet, which want to rise above you. And so I want man and woman: one fit for war and the other fit for birth, but both fit for dance in their head and legs! Lost is every day on which we have not danced. And every truth is false which does not include laughter![136]

Although it features the image of a man-warrior and a woman-mother who, Zarathustra recommends, are both better off dancing, the text was received as ambiguous. Goebbels wrote in his diary about why he banned it: "Dance rehearsal: freely based on Nietzsche, a bad, contrived and affected piece. I forbid much of it. It is all so intellectual. I do not like that. It goes around dressed in our clothes and has nothing whatever to do with us."[137] Instead of politically invested symbols and a clear object of worship (the Führer), the work promoted a mystical humanity through the dancer's attitude of being turned inward, after which Goebbels banned the usage of the words "cult" and "mystical." In a word, Laban's consecration play, with its best intentions to celebrate the occasion, was too "open" to qualify for the political ideology of Nazism in that phase. After 1937, all mass parades using mass dancing were banned, and marching as well as propaganda through radio and TV took their place.

Why exactly was Laban's last choric play censored as unsuitable and withdrawn from the program when until then it had served the purposes of Nazi propaganda so well? The answer lies in the gap between aesthetic and political ideologies, where Laban's political unconscious no longer fit the official line of Nazi movement. In the early stage of building National Socialism in Germany, Laban's movement choirs served an ideological purpose through their communitarian spirit. They performed an immanent desubjectivation of the individual toward a transcendent, suprapersonal level. The moment National Socialism became the official state ideology (after 1933), a political consciousness was required where the individuals submit to the transcendent sovereign power of the Führer and march in a Nazi *Gemeinschaftstanz*. In that moment, Laban's social choreography wasn't politically conscious enough to enact this political order, and thus it collapsed ideologically. Laban's indignation at Goebbels' censorship attests to his unawareness of the political unconscious that his choreographies had hitherto possessed.

The genealogy of mass dancing in communist parades has a reverse point of departure than Laban's, a kind of political consciousness. In the period immediately after the October Revolution, the Proletkult movement in Russia organized mass spectacles where lessons of the revolution were rehearsed.[138] In these spectacles, the events from not only the October Revolution but also the French Revolution and the Paris Commune were reenacted at authentic historic sites, mingling amateurs and professional performers, respectively, in the roles of the good and the bad actors of the historical stage while tens of thousands of spectators gathered and often interfered to prevent the negative historical characters from acting against the revolution. Alongside this tradition, we can

---

136 | Quoted in Kew, p. 80. *Wir Tanzen* (Berlin: Reichsbund fur Gemeinschaftstanz in der Reichstheater-kammer, 1936), no page indicated.

137 | Ibid., 81.

138 | For an outstanding analysis of three key mass spectacles after the October Revolution, see *The Mystery of Freed Labor, In Favor of A World Commune*, and the famous *The Storming of the Winter Palace*, all realized between May 1 and November 7, 1920, with 200 to 3000 performers. See also František Deák, "Russian Mass Spectacles," in "Political Theatre Issue," special issue, *The Drama Review* 19, no. 2 (1975): 7–22.

find counterparts to mass dancing in German *Freikörperkultur* and *Festkultur*, in the USSR (*fizkultura*), and in Czechoslovakia (*Sokoli*, the falcons), whereby the New Soviet Man was celebrated or panslavic nationalism was built.[139] Although these dances rivaled the Nazi *Gemeinschaftstanz* in terms of massiveness, they didn't manifest a martial character or war motives (e.g. the mourning of the dead soldier) as did their German counterparts. On the contrary, they celebrated the unity of youth as the best representative of the nation in an aestheticized life geard to the future.

In the second, socialist era of Yugoslavia, formed under Tito's leadership after WWII, the same mass celebrations were practiced on several occasions (May Day, the Five-Year Plan, etc.), and a peculiar place is occupied by *Slet*, the youth parade in honor of Tito's birthday, held every twenty-fifth of May. *Slet* consisted of carrying the relay baton of youth (*štafeta mladosti*) from the extreme north-western point to the south-eastern point of the country, where youths from six republics and two provinces exchanged it. On May 25, thousands of youths, pioneers (elementary school pupils), and students of the military army performed mass choreographies in the largest stadium in the capital, Belgrade, (*Stadion JNA*, or the Stadium of the Yugoslav National Army). The spectacle displayed the roles of workers, youth, children, sportsmen, and soldiers in mass ornaments such as the flag, the five-pointed star, crops as the emblem of peasants, the factory as the emblem of workers, and so on. A special act in the dramaturgy of the event was the climactic moment when an elected youth, typically an excellent student, hands over the relay baton to Tito, wishing him a happy birthday. The mission of *Slet* is best summarized in Tito's oft-quoted speech:

> What we want of our younger generation is to be physically and mentally able and strong and versatile—developed—all round. You do know why this is important—we are building socialism. And socialism is not static, but something that needs to be constantly developed. It is up to you, the youth, to carry out that development forward into the future. And we, the older generation, are going to be happy to watch you walk the paths that we started and which we walked.[140]

The social choreography of *Slet* staged a triangular bond between the people performing and watching the performance, the revolution as the object of the mass movement, and the leader whose honor was a moral and political pledge of revolutionary zeal.[141] The political consciousness of *Slet* consisted in voluntary subjectivation, where representing the ideals of revolution was a method of building and preserving state ideology. The ideology of the state didn't only involve socialism, but also "brotherhood and unity" (*bratstvo i jedinstvo*) among the ethnically varying peoples and minorities that constituted Yugoslavia.

In 1987, seven years after his death, *Slet* was still performed in hommage to Tito, whose place was thereafter taken by the political delegates of six republics. The then-president of the Young Communist League of Yugoslavia (in Serbo-Croatian, *SKOJ*, *Savez komunističke omladine Jugoslavije*), Hašim Redžepi, received the baton instead of Tito.[142] The second

139 | Cf. Frances A. Hellebrandt and Jiří Kral, "Scientific Work of the Tenth Sokol Festival," *Science*, n.s., 89, no. 2314 (1939): 413–15.
140 | "Tito o fizičkoj kulturi i sportu," *Glas Istre* Pts. 1, 3 & 4, May 4–6, 1978.
141 | This interpretation originates from a conversation with Marta Popivoda as part of her research for the documentary archive film *Yugoslavia: How Ideas Moved Our Collective Body*.
142 | Excerpts from the broadcast of *Slet* 1987 on Radio-Television Belgrade are featured in Popivoda's film.

to last celebration began to hint at a breakdown. The recording of the broadcast event on Radio-Television Belgrade shows signs and warnings of the upcoming collapse of Yugoslavia, but these signs are displayed choreographically: an eclectic mix of folk dances and generic dances to Yugoslav pop and rock music, confusion among dancers about the ornament they are supposed to make, sloppy dance routines, and close-ups on an overall sense of inertia, arbitrariness, and lazy indifference felt among thousands of bodies. The real symptom of the ideological deregulation is evidenced by a scene which deviates the farthest from the mission of *Slet*, a kind of "theater in theater" where, as the commentator explains, two hundred and fifty particular characters from European history (members of all classes, "from beggars to aristocrats") are represented in their representative fictive dances. Medieval knights and their ladies, noble gentlemen and butlers, etc., form a fragmented multitude which has nothing to do with the history of the SFRY, its state symbols, or socialism. The words of the song, sung by the Yugoslav pop star Đorđe Balašević—"This old orchestra that always plays the same tune / never changes / is always the first on the song list"—allude to those discontent with the one-party political system. The scene shows how *Slet* tries to preserve its choreographic form despite its aesthetic lapses while it is emptied of the ideology that had animated it in the first place. The discrepancy between the choreographic and the ideological is confirmed in the textual messages projected on a screen on the stadium and remarked on by the TV commentators, who wonder, for example, why one dance splits into eight different folk dances:

> It seems like we are not as united as we should be . . . This is a warning about the current political situation, albeit in a playful, dancy message . . . All this is to remind us that we live in the same backyard, which will become terribly small if we parcel it out with gates or wires . . . The message on the display says: "Every nationalism is equally dangereous, even ours."

The *Slet* from 1987 not only evinces signs of the collapse of the state ideology of brotherhood and unity that inspirited the mass dancing of youth in socialist Yugoslavia; it also shows how its logic of political consciousness allows it to narrate, in the form of aphoristic allusions, a message of warning about the political disunity in a seemingly ideological *unisono* of mass dancing.

Three conclusions for our method can be drawn from these two cases of social choreography in collapse. First, social choreography can't be determined as exclusively performative, as devoid of any register of representation or even mimesis. Second, it rarely operates without a textual support, which often yields a more complex relationship between the political unconscious, or that which manifests itself as an ideological or political contradiction; and the political consciousness, which links ideology with a political program. Third, besides its function in the rise of the cultural hegemony of the bourgeoisie in Western culture, choreography has been used as an instrument of state ideology in socialism, where it does precisely what Hewitt ascribes to it: it rehearses a social order, but in a representational and politically conscious manner. The contradiction within such a configuration of the aesthetical, ideological, and political arises in the disjunction of the three, to which the above two cases testify.

Returning to the question of social choreography as a critical method, perhaps we can now give a more well-rounded and conclusive answer. Social choreography can account, at best, for how a social order is introduced, rehearsed, perpetuated, or shaken in the aesthetic realm, where movements of and relations between bodies enrich our sense of ideology's operation. In order to examine how one social order collapses and gives way to another and how the transition between them can develop, we need to complement our analysis of the method of social choreography with the model "social drama," which is the subject of the next chapter.

PROCEDURALISM: FROM PERFORMANCE TO CHOREOGRAPHY

All cases considered above are historical, which makes them suitable for elaborating social choreography as a method in its own right. The next challenge is to investigate contemporary practices of social choreography, which could possibly help us learn about ideology today. Here is a somewhat bold claim that we will test in this section: is "proceduralism" the form of social choreography that instills liberal democracy as the ruling ideology today?

Let's begin by reading a peculiar document: *Choreography: Webster's Timeline History 1710–2007*, a book of less than a hundred pages, thin for the century-long time scope it is supposed to cover. The edition is software-generated, and according to the full signature on the book cover, its editorial authorship is attributed to Professor Philip M. Parker, Ph.D., Chaired Professor of Management Science at INSEAD (Singapore and Fontainebleau, France). The book traces all published uses of the word "choreography" in print or news media. Our interest in browsing through this curious index was to extract those recent uses of the word (since 2000) that would be the remotest from dance and performance. Three fields where "choreography" serves as a technical term are registered: molecular biology, information technology, and diplomacy, as the following examples will illustrate:

> "Chromosome *choreography*: the meiotic ballet" appears in *Science* written by S. L. Page and R. S. Hawley. Published on August 8, 2003.[143]

> Shirmer S. G., "Quantum *choreography*: making molecules dance to technology's tune?" published in *Philosophical Transactions: Series A, Mathematical, Physical, and Engineering Sciences*, vol. 364, no. 1849, on December 15, 2006.[144]

> "Patterns: serial and parallel processes for process *choreography* and workflow." Publisher: IBM International Technical Support Organization (Research Triangle Park, NC). Published in 2004.[145]

> Iran News, Feb 22, 2005, headline Bush says Notion of Attack on Iran 'Ridiculous': "Despite the careful *choreography*, the new tone and the desire on both sides to turn the page, some European officials are still wondering if Mr. Bush means what he says".[146]

143 | Philip M. Parker, *Choreography: Webster's Timeline History 1710–2007* (San Diego: ICON Group International, 2009), 55.
144 | Ibid., 63.
145 | Ibid., 56.
146 | Ibid., 60.

Olympics in Sidney – News, August 2004: "Unprecedented Security Measures in Place Ahead of Olympics Opening Ceremony" "This is a massively complex security operation involving, of course, a huge array of countries, all of which are coming with their own security details, but, also, specific countries and NATO have been engaged to provide security. So, yes, there is some diplomacy. There's a lot of security, but, again, it's the Greeks doing the *choreography*. Greece is in charge. This is absolutely a Greek lead and a Greek security operation."[147] [our italics]

The currency that "performance" as a technical term had in the 1990s seems now to be replaced by "choreography." Comparing their usages, we can infer that performance denotes competence, ability to execute, and achievement, while choreography designates dynamic patterns of the complicated yet seamless organization of many heterogeneous elements in motion. Choreography stresses the design of procedures that regulate a process—chemical, physical, algorithmic, political, and diplomatic, in the examples above. This observation resonates with choreographers' and performance-makers' current theoretical, self-reflective obsession with methods, procedures, formats, and scores. Two statements amidst a plethora of interviews, manifestos, and other types of writings in contemporary dance are eloquent here. The choreographer Eleanor Bauer writes:

What do you do when you get in the studio? There's nothing to do there! The empty room gives us nothing, nothing but space and time. A sterile luxury. Advantages of having methods we are aware of using are that we have things to do when we get into the studio and that the work is stronger than the constant shifting of our interest, confidence, and motivation.[148]

The choreographer Andros Zins-Browne remarks that "most good pieces are the writing of a methodology in their production."[149]

Given how choreography is defined by the heterogeneous discourses above, should it be rethought from the perspective of a dramaturgy of procedures, as a kind of operative reason? This implies investigating "procedurality" in various terms that it circulates within: "democratic proceduralism" as a concept of political legitimacy, "procedural rhetorics" as the widely acclaimed and controversial videogame theory, "procedural knowledge" as that which artists are taught in art education. The relation between choreography and proceduralism arises from two premises. The first states that the expanded practice of choreography entails a shift from the bias of the body and embodiment to procedures, or how processes are structured and operated in time. The second holds that procedures aren't just instruments of governance; by and large, they define actions and attitudes in general, which allows us to treat them as a logic, a thinking model, an ideological apparatus. Unpacking the aforementioned registers of procedurality may help us understand what choreography means when it is used outside the strictly artistic and aesthetic realm of dance/performance.

The first register tackles "democratic proceduralism." According to the extreme position in liberal democracy—the normative definition of democractic legitimacy—democracy is said to be a procedure. Fabienne Peter, who specializes in political and moral philosophy, defines it as follows: "Democratic decisions are legitimate as long as they are the result

147 | Parker, 57.
148 | Bojana Cvejić, "In the Making of the Making of: The Practice of Rendering Performance Virtual," in "Goat Tracks of Self-Education," special issue, *TkH*, no. 15 (2008): 29.
149 | Ibid.

of an appropriately constrained process of democratic decision-making."[150] The legitimacy of the outcomes of a (political) process depends only on the fairness of the decision-making process, not on the quality of the outcomes it produces. This view is justified by the claim that there is no shared standard for assessing the quality of the outcomes, and deep disagreement about reasons for and against proposals will always remain.[151] The neoliberal version of the same arguments is, as usual, more compellingly instrumentalist than the liberalist tradition. To paraphrase Stephen Chilton,[152] intercourse needs to be regulated even through imperfect norms, because the journey must serve a practical need. An infinite journey, which is a collective process of creation or any kind of decision-making, however enjoyable, still does not "get us to our destination." There's much to approve in all this, argues Chilton, because proceduralism ensures decisions. It prevents participants from employing the strategy of infinite delay, and it avoids having "energies consumed" by infinitely long discussions of an infinite variety of issues. "Outcomes are by their nature open to dispute, but processes need not be."[153]

The second register featuring procedurality, "procedural rhetoric," is a videogame theory conceived by Ian Bogost that is based on the following thesis:

> Procedurality refers to a way of creating, explaining, or understanding processes. And processes define the way things work: the methods, techniques, and logics that drive the operation of systems, from mechanical systems like engines to organizational systems like high schools to conceptual systems like religious faith. Rhetoric refers to effective and persuasive expression. Procedural rhetoric, then, is a practice of using processes persuasively. [154]

Procedural rhetoric has purchase beyond the ontology of games, where a critical debate has been raised.[155] The Whiteheadian philosopher and cultural theorist Steven Shaviro

150 | Fabienne Peter, "Political Legitimacy," *Stanford Encyclopedia of Philosophy*, April 29, 2010, http://plato.stanford.edu/entries/legitimacy/.

151 | This view is slightly modified in the so-called deliberative rational account of epistemic proceduralism (Jürgen Habermas), where the legitimacy of democratic decisions doesn't only depend on procedural values but also on the so-called substantive quality of the outcomes generated by the procedures. Habermas argues for deliberative politics on the basis of his ideal of rational discussion: "Deliberative politics acquires its legitimating force from the discursive structure of an opinion . . . because citizens expect its results to have a reasonable *quality.*" Jürgen Habermas, *Between Facts and Norms*, trans. William Rehg (Cambridge, MA: MIT Press, 1996), 304. Deliberative decision-making processes, if appropriately shaped, are uniquely able to reach rationally justified decisions that everyone has reasons to endorse. But we should understand what deliberation means: it is less a matter of settling disputes over the cognitive validity of competing proposals than a matter of developing legal frameworks within which citizens can continue to cooperate despite disagreements about what is right or good.

152 | Stephen Chilton, "The Problem of Agreement in Republicanism, Proceduralism, and the Mature Dewey: A 'Two Moments of Discourse Ethics' Analysis," *Steve Chilton's Home Page*, last modified November 5, 2001, http://www.d.umn.edu/~schilton/Articles/Tilburg.html.

153 | Ibid.

154 | Ian Bogost, *Persuasive Games: The Expressive Power of Videogames* (Cambridge, MA: MIT Press, 2007).

155 | Miguel Sicart's ludological defense of playfulness, the agency of player, and the act and experience of the game as a play, against rule-determinism, which centers game on its design, is weak because it tends to morally redeem itself through the same, in fact epistemically proceduralist, arguments that hold that games are played in interaction through the negotiation, appropriation, and self-expression of the player, a claim which he draws from critical theory perspectives as well as from Johan Huizinga, Roger Caillois, and Eugen Fink. Miguel Sicart, "Against Procedurality," *Game Studies* 11, no. 3 (2011), http://gamestudies.org/1103/articles/sicart_ap.

raises a philosophical objection of ontological priority: "All procedures are in fact processes, but not all processes are procedures."[156] While Whiteheadian process philosophy invests in a metaphysical notion of process, Bogost's emphasis on procedures is illuminating when used as a tool of ideological analysis. It asserts procedurality as the logic by which something works; therefore, Bogost's procedural rhetoric is a framework suitable for neoliberalism, in which it belongs. Social choreography, then, implies a knowledge of procedures (and tools to apply them) which comprehends a complex design of elements to be organized, as Webster's index shows. Proceduralism forces us, like neoliberalism, to ask if there is any material production that can't be subsumed under procedures. What happens when procedures are lacking? Can we think social choreography without emphasis on the procedures? Do we need to crack open social choreography in order to do a proper critique of procedurality?

In *Living in the End Times*, Žižek targets procedurality as an ideology which prevents any revolt against capitalism.[157] He writes that our political consciousness is shackled by questions like the following, questions which form the legal framework of an empty concept of freedom: Does a country have free elections? Are its judges independent? Is its press free from hidden pressures? Does it respect human rights? The Marxist answer would be that the key to actual freedom resides in the "apolitical" network of social relations, from the market to the family, which can be transformed not by any political procedure, but rather by class struggle:

> We do not vote on who owns what, or about relations in the factory, and so on—such matters remain outside the sphere of the political, and it is illusory to expect that one will effectively change things by "extending" democracy into the economic sphere. . . . Radical changes in this domain need to be made outside the sphere of legal "rights."[158]

He thereby concludes that the acceptance of democratic mechanisms as providing the only framework for all possible change is the "democratic illusion" which prevents any radical transformation of capitalist relations.

Although he comes from quite a different theoretical orientation than Marxism, the sociologist Bruno Latour conducts a similar critique of proceduralism in an interview. Following Lippmann and Dewey, he posits that the public sphere arises in the exploration of the unintended consequences of actions that would remain private.

> The private is everything that is formatted, already established, everything that has known consequences of action. It's arbitrated and there's a protocol for every action; there is a habit of thought. . . . An issue becomes public when there is no knowledge of what to do, so the issue is dealt without knowledge, like groping in the dark, fumbling blind: *tâtonner*. That's why phantom public: something that appears and might disappear, so long as we don't develop instruments to treat it; but the departure is no instruments, no procedures, new protocols have to be found. This is the ephemeral, exceptional moment of politics. Because political science

---

156 | Steven Shaviro, "Processes and Powers," *The Pinocchio Theory* (blog), *shaviro.com*, August 18, 2011, http://www.shaviro.com/Blog/?p=995.
157 | Slavoj Žižek, *Living in the End Times* (London: Verso, 2010).
158 | Slavoj Žižek, "The Jacobin Spirit," *Jacobin*, no. 3-4 (2011), http://jacobinmag.com/summer-2011/the-jacobin-spirit/.

> teaches politicians procedures, how to do everything to avoid politics. Let's forget about politics and get good management: fight against corruption, and for rankings, standardizations, procedures, the masses of European good practices.[159]

It might be difficult, even impossible, to disentangle choreography from procedurality entirely. But it is possible, as we would like to propose here, to distinguish three operations in social choreography by which it can be transformed from a normative practice as a phenomenon into a critical model. The first is the recognition of regulatory procedures by which social choreography is normative. The second is deregulation, where the procedural knowledge of a social choreography is instrumentalized for another goal or process. (*Slet* from 1987 would be a case in point here.) The third is intervention, the rupture of procedures, and prescription that involves a direct and urgent application of a principle rather than a procedure. The last operation implies a thorough rethinking of politics, proposed by Peter Hallward on the basis of Alain Badiou's theory of event. Hallward's call for a "prescriptive practice of politics" from 2005 sounds prophetic in relation to the rising protests and riots against social injustice held by students, Indignados, the Occupy movement, or the London mob from summer 2011:

> Against alignment with the way of the world, against withdrawal from engagement with the world, it is time to reformulate a prescriptive practice of politics. Prescription is first and foremost an anticipation of its subsequent power, a commitment to its consequences.[160]

In the current protests where the public sphere is rising up, or in the riots of the "lawless mob," the "rabble," the crowd, we can discern a messy, uncontrolled choreography that breaks the law protecting private property. It doesn't proffer a political ideology in its conscious manifestation, but it does disrupt normative procedures.

159 | Bojana Cvejić, Marta Popivoda, and Ana Vujanović, "Interview with Bruno Latour," in "Art and the Public Good," special issue, *TkH*, no. 20 (2012): 72–81.
160 | Peter Hallward, "The Politics of Prescription," *The South Atlantic Quarterly* 104, no. 4 (2005): 770.

We established social choreography in order to analyze how a social order is instilled, rehearsed, and trained by means of aesthetic ideology. But in order to explain how the social order can also be considered, breached, and changed, we must introduce the concept of the social drama. We find it complementary to the social choreography, since it emphasizes the critical moments of a conflictual society when the social structure as we know it collapses, opening a "betwixt and between" space where we can observe mass public performances of the reconfiguration of a social order.

REVISITING THE METHOD
OF SOCIAL DRAMA

Let us first briefly explain our reasons for reviving a—what some might call dated—concept in order to explain the current situation of the public sphere. Social drama as a theoretical notion stems from social anthropology and has been used in performance studies, where it operated as one of the foundational concepts for the emerging field of study in the late 1960s and 1970s. The term was coined by Victor Turner in the late 1950s and signified both a social phenomenon and a method for analyzing social processes, a method which focused on cultural performances: mass gatherings, rituals, carnivals, large-scale cultural events, and other collective, symbolic actions in public space. Social anthropology of this kind, together with a few other approaches, most of which employ theatrical vocabulary in theories of social life, like those of Roger Caillois, Clifford Geertz, Erving Goffman, and others, was connected to experimental theater practices and discourses on dramaturgy, on acting, and on the social and anthropological dimensions of theater. This groundbreaking intersection resulted in performance studies, a field concerned with broadening the traditional discipline of theater and constituting the field of performing arts while being invested in the research of performance as a human social practice that takes place in art, ordinary life, politics, culture, and so on. This two-sidedness, which has been encouraged by Richard Schechner, one of the founders of the discipline, as well as by many others, provoked much confusion. And soon after its initial phase, performance studies began to appear as an "everything is performance" approach, which sparked criticism that deemed it an academic discipline in lack of a methodology, and even of an object of study.

In the course of this process, social drama analysis (and related concepts) from the 1960s were gradually put aside for being inappropriate for the new climate of the 1980s–90s, a time colored by cultural studies, when everything was subsumed under culture, conflating art, politics, culture, work, and private life. In this framework, performance studies joined investigations on cultural identities, offering explanations for how they are performed— the most notable of all contributions made by the discipline. At the same time, Turner himself tried to prove that social drama analysis belongs to "the postmodern turn" by emphasizing its focuses on performance in the linguistic competence/performance dichotomy, on process in the structuralist structure/process dichotomy, and on action in the anthropologist norm/behavior and ideology/practice dichotomies.[161] Nevertheless, social drama analysis, epistemically speaking, doesn't belong to the horizon of cultural studies, where the basic distinction between social and cultural/artistic performance on which it is grounded ceases to exist. Or, it does only if one begins to observe social dramas as cultural phenomena or phenomena in culture, thereby dissolving its socio-political dimension, which is the very way the social drama has commonly been used in performance studies recently. Added to the social drama's confrontation with the trend of cultural studies, a new challenge was made in the late 1990s and 2000s by theater studies: the concept of postdramatic theater, supposedly a new paradigm of international theater practice. At bottom, the postdramatic, as proposed by Hans-Thies Lehmann and developed by many other theater scholars,[162] decentralizes and hence dissolves drama as a dialectic, symbolic structure based on conflict and accordingly fragments performance, which ceases to revolve around the dramatic text, but whose various elements become "texts" (in a poststructuralist sense) in their own right. A seemingly consequential question arises here: does it still make sense to analyze public social life through the lens of social drama when, already in theater, the dramatic has been replaced with the postdramatic? The question obviously already implies a negative answer.

However, there is something intriguing to us in this epistemic history, especially since the currently prevalent conceptual platform in performance studies seems inadequate, as it abounds in metaphorical speech and is incapable of producing a discourse on performance

161 | See Victor Turner, *The Anthropology of Performance* (New York: PAJ Publications, 1988).
162 | Hans-Thies Lehmann, *Postdramatic Theater* (London: Routledge, 2006); originally published as *Postdramatisches Theater* (Frankfurt am Main: Verlag der Autoren, 1999).

that could link with current social and political debates on the public sphere, democracy, and citizenship, which are our concern. So in our search for methodological tools, we decided to look again at the social drama, not with a desire to follow Turner and merely "apply" his theory, but with the aim of examining it in our own analyses while rethinking, changing, and developing it.

From the perspective of social drama analysis, society, especially modern Western industrial and class society, is predicated on *agons*—divisions, conflicts, antagonisms— and individuals play social roles within its structure, roles fixed to their social status. As conflicts tend to be resolved in favor of the one or the other side, societal dynamism complements society's synchronic structure, its static entity, and can be seen in a dialectic between the procedures, on the one hand, of social normativization and mending conflicts and, on the other hand, social dramas that emerge when agons escalate.

The main source of such a vision of society lies in Victor Turner's notion of social drama, including the concepts of liminality and communitas.[163] Conceptual roots of the social drama lie in Arnold van Gennep's writing on rites of passage, where he started off with fieldwork and case studies and ended with a formal analysis of ritual.[164] In parallel and in close relation to Turner's work, Clifford Geertz developed the concept of "deep play," where his case study, based on formal analysis of the Balinese cockfight, took one step further toward the development of a methodological tool for understanding the role of cultural performances in the symbolization of the social.[165] Later on, liminality is contested by Jon McKenzie, who brought it closer to "liminoidity" and thus to a normative function of cultural performance in neoliberal capitalist society.[166] On the other side, arguments similar to those that Turner made in his elaboration of communitas can be traced in Jean-Luc Nancy's "inoperative community"[167] and Maurice Blanchot's "unavowable community,"[168] as well as in Giorgio Agamben's "coming community,"[169] while Roberto Esposito used the same term, communitas, to question the social community as such by a critical analysis that emphasizes an impossibility of immunization among human beings bonded in community.[170]

As a social phenomenon or artifact, social drama is a unit of social process that arises in conflict situations. Turner described it thus:

163 | Victor Turner, *The Ritual Process: Structure and Anti-Structure* (New York: Aldine de Gruyter, 1969); *Schism and Continuity in an African Society: A Study of Ndembu Village Life* (Manchester: Manchester University Press ND, 1972); *From Ritual to Theater: The Human Seriousness of Play* (New York: PAJ Publications, 1974); *Drama, Fields, and Metaphors: Symbolic Action in Human Society* (Ithaca, NY: Cornell University Press, 1975); *The Anthropology of Performance* (New York: PAJ Publications, 1988).

164 | Arnold van Gennep, *The Rites of Passage* (London: Routledge, 1977); originally published as *Les rites du passage* (Paris: E. Nourry, 1909).

165 | Clifford Geertz, "Deep Play: Notes on the Balinese Cockfight," in *The Interpretation of Cultures* (New York: Basic Books, 1973).

166 | Jon Mckenzie, *Perform or Else: From Discipline to Performance* (New York: Routledge, 2011).

167 | Jean-Luc Nancy, *Being Singular Plural* (Palo Alto, CA: Stanford University Press, 2000); *The Inoperative Community* (Minneapolis: University of Minnesota Press, 1991).

168 | Maurice Blanchot, *The Unavowable Community* (Barrytown, NY: Barrytown, 2006); originally published as *La Communauté inavouable* (Paris: Éditions de Minuit, 1983).

169 | Giorgio Agamben, *The Coming Community* (Minneapolis: University of Minnesota Press, 1993).

170 | Roberto Esposito, *Communitas: The Origin and Destiny of Community* (Palo Alto, CA: Stanford University Press, 2010).

> A limited area of transparency on the otherwise opaque surface of regular, uneventful social life. In the social drama latent conflicts become manifest, and kinship ties, whose significance is not obvious in genealogies, emerge into key importance. Through the social drama we are enabled to observe the crucial principles of the social structure in their operation, and their relative dominance at successive points in time.[171]

In socio-dramaturgical terms, Turner identified four stages of social drama: break with regular, norm-governed social relations; crisis, which is a threshold between the stable states of society, with the rambling characteristic of the forum; redressive action, which is still an in-between stage of legal or ritualistic mediations, negotiations, and resolutions; and restoration or reintegration, which comes either by healing the breach by reintegration of the social group who enacted the break or by "schismogenesis" where there is a recognition of the social schism that cannot be repaired.[172] In Turner, the crisis and the redress are the phases that are structured as social performances in public, while Schechner—paying more attention to the aspects of making social principles transparent, of manifesting and bringing social conflicts into sight—emphasizes performative aspects of social drama in general and interprets Turner's concept in the following way:

> Victor Turner (1974) analyzes "social dramas" using theatrical terminology to describe how disharmonic or crisis situations are dealt with. These situations—arguments, combats, rites of passage—are inherently dramatic because participants not only do things, they *show themselves and others what they are doing or have done*; actions take on a reflexive and performed-for-an-audience aspect.[173]

COMMUNITAS AND LIMINALITY

Within social dramas, there are two categories that we would like to single out as crucial for analyzing public performances of ideology: liminality and communitas.[174] They both relate to the social structure, but they do so in an ambivalent way—as a rupture that comes from its interstices, edges, margins. Turner's point of departure is the classical Marxist base/superstructure division of social structure. Thus he generally locates social drama with its public rituals[175] in the superstructure. However, for him the superstructure

171 | Turner, *Schism and Continuity in an African Society*, 93; Turner, "Anthropology of Performance," in *The Anthropology of Performance* (New York: PAJ Publications, 1987), http://erikapaterson08.pbworks.com/f/Antrophology%20of%20performance(2).pdf, p.1.

172 | See Victor Turner, "The Concept of Social Drama" in *Schism and Continuity in an African Society*, 91–95; Turner, "Anthropology of performance" in *The Anthropology of Performance*, http://erikapaterson08.pbworks.com/f/Antrophology%20of%20performance(2).pdf, pp. 4–5. This socio-dramaturgical scheme suggests that Turner's social drama is modeled on the classical Greek and later European concept of theater, or, as Turner himself would imply, that the European concept of theater as a form of cultural-artistic performance is modeled on the structure of social drama characteristic for European society.

173 | Richard Schechner, "Transformances," in *Performance Theory* (London: Routledge, 2003), 186.

174 | See esp. Victor Turner, "Liminality and Communitas," in *The Ritual Process: Structure and Anti-Structure*, 95–131.

175 | For the sake of clarity, we need to explain that for Turner the ritual is not a standardized unit act (like ceremony), but the performance of a complex sequence of symbolic acts, or, even more specifically, a "transformative performance revealing major classifications, categories, and contradictions of cultural processes."

is where the social structure may be reflected and changed rather than merely reflected and reproduced. Furthermore, Turner emphasizes that liminality and communitas do not simply belong to the regular social superstructure, but instead appear at the (seemingly) irrelevant and inferior edges of social structure as a proto-, meta-, or even an anti-structure rather than as a superstructure, which is where their transformative potential lies.

The term liminality is derived from the Latin *limen*, which means threshold. Van Gennep was the first to use the term in the sense we use it today, analyzing rites of passage, like rituals of initiation, and their role in constructing social subjectivity. Turner elaborated the term more and in a broader social perspective and made it a methodological concept. For him, the liminal is "the moment in and out of time," a state in which a society is restructured, reclassified, and where social positions, roles, and statuses are redistributed. In terms of a wider social dramaturgy, the liminal is the moment of discontinuity of historical time in which social drama takes place, causing standstill and the collapse of the existing social order. Therefore, rituals and other performances belonging to the liminal moment are those practices where social structure is breached, reflected, and restructured by means of collective actions in public that presuppose affective-experiential aspects of bodily movement and their symbolization, which, instead of relying on preexisting language and symbols, advances new ones.

However, in modern societies after the Industrial Revolution, liminal practices are more often liminoid, being the results of professional cultural-artistic work and the professionalization of human play[176]—which gains its momentum today, alongside the capitalization of both play and leisure time, in neoliberal capitalist society's favoring of immaterial labor and the post-Fordist organization of production. Already in his time, Turner, coming from his Marxist-Catholic perspective, called it "Protestant ethics," where one's whole life is subsumed under work and thus lacking the time and space for reflection and, accordingly, for change. The liminoid practices resemble the liminal ones but may be both liminal and, more often, pseudo-liminal, promising a transformation but in fact only homeopathically treating the endangered social equilibrium. The question, which was the basic dilemma of Jon McKenzie's book *Perform or Else,* is how to define the cultural-artistic performance today, even when it comes to, for instance, a radically critical theatrical performance or, more broadly still, big rave concerts and parties from the 1990s—as a normative and hence servile or as a potentially transformative practice. The reason for the weak transformative potential and usual pseudo-liminality of liminoid cultural performances would amount precisely to their pertaining in and to the system of production, where they, firstly, become "socially relevant" and, secondly, where a certain (dominant) ideology operates but is never shown and observed in its operations.

Communitas (the Latin term for community) is a more comprehensive notion and deserves a more extensive elaboration. As a concept advanced by Turner, it is not the social community as such, but an unstructured rudimentary community that emerges in the liminal period, a potential community, a community that is becoming. Although his approaches and frame of reference are different, Roberto Esposito established a similar point of departure when he discusses the origins of community, re-employing the term communitas. However, while in Turner's social anthropology communitas has a positive

176 | See Victor Turner, "Liminal to Liminoid, in Play, Flow, and Ritual" in *From Ritual to Theater: The Human Seriousness of Play,* 20–61.

connotation of togetherness—the common, and equality among people when social order, property, and social roles are suspended—in Esposito, who conducted a philosophical and etymological analysis of the term starting with the term *munus* (gift and duty) and who brought the discussion to the terrain of ontology, what lies at the core of community is more the lack, void, duty and obligation rather than the common (shared property or "thing") that is shared.

According to Turner, the basic types of communitas or sometimes also considered as the phases of a communitas are:

• The spontaneous or existential communitas, which breaches the norm-governed social structure and directly confronts it. It is immediate and usually short-lasting. Its main quality and social power is the experience of participation

• The ideological communitas, which comprises theory and history, conceptualizing previous communities. It may offer a utopian model of society (commonly based on the experience of communitas).

• The normative communitas, which is organized into a perduring social system and can thus be very slow and long-lasting. It may be imposed or ordered.[177]

Among these, the spontaneous communitas clearly resides in the domain of anti-structure, while the ideological and normative communitates already belong to a certain extent to the social structure, but nevertheless also rely on the attributes of the structurally inferior. We will return to this issue later when discussing the ideological practice of communitas.

As a rudimentary proto-community, communitas is always seen as a danger brought into the society through the "powers of the weak," of the precarious, of the inferior who don't fit well in the social structure. The foremost reason lies, in both Turner's and Esposito's views, in the fact that communitas fundamentally remains in opposition to the (supposed) *immunitas* of the structured social community. Within the current uprisings under the names Indignados or Occupy we can recognize the figure of Turner's "powers of the weak," nowadays associated more with the expression of an affect—indignation or outrage— than with an ideological view and a corresponding political program. In the post-9/11 era of the Bush regime and wars in Afghanistan and Iraq, the trend was to analyze the politics of "fear" in order to explain the mechanism of pre-emptive action which claimed the imminent threat of terrorist attack and thus reversed the virtual effect into an actual cause of security operations.[178] Together with a list of diverse social and political reasons for personal outrage (the growing gap between the rich and the poor, the treatment of illegal immigrants in France, the limitations on the freedom of press, environmental destruction, and so forth), Stéphane Hessel's call *"Indignez-vous"* lent a name to the social affect within which the Indignados and Occupy movements arose: a general and spontaneously expressed sense of dissatisfaction, a call for nonviolent insurrection. The question we will pursue here is whether a social affect is just a symptom of insurrection or the ideological expression thereof—which might lead to a new social formation.

---

177 | See Victor Turner, *The Ritual Process: Structure and Anti-Structure*, 132 and after, esp. "Ideological and Spontaneous Communitas," 134–41.
178 | See Brian Massumi, "Fear (The Spectrum Said)," *Positions* 13, no. 1 (2005): 31–48; Cf. the edited collection of essays Massumi, ed., *The Politics of Everyday Fear* (Minneapolis: University of Minnesota Press, 1993), which particularly focuses on the culture of the neoconservative Reaganite and Thatcherist turns.

The issue of immunization thereby places communitas in medias res of the ongoing dramas of neoliberal society as they arise from growing precarity associated with terrorism, insecurity, the economic crisis, and austerity measures. The notion of immunity, apprehended as a protection from disease, from common law, or from risks that threaten the community, has a long tradition and has reappeared in recent theoretical, political, and biopolitical understandings of the social community. At bottom, immunity is predicated on the thesis that the human being is, from birth, dependent on the social, where social bonds have two different yet reconcilable faces: fear associated with a "nonimmunity," that is, the vulnerability of the human being exposed to others who all share the capacity to cause her death, and vice versa; and the processes and instruments of immunization that protect human beings from one another. What is characteristic for our times in this regard is probably explained best by Isabell Lorey,[179] who further develops Judith Butler's theses from *Precarious Life* and *Frames of War,* where Butler contests the current "ontology of individualism" on the grounds that it overlooks the ontological precariousness of human life and the human body, namely, that they are unable to function autonomously and independently.[180] Lorey recognizes that in the course of history these instruments of immunization were never used equally, that they were instead used predominantly to protect certain individuals from the risks to which the rest of society is exposed. This consequently leads to competitiveness and the projection of precariousness into unprotected social margins. Lorey therefore distinguishes three registers of precarity. The first is, as in Butler, the ontological precariousness of human life. The second involves precarization in the form of political or legal processes of immunizing and protecting some lives. In neoliberal capitalism today, precarization becomes an instrument of governance, instigating an overall sense of insecurity within which it can normalize differences and pacify frictions. The third register are the precarious, who appear as an effect of precarization and could become a social agency if they concentrated on what they have in common and how to change the current modes of governing. According to Lorey, the attempts of the precarious to establish the commons and change governance could be found exactly in current communitates: the ¡Democracia Real YA! movement in Spain or the movement of the Outraged in Athens.[181] Why in communitas? Let us return to the basic references. If communitas as an anti- and proto-community that springs from the breach of norm-governed social community between or among individuals is "what all of us believe we share," for Turner it is a positive category, a sharing of the common as an experience of solidarity and equality where the very exigency of immunity is abolished. Communitas stops the process of immunization in the moment when it also puts a stop to a role-play[182] that characterizes regular social life in its ties to social status.

179 | She develops her theses on immunity and precarity in numerous lectures and writings. See Isabell Lorey, *Figuren des Immunen: Elemente einer politischen Theorie* (Zurich: diaphanes, 2011); Lorey, "Identitary Immunity and Strategic Immunization: *Lépra* and Leprosy from Biblical into Medieval Times," in "translating violence," special issue of the online journal *transversal* (October 2008), http://eipcp.net/transversal/1107/lorey/en; Lorey, "Governmental Precarization" in "inventions," special edition of the online journal *transversal* (August 2011), http://eipcp.net/transversal/0811/lorey/en; Lorey, "Becoming Common: Precarization as Political Constituting," *e-flux* no. 17 (2010), http://www.e-flux.com/journal/becoming-common-precarization-as-political-constituting/.

180 | Judith Butler, *Precarious Life: The Powers of Mourning and Violence* (London: Verso, 2004); Butler, *Frames of War: When is Life Grievable?* (London: Verso, 2009).

181 | See Isabell Lorey, "Non-representationist, Presentist Democracy," in "#occupy and assemble∞," special edition of the online journal *transversal* (October 2011), http://eipcp.net/transversal/1011/lorey/en.

182 | For more about social roles as defined by Erving Goffman, to whom Turner refers, see Part 3 in this book: "The Self and the Public," Chapter 6: "Performance of the Self: A History in Theory."

Since social roles thereby reproduce precarization as a governmental instrument and concurrently maintain differences and competiveness, contemporary communitates, by suspending role-play, also suspend the normalization of precarization and start looking at what the "ninety-nine percent" of the precarious have in common. On the other hand, Esposito—who, as we said, has a different notion of communitas and yet nevertheless also addresses the origin of social community—explains communitas by the negative, by sharing "no-thing," whereby duty, sacrifice, obligation, reciprocal gift-giving and debt appear, keeping us together and abolishing the immunity.[183] In his book *Immunitas: The Protection and Negation of Life* he conducted the same etymological analysis of immunitas as he did in the case of communitas.[184] First of all, he shows that they share the same etymological root (*munus*), but second of all, he emphasizes that their relations to munus are diametrical. Since immunitas indicates exemption and privilege of the exemption, the one who is immune is freed from *munus* and owes nothing to anyone, therefore establishing her position as particularity in difference to others; whereby communitas, with its abolishing borders between individuals through sharing *munus*, is the absolute antonym of immunitas.[185]

In macroterms, Turner's wholeness and Esposito's lack are the two poles between which we propose to analyze the collective dimension of communitas, but without seeking to alleviate the tension; since our standpoint is that communitas per se is neither a positive nor a negative but rather a methodological term by which one can examine how we, contemporary citizens, can be together in a collective situation where the social order—the community as we currently know it—with its social roles and statuses is resisted and suspended.

THE IDEOLOGICAL PRACTICE OF COMMUNITAS: INDIVIDUALISM AND COLLECTIVISM

The problematic unfolded above is especially important from an ideological stance on the configuration of the public. It points out that in modern and contemporary capitalist societies, where community is predicated on individualism and the social structure

183 | "As the complex though equally unambiguous etymology that we have till now undertaken demonstrates, the *munus* that the *communitas* shares isn't a property or a possession [*appartenenza*]. It isn't having, but on the contrary, is a debt, a pledge, a gift that is to be given, and that therefore will establish a lack. The subjects of community are united by an 'obligation,' in the sense that we say 'I owe *you* something,' but not 'you owe *me* something.'" Roberto Esposito, *Communitas*, 6. See also Esposito, "The Immunization Paradigm," *diacritics* 36, no. 2 (2006): 23–48; and Esposito, *Immunitas: The Protection and Negation of Life* (Hoboken, NJ: John Wiley & Sons, 2011).
184 | See "Introduction" in *Immunitas*, 1–21.
185 | This addresses only communitas, while modern society tends to integrate immunitas, so much so that Esposito, relying mostly on Bataille, sees the community based on Hobbesian premises (including fear) as an immunitas where everyone is protected from everyone else. By stressing the antinomy communitas/immunitas, he in fact criticizes the community predicated on the idea of immunity instead of on the idea of obligation and care for one another. See especially Roberto Esposito, "Fear," in *Communitas*, 20–41.

is, according to Turner, closely connected to property,[186] communitas appears as a liminal passage of the collective, of the "in-common," of a rupture of collectivism. In its unstructured and uncompleted state, which we come across in communitas, collectivism functions as the cohesion of the precarious, of the weak and equal. The undecidability of these "betwixt and in-between" collective moments appears threatening to the existing social order—a point that can be observed in Occupy protests as well as in the recent conflicts and uprisings in Arab countries. Reverberating with Turner's vocabulary, in her interpretation of the Occupy movement, Judith Butler explains:

> Demonstrations are one of the few ways that police power is overcome, especially when they become too large and too mobile to be contained by police power, and when they have the resources to regenerate themselves. Perhaps these are anarchist moments or anarchist passages, when the legitimacy of a regime is called into question, but when no new regime has yet come to take its place. This time of the interval is the time of the popular will, not a single will, not a unitary will, but one that is characterized by an alliance with the performative power to lay claim to the public in a way that is not yet codified into law, and that can never be fully codified into law.[187]

The collectivity that emerges in Occupy is incomplete, "never fully codified," as it dwells in mass dissatisfaction and disagreement without projecting a new social order. But being incomplete and outraged is what makes it an elusive, spectral enemy in the eyes of the existing social order, an enemy not easily represented and identified and hence struggled against; it is what therefore opens an enormous space for misrepresentations and hysterical reactions on the part of an endangered society.

The relations between the collective and the individual should be examined further within the internal organization of communitas, wherein we will try to find an answer to the question of who the subject of communitas is, the subject that it brings into the public sphere. Communitas is a social composition where individual distinctions are not completely erased in totalitarian collectivist unison but are subsumed under a collective action or experience of "being together."[188]

> Extreme individualism only understands a part of man. Extreme collectivism only understands man as a part. Communitas is the implicit law of wholeness arising out of relations between totalities. But communitas is intrinsically dynamic, never quite being realized. It is not being realized precisely because individuals and collectivities try to impose their cognitive schemata on one another.[189]

Here we can see that for Turner the individual and the collective are still situated in a binary opposition, even when it comes to communitas, although he—by emphasizing the dynamism of communitas—implies a third direction where an in-between social subject is emerging on the horizon outlined by each opposite. The third direction, however, is seen

---

186 | See Turner, "Liminality and Communitas," 106, 111, 129.
187 | Judith Butler, "Bodies in Alliance and the Politics of the Street," in "#occupy and assemble∞," special issue of the online journal *transversal* (October 2011), http://eipcp.net/transversal/1011.
188 | In Turner, communitas relates more closely to camaraderie, *comitatus*, and *comitas* than to *communion*—which erases individualities and unifies them—because "being together" and a "flowing from *I* to *Thou*" are crucial here.
189 | Turner, "Anthropology of Performance," 16.

only as a moment between the realization of one or the other opposite. This is the point where we would like to augment Turner's model by claiming that while binarism is the very thing through which individualism and collectivism are defined as ideological categories of capitalist and socialist social communities, the subject that emerges from many communitates that have appeared in recent decades—in "a situation that joins in a unique epochal knot the failure of all communisms with the misery of new individualism"[190]— abandons both sides rather than simply being located between them. Here communitas brings into view a subject that can be conceptualized by what Nancy calls "the singular plural" or what Gerald Raunig terms the "condividual."[191] Raunig's neologism is pretty close to Nancy's singular plural, according to which a singularity is always a singular of a plural, belonging to it via an "and," and specific in its singularity. The notion of condividual is based on Raunig's analysis of the Italian word *condivisione*, which at the same time indicates association and sharing (*con-*) as well as the differentiation and separation of singularities (*divisione*):

> This means that my proposed neologism, condivision, becomes a term for a concatenation of singularities, which not only names their exchange, their mutual reference, their association with one another, but also impels it. In condivision, the dividual component, the division, does not indicate a tribute, a reduction, a sacrifice, but rather the possibility of an addition, an AND. Singularities and their concatenations become in condivision. It is not necessary for a community to emerge first in order to achieve the recomposition of previously separated individuals, but instead the concatenation and the singularities are co-emergent as the condividuality of condividuals.[192]

Although neither Nancy nor Raunig locate their conceptions of subject in concrete social circumstances or formations but rather indicate that they are co-emergent, we would say that if the singular plural or the condividual exists somewhere in social reality, it is the communitas.

Going further in his analysis, Turner precisely distinguishes the being-together which characterizes communitas from teamwork, which associates individuals in the execution of a task more efficiently than individually: "Here it is not teamwork in flow that is quintessential, but '*being*' together, with 'being' the operative word, not 'doing.'"[193] This thesis is close to Nancy and his ideas about the (inoperative) community.[194] For Nancy, the community (communitas in the sense we are elaborating here) is an always already lost root and essence of the society that fails to understand the singularity of a human being and its "being-in-common" and thus oscillates between individuality and particularity.

> Moreover, there is no entity or hypostasis of community because this sharing, this passage cannot be completed. Incompletion is its "principle," taking the term 'incompletion' in an active sense, however, as designating not insufficiency or lack, but the activity of sharing, the dynamic,

190 | Roberto Esposito, *Communitas*, 1.
191 | See Gerald Raunig, "Inventing Con-dividuality: An Escape Route from the Pitfalls of Community and Collectivity," in "Politicality of Performance," special issue, *TkH* no. 19 (2011): 142–8. http://www.tkh-generator.net/en/casopis/tkh-19.
192 | Ibid., 147.
193 | Victor Turner, "Liminal to Liminoid, in Play, Flow, and Ritual," in *From Ritual to Theater*, 48.
194 | With a certain approximation, he uses the term "society" to describe what Turner considers community and the term "community" in place of Turner's "communitas."

> if you will, of an uninterrupted passage through singular ruptures. That is to say, once again, a workless and inoperative activity. It is not a matter of making, producing, or instituting a community; nor is it a matter of venerating or fearing within it a sacred power—it is a matter of incompleting its sharing.[195]

As we already mentioned, within the frame of social drama, liminality and communitas do not fit smoothly into the societal superstructure; they are anti-, meta- or proto-structures that are relatively free from and thus potentially threatening to the social structure. Yet when Turner speaks about liminal collective actions in the public and their performative dimension, he does so without invoking pure or transcendental freedom with its romantic attributes of emotionality, irrationality, regression to infancy, and so on. Instead he talks about breaching, subverting, and restructuring the social order, which includes, but cannot be reduced to, a cognitive and linguistic register and hence also ludism, playfulness, the experience of participation, and a discursively unstructured corporeality as constitutive elements of new models of human interaction and relation. Regardless of whether they resulted in new social orders or in reintegration into already existing ones, when we bring to mind various liminal collective actions and movements in recent history—from '68 and protests and demonstrations in late socialism to the protests in Seattle and Genoa, and now the Occupy and Indignados movements—we perceive the following: in the moment of an ideological breach brought on by social drama, the thing at stake is, on the one hand, a conjunction of bodily action in a specific spatiotemporal constellation, i.e. in a liminal moment in public space which processualizes that space, and on the other, that conjunction's symbolization. As Turner would say, it's about the point of contact between the *Weltanschauung* and *praxis*. However, the symbolization that brings new ideology is not necessarily articulated discursively in the moment of action. Generating new symbols and new language can also appear after a spontaneous communitas enters the public stage as a so-called ideological communitas; while in many cases, as Turner insists, it appears only as that which a certain communitas embodies by the very experience of being performed, by its duration and dynamics, by its organization of actions, by new voices and images, by the mise-en-scène of its use or production of public space, and so on. In Turner's view, "It is in the social drama that *Weltanschauungen* become visible, if only fragmentarily, as factors giving meaning to deeds that may seem at first sight meaningless."[196] Judith Butler stresses exactly that aspect of the Occupy gathering—it doesn't necessarily possess and promote clear ideologies or politics for the future which would define ways of being together and commonly producing and sharing public space; it claims these ways by means of participative bodies:

> The persistence of the body calls that legitimacy into question, and does so precisely through a performativity of the body that crosses language without ever quite reducing to language. In other words, it is not that bodily action and gesture have to be translated into language, but that both action and gesture signify and speak, as action and claim, and that the one is not finally extricable from the other.[197]

To sum up, liminal performances of communitas that take place within social dramas always embody an ideology that is sometimes elaborated discursively in the type or phase of communitas identified as ideological communitates, which are focused on reflection,

195 | Jean-Luc Nancy, *The Inoperative Community*, 35.
196 | Turner, "Anthropology of performance," 24.
197 | Judith Butler, "Bodies in Alliance and the Politics of the Street."

symbolization, and the discursive articulation of previously existing and currently happening communitates, and which may programmatically formulate a new model of social order. If Turner said that "*Weltanschauungen*, like all else that motivates humankind, must be performed,"[198] we have to add that the performance of communitas must also be a performance of *Weltanschauung*.

The concept of ideological corporeality can help us resolve the political and theoretical dilemma of the existence of the spontaneous communitas, a dilemma which has recurrently accompanied mass movements of resistance in recent history. Here we need to clarify or rework Turner's differentiation of three types or phases of communitas and also say that there can be no clear differentiation between spontaneous and ideological communitas where the former is to be understood as nonideological. By claiming the above and stating that the performance of communitas is a performance of *Weltanschauung*, we're not claiming that every performance is political and ideological, but we want to remind the reader that a communitas, which is a corporeal aspect of social drama, appears precisely in the escalation of a social agon that presupposes at least two sides, two elements, two entities in conflict with one another about how social order should function. Therefore, since it is not a psychological category pertaining to an individual human qua her internal dynamics, but clearly a social (hence relational) category, the social drama brings forth a communitas that antagonizes, resists, and breaches the established social order, and publicly performs a different set of ideas about living, being, and doing together. Yet we needn't hastily abandon Turner's differentiation, since it may help us in an appreciation of both corporeal (and, possibly, discursively unarticulated) and linguistic (discursively or even programmatically articulated) aspects of ideology,[199] which would conserve the possibility of a communitas that emerges without an ideological program up its sleeve and whose primary fuel is indignation at, resistance to, and breach of the already existing program, so we can name it "spontaneous." Moreover, most of the communitates in history emerged in this very way, and these superimpositions and intertwinings of ideological corporeality, these generations of new language, this point of intersection between *Weltanschauung* and *praxis*—all this characterizes the communitas and sets social drama apart from social choreography in terms of its ideological operation.

SOCIAL DRAMA IN
NEOLIBERAL SOCIETY:
THE DRAMATIC VS.
THE POSTDRAMATIC

The last issue we want to address regarding social drama analysis starts with the following question: is social drama still useful in analyzing processes in our current society as well as the constitution of community through mass public performances? Or, in other words, what is implied if we abandon the concept of social drama and in return shift to a framework of "social postdrama"?

198 | Turner, "Anthropology of performance," 19.
199 | Indeed, in his differentiation, Turner himself describes the ideological communitas in terms of "explicitly formulated views on how men may best live together in comradely harmony," Turner, "Ideological and Spontaneous Communitas," in *The Ritual Process*, 134.

After all we have said about social drama, we would like to begin reflecting on that issue with a brief juxtaposition: the dramatic is predicated on such categories as agon, antagonism, protagonists, and antagonists, while the postdramatic indicates fragmentation and dispersion of the conflict as well as pluralism of positions, anticipating complementarity and, in the last instance, a non-conflictual or consensual societal organization. Politically speaking, the postdramatic as it is formulated in theater studies is to a degree close to the recent agonist political theories. More specifically, we could associate it with the "agonistic democracy" proposed by Chantal Mouffe,[200] which conceives of the political as the "space of power, conflict, and antagonism" but advocates a sublimation of the political whereby the antagonism has to be transformed into an agonism, focusing on the positive aspects of the conflicts and their affective motives while promoting liberalism and pluralism. For Mouffe—who takes the notion of (value) pluralism from Max Weber (as well as from Foucault) and the notion of antagonism from Carl Schmitt (and not Marx)—the pluralism both underlies antagonism and is a way to manage conflicts without aiming to eliminate the others (antagonists as (class) enemies), but rather to understand them as our "adversaries."

Although Mouffe's theory is far more complex, we shall take a step back here and ponder a basic question it provokes: how can we understand the agonism in our deeply antagonistic capitalist society? It may be that agonistic pluralism as well as pluralism in recent socio-political discourse addresses and can explain only one moment of a conflictual society, the moment of equal coexistence and public co-presence of the entities in conflict, when the tension between those entities is manageable and can be discussed or even celebrated as proof of a liberal and pluralistic democratic public sphere. However, in terms of the public performance of citizenship, this viewpoint presupposes an absolute parrhesia in a "radically democratic" society. On the one hand, the current neoliberal democratic society can be hardly described in these terms, and on the other, we doubted this very vision in the first part of the book by introducing Foucault's skeptical claim that real parrhesia in fact cannot exist where real democracy exists.[201] Furthermore, in terms of the macroideological and macropolitical performance, the moment to which agonistic pluralism refers is actually the moment before one or another social force wins and instills the social order that it advocated in the conflict. All this turns agonistic pluralism as a theoretical-political proposal as well as pluralism as neoliberal socio-political discourse into a rather ahistorical perspective on conflictual society; otherwise, if we are to challenge it historically, we would dare say that it is a politically conservative perspective that advocates and maintains the social status quo. Agonistic pluralism functions in this way since it neglects the point that pluralism is itself limited through that which can be done within existing political institutions, which are constitutive of the existing order, and due to which antagonistic protests, violence, and revolutions occur in a conflictual society. Therefore, agonistic pluralism as an ideological formation prevents the real existing social conflicts from escalating into social drama by dissolving them into a postdramatic pluralism of an endless present.

200 | See Chantal Mouffe, *On the Political* (London: Routledge, 2005); Mouffe, *Deliberative Democracy or Agonistic Pluralism* (Vienna: Institute for Advanced Studies, 2000); Mouffe, "Artistic Activism and Agonistic Spaces," *Art & Research* 1, no. 2 (2007); Nico Carpentier and Bart Cammaerts, "Hegemony, democracy, agonism and journalism: An interview with Chantal Mouffe," *Journalism Studies* 7, no. 6 (2006): 964–75.
201 | See Part 1 of this book, "The Public Sphere and Its Discontents," Chapter 2, "Can We Only Perform the Public Now?"

Starting with this critical assumption and transporting it into the terrain of current social conditions, we would thus argue that the contestation or rejection of the social drama as an explanatory model suggests that contemporary neoliberal capitalist society has already achieved consensus regarding its foundational structure, or in other words, has already been plural, its conflicts multifold and dispersed, its current social divisions and partitions never fundamental and therefore manageable. As it is indeed the main discourse of neoliberal capitalism, the postdramatic is apparently more appropriate today than the dramatic simply because it uses the same vocabulary and the same performative mode, thus going hand in hand with the hegemonic social discourse.[202] Our critical stance asserts that we need social drama analysis today precisely on account of this adequacy of the postdramatic. Whereas social drama analysis insists on the conflictual yet opaque basis of society, on a need for rendering the conflicts visible, manifest, transparent, for showing "the crucial principles of the social structure in their operation" while also insisting on the possibility of change, the discourse of postdramatic theater and further social postdramatic models provides us instead with tools for leveling and blurring the conflicts in the plurality of the complementary.

Extending the aforementioned ahistoricity, or conservativism, of agonistic pluralism, our claim is predicated on the following thesis: Although neoliberal capitalist society performs, more or less consistently, pluralism in public, it does so only when its basic structural premises of (neo)liberalism, democracy, and capitalism go unquestioned. And vice versa. As soon as its premises are contested or rejected, it is incapable of maintaining such a performance in the public sphere. This indicates that neoliberal pluralism in its totality is possible only by virtue of the acceptance—or, in other words, prior instillment—of the basis of social order and its values, ideas, images, and discourses. This social conditioning makes pluralism truly postdramatic, but in an unexpected way: it came after a social drama. On the other hand, it simultaneously makes pluralism an ideological category, which is inherent to a particular social order that sees itself as the horizon of the possible rather than as a category that can (plurally) discuss the social order itself. In a word, pluralism as an ideological and political conception and practice encourages every discussion, except for the discussion of pluralism. The same is true for the postdramatic, whose power to interpret current society is weak because its reproduction of the dominant social discourse offers a symptomatology—a "diagnosis of time" (*Zeitdiagnose*)—instead of an explanatory model of the society. Continuing in this direction, we would claim that social drama analysis could also help us shift from Cultural Studies' keen interest in identitarian micropolitics, wherein conflicts are dispersed and managed without posing a threat, as defined by a wider socio-political perspective, to the social order. This is the perspective from which we can reopen crucial macropolitical issues of the very social order, asking if there is any public concern or good, any common world, anything-in-common around which the common world is constructed or around which we can construct it. This is also the point where the discipline of performance studies can repoliticize its methodology and open a new chapter in the analysis of the performativity of social life by placing a stronger focus on how social order relates to its ideological formations performed in public, a direction which it has rather neglected in the turbulence of the last twenty years.

GAZIMESTAN (KOSOVO),

202 | Neither Hans-Thies Lehmann in theater studies nor Chantal Mouffe in political theory make, at least intentionally, this claim. Mouffe's standpoint rests on new-left social democracy while Lehmann's is indifferent to explicit political positioning. Their discursive platforms nevertheless share a similar ideological horizon that is informed by, or at least akin to neoliberal capitalist social order.

1989: COMMUNITAS AS
THE NEGATIVE

We would now like to turn our attention to a highly controversial case in the context of Yugoslavia—a mass gathering and a social and cultural performance that happened on June 28, 1989, at Gazimestan in Kosovo. The event was the focal point for a year-long celebration of the six hundredth anniversary of the historical Battle of Kosovo and consisted of a mass gathering of approximately 1.5 million people as well as a cultural-artistic program including the performance of the musical drama *The Passion of the Saint Prince Lazar* and the delivery of a speech by Slobodan Milošević.[203] It is important to say that the event at Gazimestan took place amidst the biggest social drama in Yugoslavia after World War II: on a wider scale, the moment of revolution in European real-socialist states, the fall of the Berlin Wall, and the collapse of the ideology of communism; and in the local context, the era of late socialism marked by the economic crisis, demands for democratization, and the change in communist leadership, as well as worsened relations between Yugoslav republics, exacerbated by mounting nationalism.

In the huge Battle of Kosovo between the Serbian and Ottoman armies and the ensuing massacre, the majority of fighters on both sides were wiped out. Both the Serbian Prince Lazar and Sultan Murad I were killed, after which one of three Serbian commanders (Vuk Branković) left the field in order to save his people, and the armies finally retreated. According to some historians, the battle ended without a clear victor; according to others, victory is attributed to the Ottoman Empire; while according to some minoritarian histories and the report of Vlatko Vuković Kosača, also a Serbian commander, it was a Serbian victory. Regardless of the outcome of the battle, the loss on the Serbian side was irrecuperable, since in the following years most Serbian principalities became Turkish vassals, which marked Serbia's final defeat as well as the beginning of Turkish expansion into Europe. Since the battle was poorly documented at the time, its history has remained a mixture of ambiguous stories, legends, myths, and poems. As a social macronarrative, it was first revived in the nineteenth century, when Serbia was still under Ottoman rule, as part of its national awakening and independence movement, and again in 1989 in the midst of the conflicts between Albanians and Serbs in Kosovo, the same year that Slobodan Milošević became president of the Socialist Republic of Serbia and the Serbian parliament approved the constitutional amendments (29, 31, 33, 43, 47) reducing the autonomy of Kosovo (then an autonomous province of Serbia).

The most controversial part of the event is Milošević's speech. On the one hand, it was severely criticized by the international news media, by Yugoslav politicians from other republics, and Serbian communists and anti-nationalists for being univocally nationalistic, for inciting the war, and heralding the dissolution of the SFRY. (Actually, only nationalists have considered it non-nationalistic.) On the other hand, a close reading and discursive analysis that we carried out indicates that the speech is not that unambiguous, as it mostly employed socialist rhetoric with much smaller parts that can be indentified as nationalistic. The following segments stand out as nationalistic:

> Through the play of history and life, it seems as if Serbia has, precisely in this year, in 1989,

203 | Video footage of the celebration is available online. "Gazimestan, 600th anniversary of the Kosovo polje battle," from Internet Archive, MPEG video, 71:26, http://archive.org/details/Gazimestan600thAnniversaryOfTheKosovoPoljeBattle.

regained its state and its dignity and thus has celebrated an event of the distant past which has a great historical and symbolic significance for its future. [...]

Disunity among Serb officials made Serbia lag behind and their inferiority humiliated Serbia. Therefore, no place in Serbia is better suited for saying this than the field of Kosovo and no place in Serbia is better suited than the field of Kosovo for saying that unity in Serbia will bring prosperity to the Serbian people in Serbia and each one of its citizens, irrespective of his national or religious affiliation. [...]

I am convinced that this awareness of harmony and unity will make it possible for Serbia not only to function as a state but to function as a successful state. Therefore I think that it makes sense to say this here in Kosovo, where that disunity once upon a time tragically pushed back Serbia for centuries and endangered it, and where renewed unity may advance it and may return dignity to it. [...]

Six centuries later, now, we are being again engaged in battles and are facing battles. They are not armed battles, although such things cannot be excluded yet. However, regardless of what kind of battles they are, they cannot be won without resolve, bravery, and sacrifice, without the noble qualities that were present here in the field of Kosovo in the days past. [...][204]

Besides the paragraphs quoted above, in the rest of the sixteen minute long speech Milošević uses rather typical socialist phrases, late socialist bureaucratic rhetoric, the language of multiculturalism, pro-European vocabulary, and metaphoric, poetic speech. Indicatively, however, the only national or ethnic mentioned used in the speech is "Serbs," while Albanians (as well as Croats, Slovenes, Montenegrins, and Macedonians, all of whom were recognized in the time of Yugoslavia as constitutional nations) are always referred to as "the others."

As far as its discursive structure is concerned, we identify three parts in the speech. The central one,[205] typically socialist and containing no deviations or ambiguous references, speaks about the crisis in Yugoslavia, the advantages of socialism, and the need to preserve Yugoslavia as a socialist and multicultural society. The paradigmatic paragraph from this part reads as follows:

Socialism in particular, being a progressive and just democratic society, should not allow people

204 | English translation of "Slobodan Milošević's 1989 St. Vitus Day Speech," "compiled by the National Technical Information Service of the Department of Commerce of the U.S." *slobodan-milosevic.org*, http://www.slobodan-Milošević. org/spch-kosovo1989.htm. When he speaks about regaining the state and dignity of Serbia, Milošević refers to the constitutional amendments approved in March 1989. When he refers to the disunity of Serbian leaders, he means the disunity (and Vuk Branković's betrayal) that supposedly occurred in 1389, at the same time alluding to then-current disunities, since he was in conflict with some other Serbian communist leaders. The last quotation is a part of the paragraph that continues with: "Our chief battle now concerns implementing the economic, political, cultural and general social prosperity, finding a quicker and more successful approach to a civilization in which people will live in the twenty-first century. For this battle, we certainly need heroism, of course of a somewhat different kind, but that courage without which nothing serious and great can be achieved remains unchanged and remains urgently necessary."
205 | Starting with "Serbia has never had only Serbs living in it" and ending with "Therefore it is the obligation of the people to remove disunity, so that they may protect themselves from defeats, failures, and stagnation in the future."

> to be divided in the national and religious respect. The only differences one can and should allow in socialism are between hard working people and idlers and between honest people and dishonest people. Therefore, all people in Serbia who live from their own work, honestly, respecting other people and other nations, are in their own republic.

Apart from employing socialist discourse in the speech's central part, Milošević opens the speech by greeting the mass with the typically communist call "Comrades!"[206] and ends with, "Let the memory of Kosovo heroism live forever! Long live Serbia! Long live Yugoslavia! Long live peace and brotherhood among peoples!" The last line is a paraphrase of the motto of the SFRY, "brotherhood and unity." In difference to the central part, the first part of the speech contains a lot of national references and amounts mostly to a fictionalized history of the Serbian people marked by disunity among their leaders, which started already at the Battle of Kosovo and had just come to an end, finally giving Serbs cause for optimism about their future. The third part is the most ambiguous; it comprises both the call to nationalism and a pro-European vocabulary. Here Milošević identifies three conditions for a prosperous future for Serbia: patriotism (national pride, dignity, unity, not excluding even "armed battles"); the acceptance of "European values" ("Six centuries ago, Serbia heroically defended itself in the field of Kosovo, but it also defended Europe. Serbia was at that time the bastion that defended the European culture, religion, and European society in general."); and a universal, progressivist "implementation of the economic, political, cultural, and general social prosperity." All this makes the speech hybrid and controversial rather than univocally nationalistic. However, in the social reality of Yugoslavia, it acquired the illocutionary power to call Serbian citizens to nationalism. But for a more profound understanding of how and why this happened, we need to move from the discursive analysis of the speech to a performance analysis of the entire event.

Gazimestan can be observed as a paradigmatic liminal performance occurring within social drama and bringing, in a controversial way, a new communitas into the Yugoslav public sphere. Approximately 1.5 million people, who gathered to celebrate the anniversary and the famous Milošević's speech, marked the public inception of a long-term normative communitas in Serbia, one based on national (Serbian) and religious (Orthodox) values. In the following years it instituted itself more and more, gradually occupying the public sphere and entirely changing both the social context of socialist Yugoslavia, where nationalism was a taboo, and, to a certain extent, religion. Focusing on material aspects of the event, we need to explain that Kosovo at that time was a multiethnic province of Serbia were Albanians were in the majority while Serbs were a minority reduced to less than 200,000 citizens.[207] And the organizers of the Gazimestan event—without advertising or referring to it as an ideological or political gesture—brought 1.5 million people, almost exclusively Serbs from Serbia, other republics, and from the Serbian diaspora worldwide, to physically participate on Kosovan territory in the event. The number and physical presence of the "Serbian bodies" in Kosovo truly "speaks for itself" in terms which identify an ideological and political corporeality as akin to that which Judith Butler identifies as the production of public space by bodies gathered together.

---

206 | For passages not included in the translation, see video documentation of Milošević's speech in Serbo-Croat, "Gazimestan, 600th anniversary of the Kosovo polje battle," video from Internet Archive, http://archive.org/details/Gazimestan600thAnniversaryOfTheKosovoPoljeBattle.

207 | According to the census from 1981—1,226,735 (77.4%) Albanians and 209,498 (13.2%) Serbs; according to the census from 1991—1,596,072 (81.6%) Albanians and 194,190 (9.9%) Serbs.

In the course of the event, the new public space in Yugoslavia was thus formed primarily between or among the bodies co-present in alliance at Gazimestan in Kosovo. In addition, the event took place in a symbolically heavily laden spot. Gazimestan is a hill near Priština with a commemorative monument dedicated to the Battle of Kosovo. Gazimestan means "the place of the (war) hero" and is composed of the Turkish word *gazi* (hero) and Serbian *mesto* (place). At the monument the infamous "Kosovo Course" uttered by Prince Lazar is inscribed, which curses all Serbs who failed to come to Kosovo to fight for Serbia. Apart from this direct symbolism, it is worth mentioning that since the battle is not seen as a battle only between Serbs and Turks but also between Christians and Muslims, the story could have been smoothly extrapolated and reused in the then ongoing conflicts between Serbs (Christians) and Albanians (Muslims) in Kosovo.

Keeping this contextual framework in mind, it is now easier to understand how Milošević's speech, which itself is not extremely nationalistic, functioned as a nationalist hailing. The crucial matter is an indeed liminal moment in which the event took place: the speech was delivered in the time when socialist ideology was exhausted, being too familiar, heard too many times, too bureaucratic, and finally reduced to empty signifiers. In such a moment, the major part of the speech employing socialist ideas, vocabulary, and rhetorics was heard much less than the then-new patriotic and nationalist discourse. In fact, it served as a neutral and common background for the emergence of new ideas rather than as their counterpoint. Therefore it comes as no surprise that the gathered mass in that liminal moment reacted to the speech exactly as they did, responding only to the nationalistic parts and to patriotic references, thus giving an additional illocutionary power to Milošević's speech and making the whole event a ritual of collective national initiation. The reactions were in fact an ideological continuation and consolidation of the performance of the crowd itself, who, though confusingly mixing both SFRY and Serbian symbols, banners, and posters, was most of the time singing Serbian patriotic and nationalistic songs, like "Who Says, Who Lies [that] Serbia Is Small?"—which could not be forbidden or relegated to the level of "private matter" any more because they were now being sung publically by 1.5 million voices. The same mechanism can be observed in the stage design where the official program took place, which bore three flags and a symbol between them. All three flags belonged to socialist iconography: the flag of the SFRY, the flag of the Socialist Republic of Serbia, and the flag of the Communist Party of Yugoslavia. Between these flags was the golden logo of the event: "600" with "1389–1989" filling the last zero, which, as a whole, somewhat resembles the Orthodox cross with the symbol of a fourfold "S" in the Cyrillic letter ("C"), designating the slogan "Only unity (concord) saves the Serbs." This logo was the most remarkable element of the display, again since the flags were perceived as the conventional iconography of an official public event. And this is how the materiality of the context and of the event enacted a "performative turn" of its linguistic, locutory register, which should not be neglected when observing and analyzing its social functioning. And only at this point can we fully understand what Milošević's speech *did with words*: it interpellated the citizens of Serbia as Serbs. The ideological transformation of workers as citizens of a socialist republic into a nationally identified people is crucial here and turns the event into a genuine socio-political ritual. Moreover, this ideological performative had its real political consequences, since in the near future it will hail ethnic Serb citizens of other Yugoslav republics (especially Croatia and Bosnia and Herzegovina) and unite them under the idea of a Serbian people, without which the civil wars in former Yugoslavia wouldn't have been possible.

We would end this analysis with a few remarks about the communitas that was emerging during the Gazimestan event and which normativized itself during the 1990s. The question of whether it was a spontaneous or ideological communitas, which has often appeared in interpretations of the event, is, we hope, already answered in general. So we could only repeat here that it doesn't matter whether it was a spontaneous and grassroots communitas that didn't have a clear ideological program and saw Milošević as the one who would legitimize it, or if it was, from the outset, organized and "commissioned" by the Milošević-led state in order to implement a new ideology and prepare the terrain for his political decisions of the near future. It does not really matter since the event and the gathered mass already ritualistically embodied its ideology, bringing it to the Yugoslav public in a spectacular way and completely changing its landscape.

In this case there arises an even more challenging and far-reaching question: the question of the void versus the wholeness as the basis of communitas. In the recent history of Yugoslavia and Serbia, Gazimestan almost illustratively functioned as a ritualistic return to the lost (and mythic, probably never existing) roots of a Serbian community. It occurred in the moment when the conflicts among Albanians and Serbs in Kosovo escalated into the social symptom. Thinking further about the roots of the community, Turner's enthusiasm about the power of the weak and equal as a reminder of social wholeness cannot help us, for it seems that only Esposito's somewhat "dark" perspective could explain why in that situation the Battle of Kosovo played the central role. The battle—paradoxically, at first glance—is not a Serbian victory that is to be celebrated and used as fuel for national pride, but a traumatic point in Serbian history, not only because its Prince was killed, together with a huge number of Serbian men, but also because in the aftermath of the battle the independent Serbian state fell and failed to defend Christian Europe. Therefore, embedding the battle in the symbolic core of the new Serbian community based on the "scapegoat national identity"[208] means, to be sure, building the community around the hole, debt, trauma, and sacrifice. Esposito's words could explain it precisely:

> All of the stories that tell of the founding crime, the collective crime, the ritual assassination, the sacrificial victim featured in the history of civilization don't do anything else except evoke metaphorically the *delinquere* that keeps us together, in the technical sense of "to lack" and "to be wanting"; the breach, the trauma, the lacuna out of which we originate. Not the Origin but its absence, withdrawal.[209]

Continuing in this direction, we can infer that the new Serbian community grounded on the myth of Kosovo is *per definition* a negative category, a community which paradoxically arises by affirming its own negation. The Battle of Kosovo is not a thing, but rather a no-thing. And that is exactly where its enormous ideological power lies, since it is a hole that seeks to be but is never filled with a thing, a hole into which many things can be projected. This reasoning can explain how the tragic nihilism of the Serbian community celebrating its own loss, which has followed it throughout the last twenty years, makes ontological sense. And, however irrational it is or looks, history has already shown that it cannot be fought easily by the rationalist discourse of neoliberal capitalism; in turn, it can,

---

208 | The scapegoat national identity is constructed in a reactionary relation to the past, generating resistance to what its subjects understood as the position of the oppressed and deprived of inherited rights. In this particular case the sense of defeat and loss motivates an active force of retribution and revenge for the sake of a nationalist political project. See Manuel Castells, *The Power of Identity* (Oxford: Blackwell Publishers, 1997).

209 | Esposito, *Communitas*, 8.

however, be easily manipulated and abused by any political partly or social organization who would reaffirm and reproduce it to advance its rise to power and even its simplest material interests. Furthermore, the community entrapped by its own linkage to the *delinquere* cannot stand to hear the public debate about "Kosovo," even when it comes to current geopolitical questions concerning the territory of Kosovo, for every public speech about the matter is viewed through fundamental categories of "with us" or "against us." In that atmosphere every link seems too profane to be substituted for the *delinquere* that keeps the community together. However, in closing, we want to add that the community built on the myth of Kosovo is not the only one existing in Serbia, though it is the most powerful one. After it resolved the social drama of the end of socialism and dismissed socialist and communist discourses and political options, it brought a new, intense, and long-lasting antagonism onto the public scene—the antagonism between one side that promotes neoliberal democratic capitalism and the other side that advertises nationalism and conservativism and, yet, also complies with capitalism. These processes, which symbolically started at Gazimestan, also show how nationalism in Serbia emerged in the context of socialism, with socialism as its antagonistic opposition, and confirms the main thesis of this part of the book: only ideology can fight ideology. For while the last *Slets* represented a certain exhaustion of and dissatisfaction with socialism, the Gazimestan event heralded nationalism as a new ideology capable of fighting the socialist ideology and eventually defeating it.

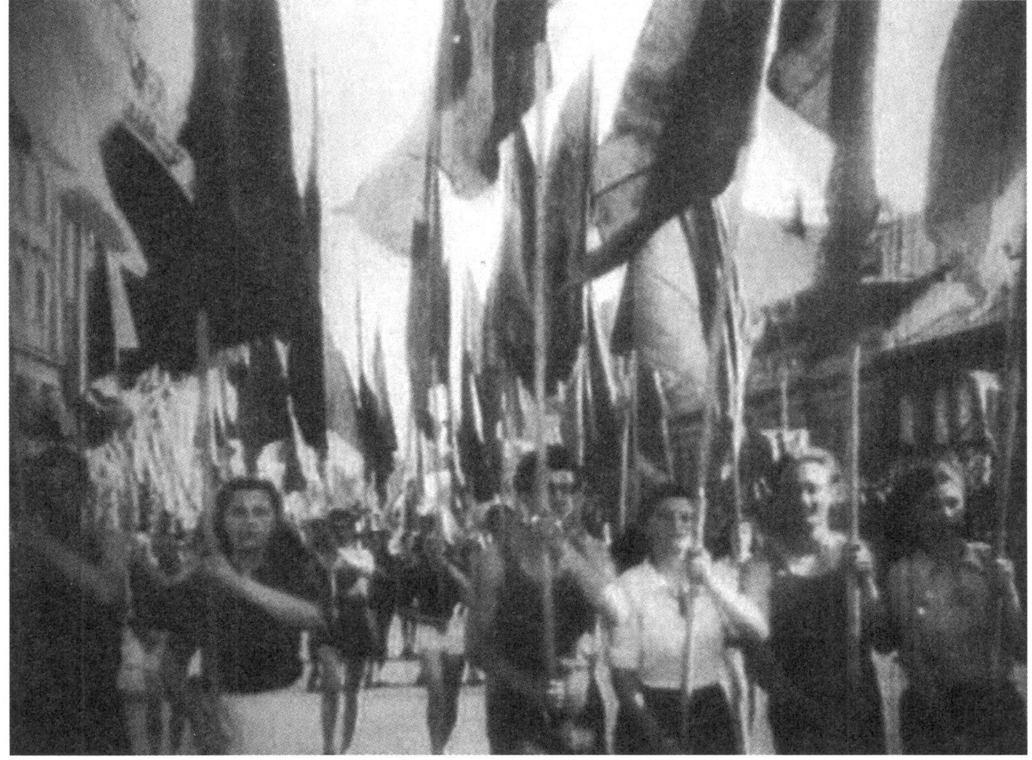

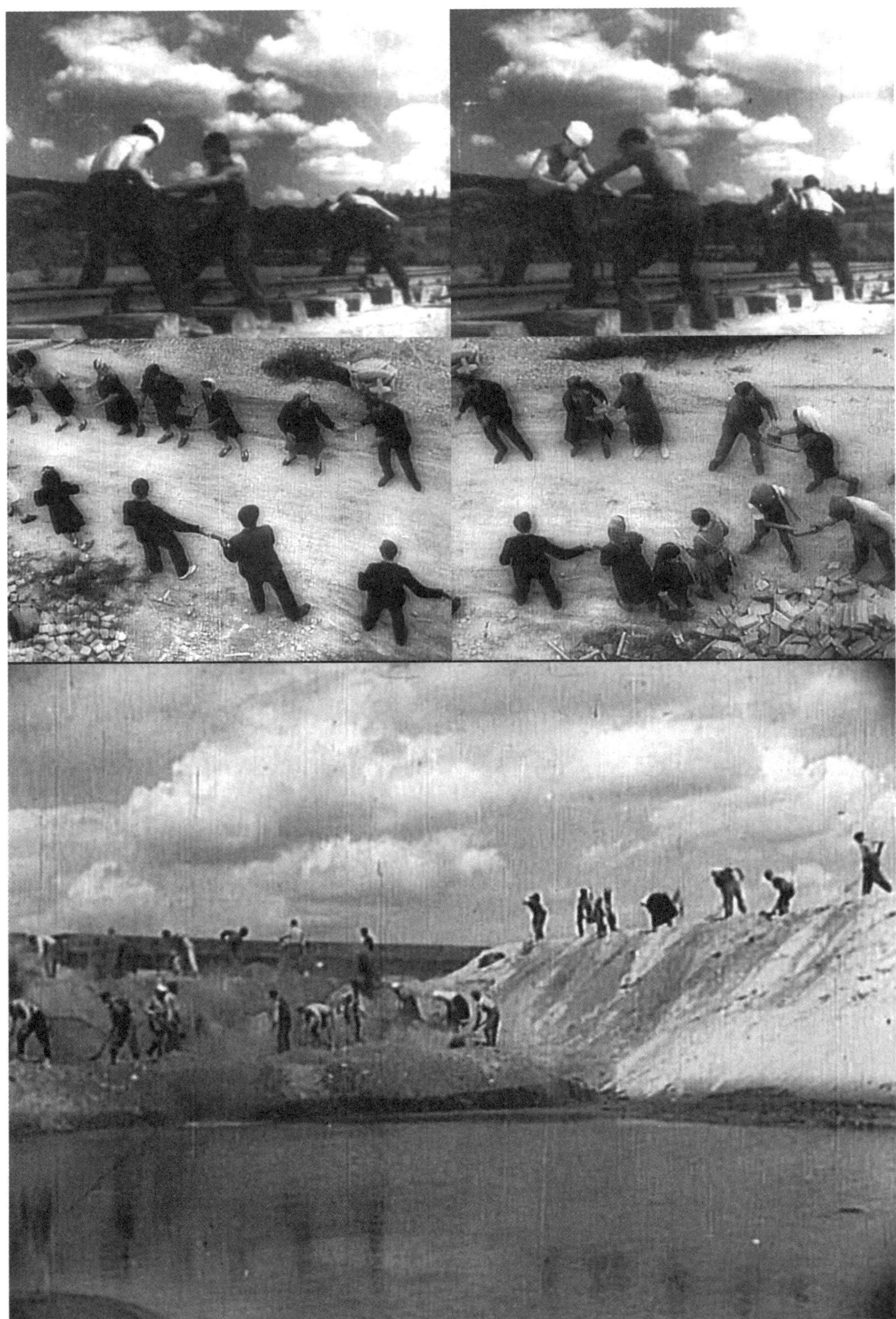

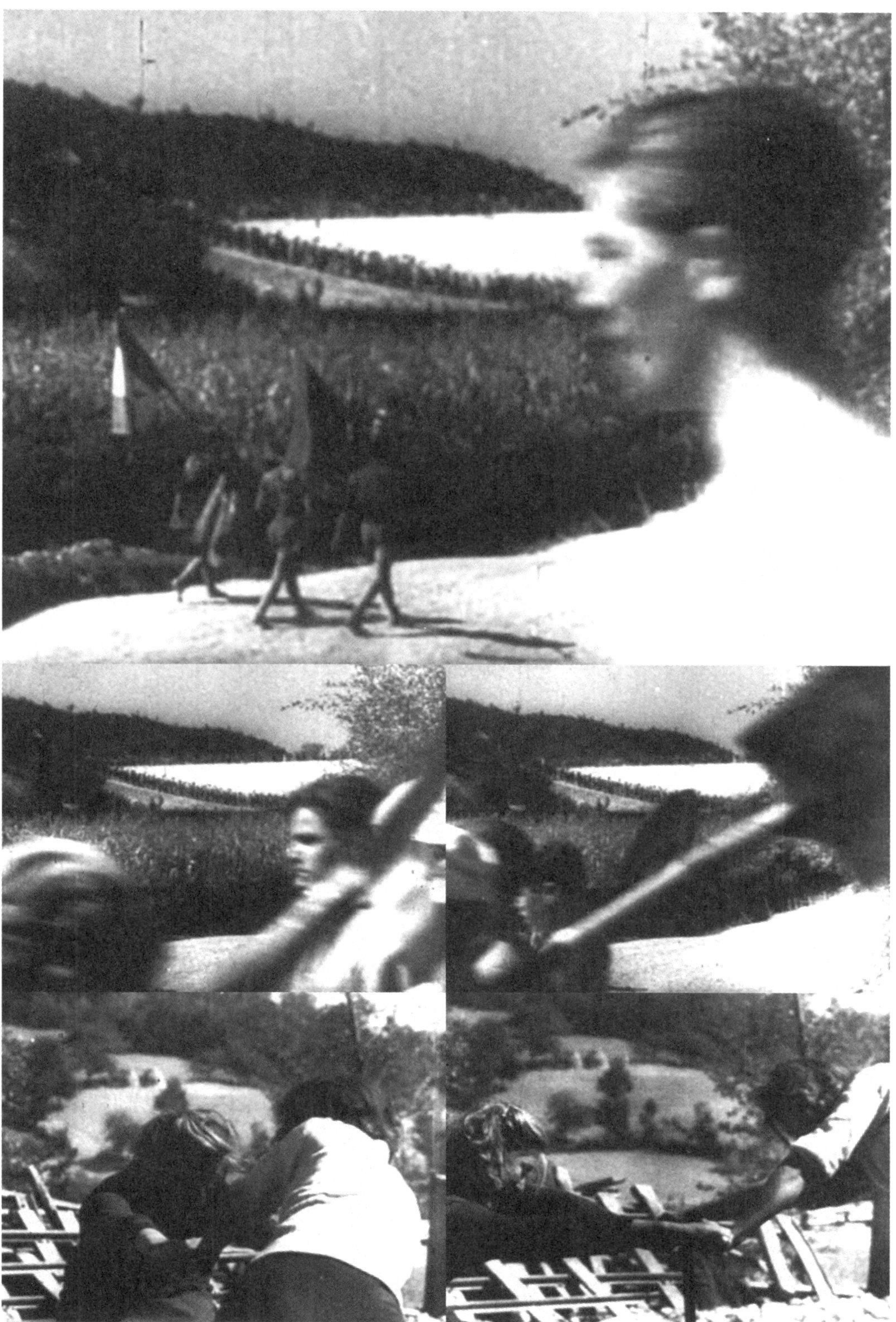

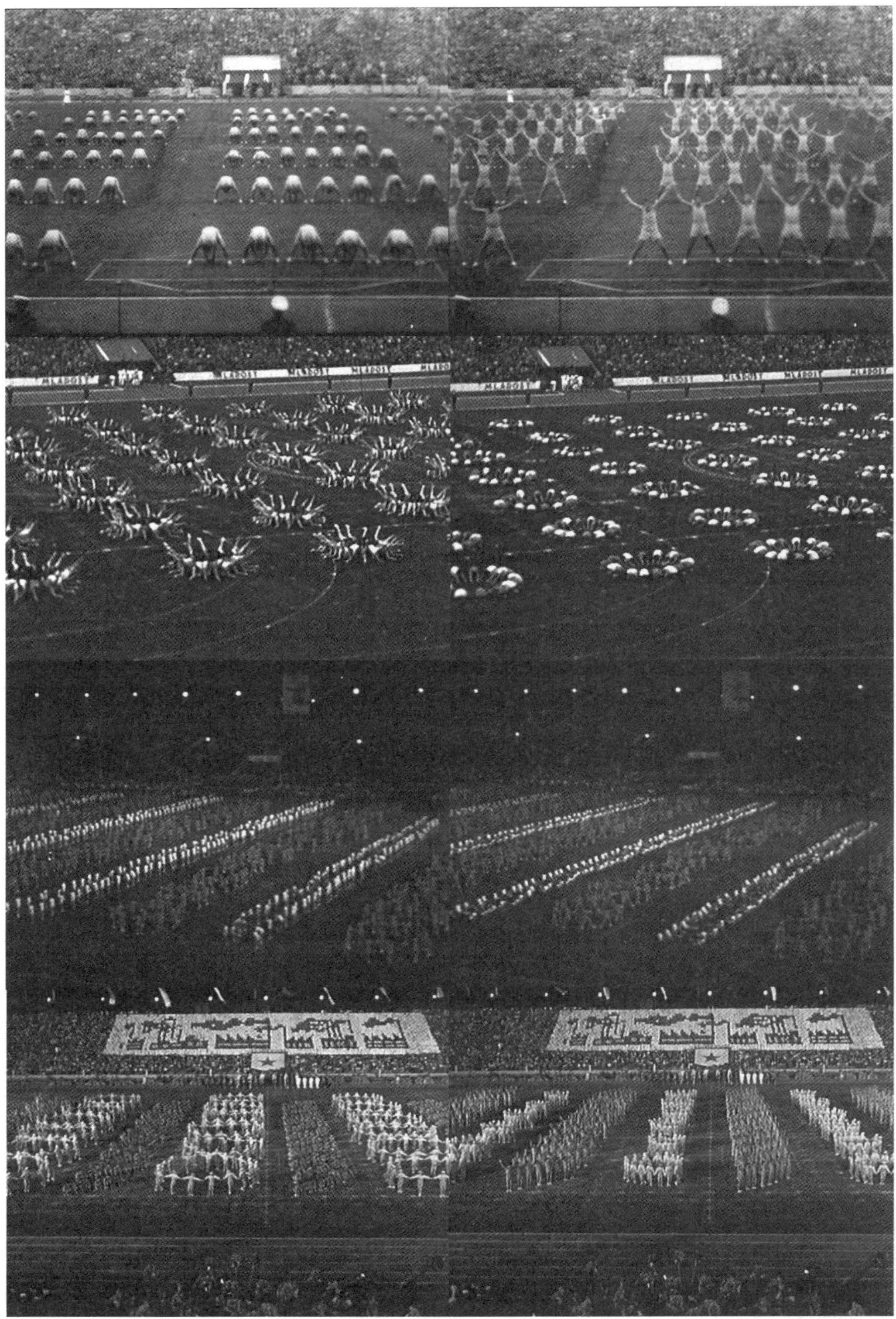

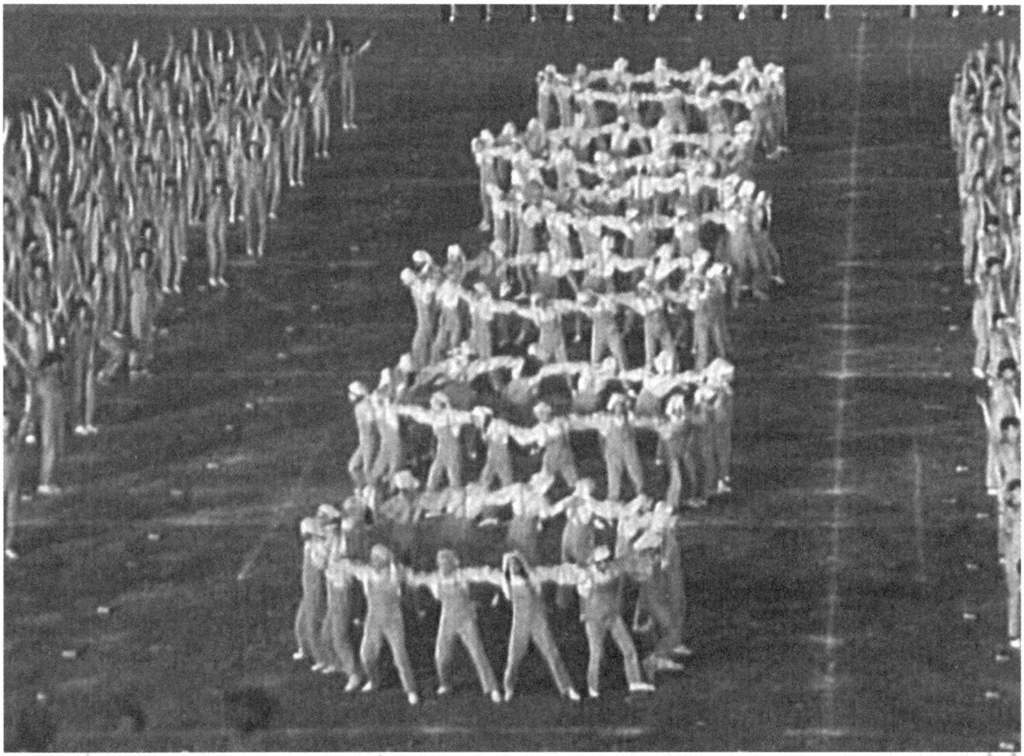

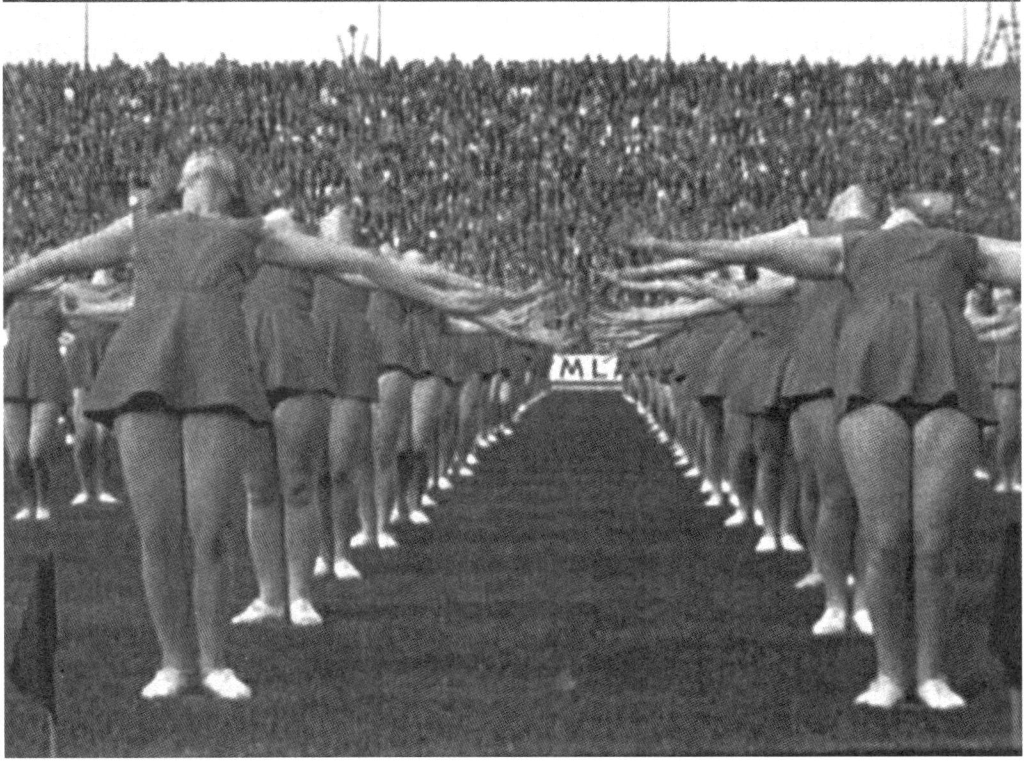

ML

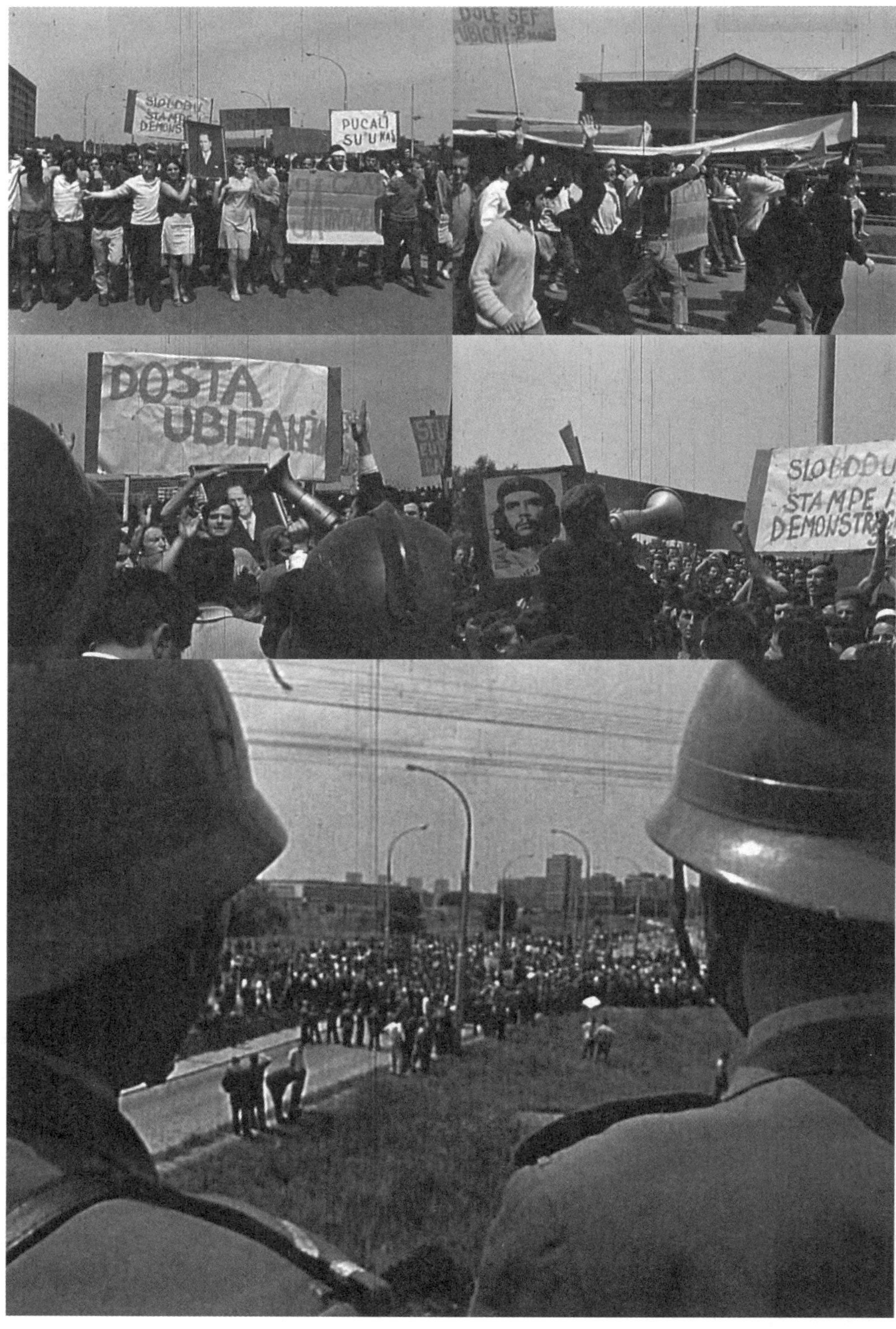

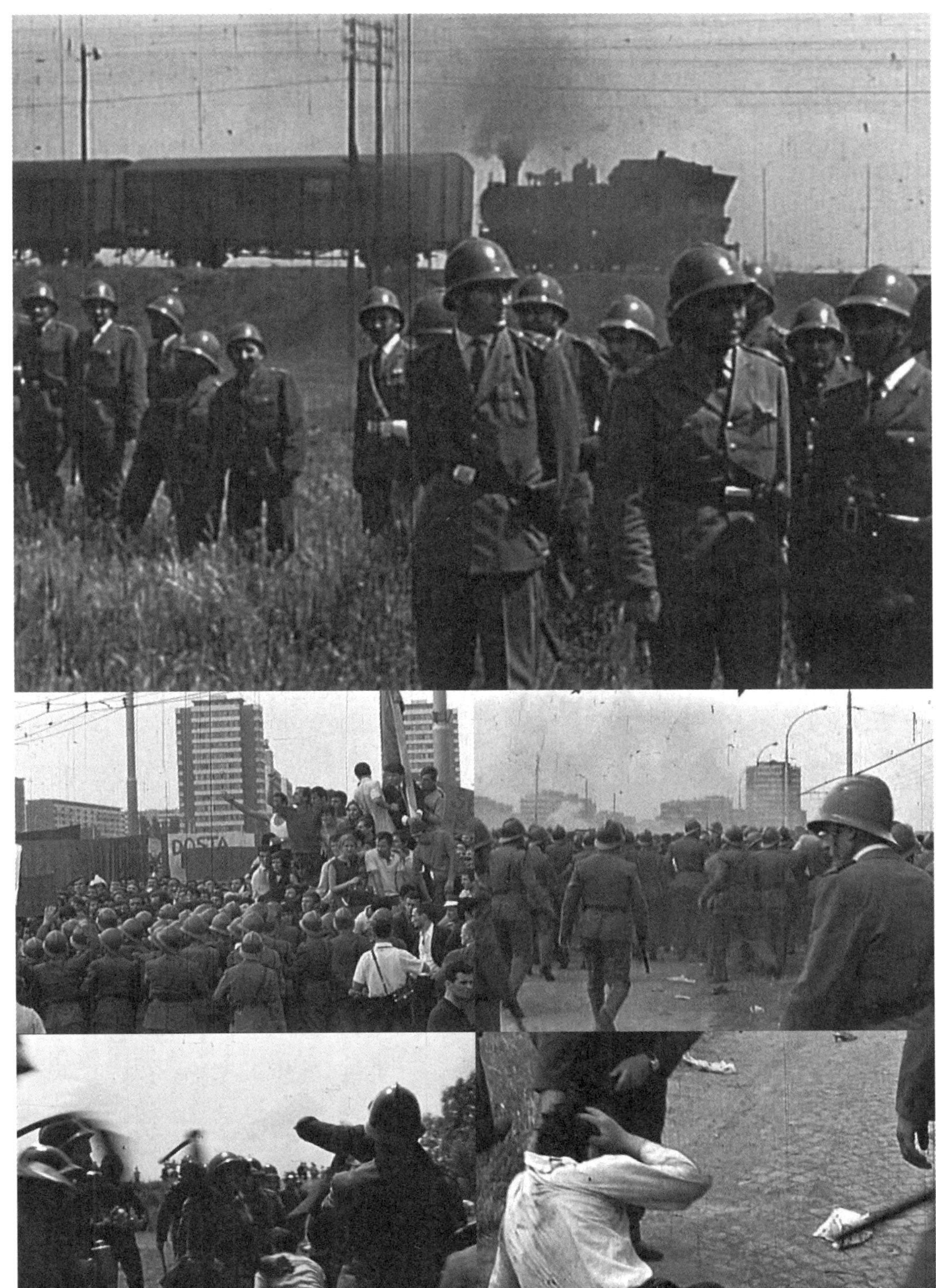

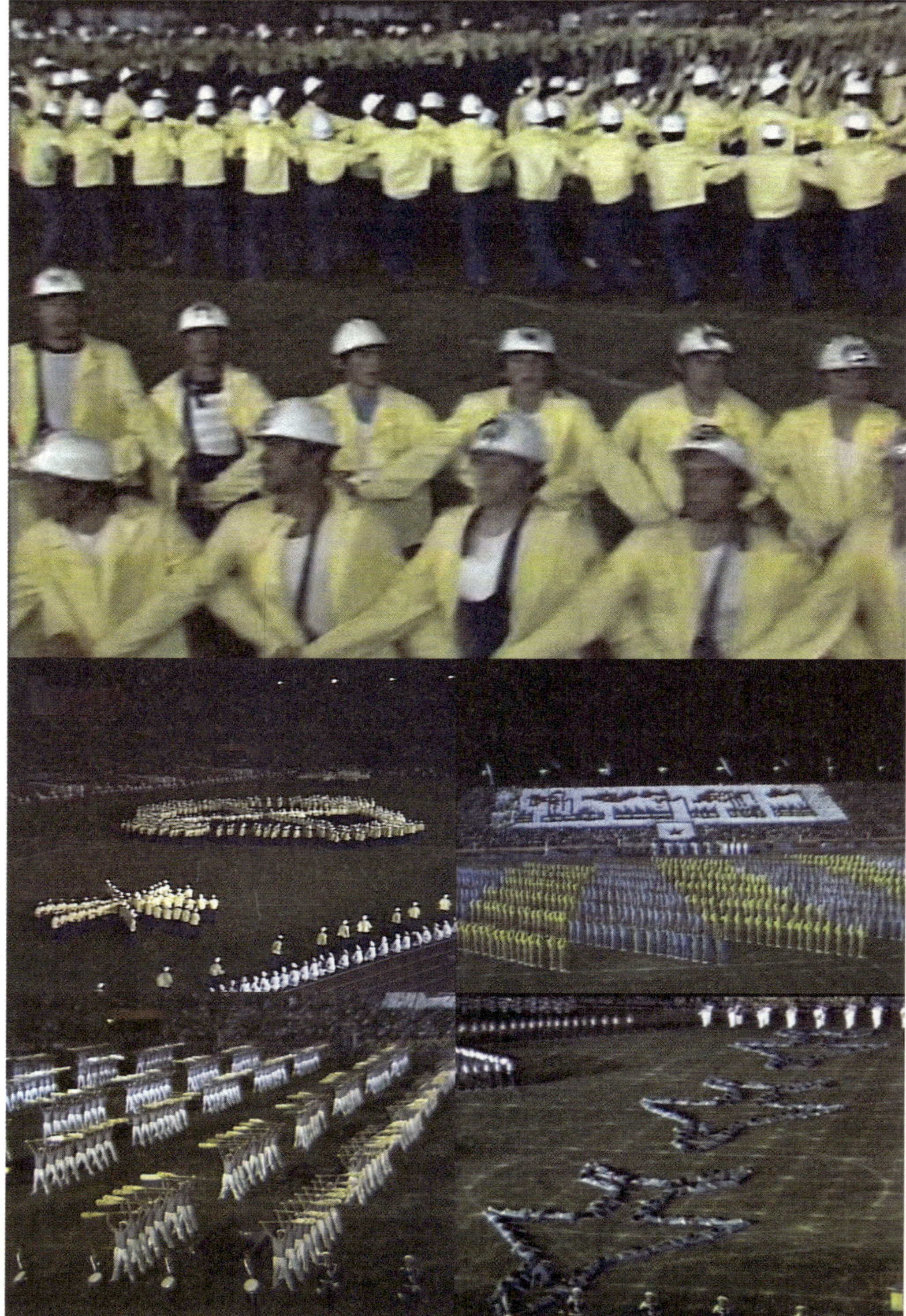

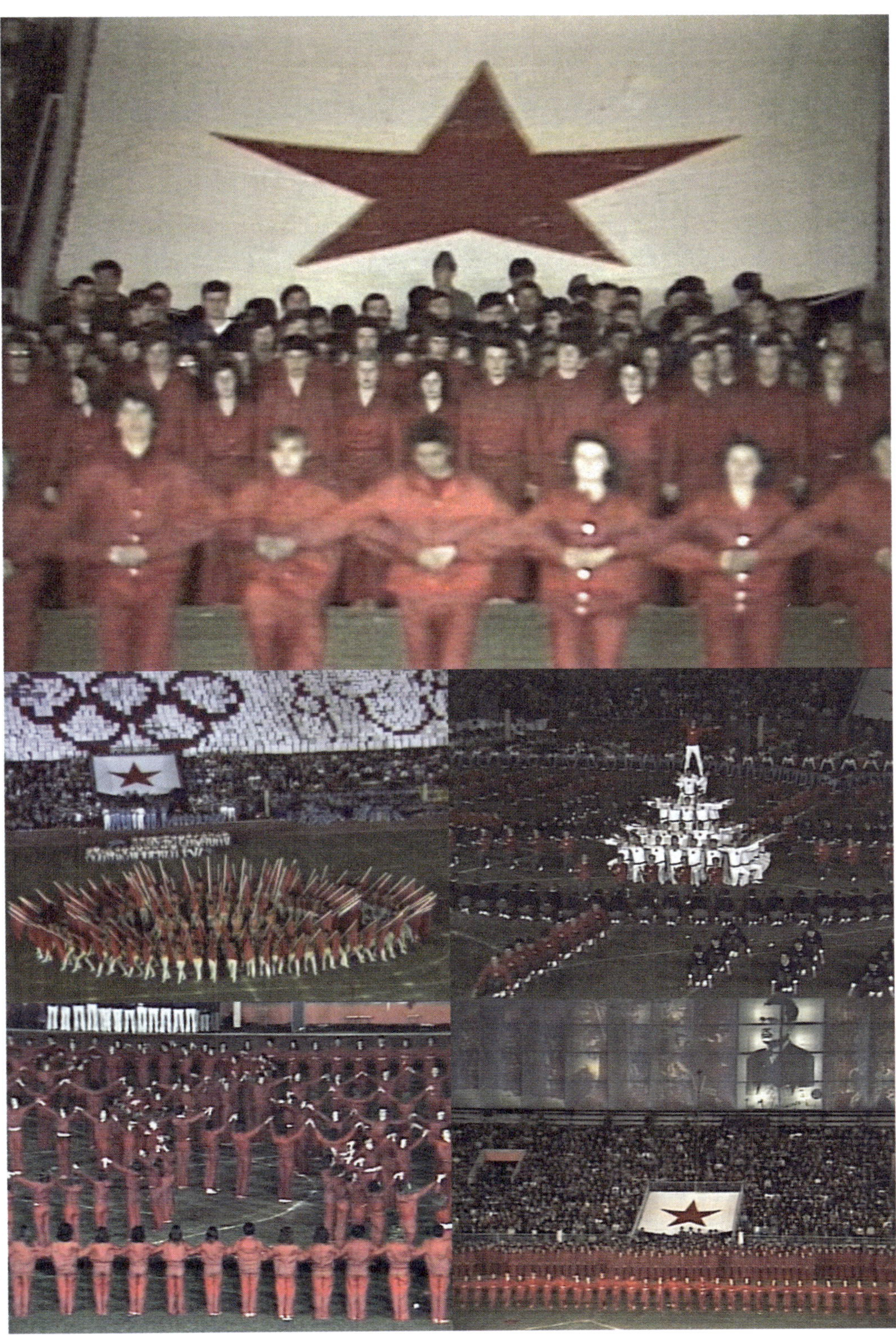

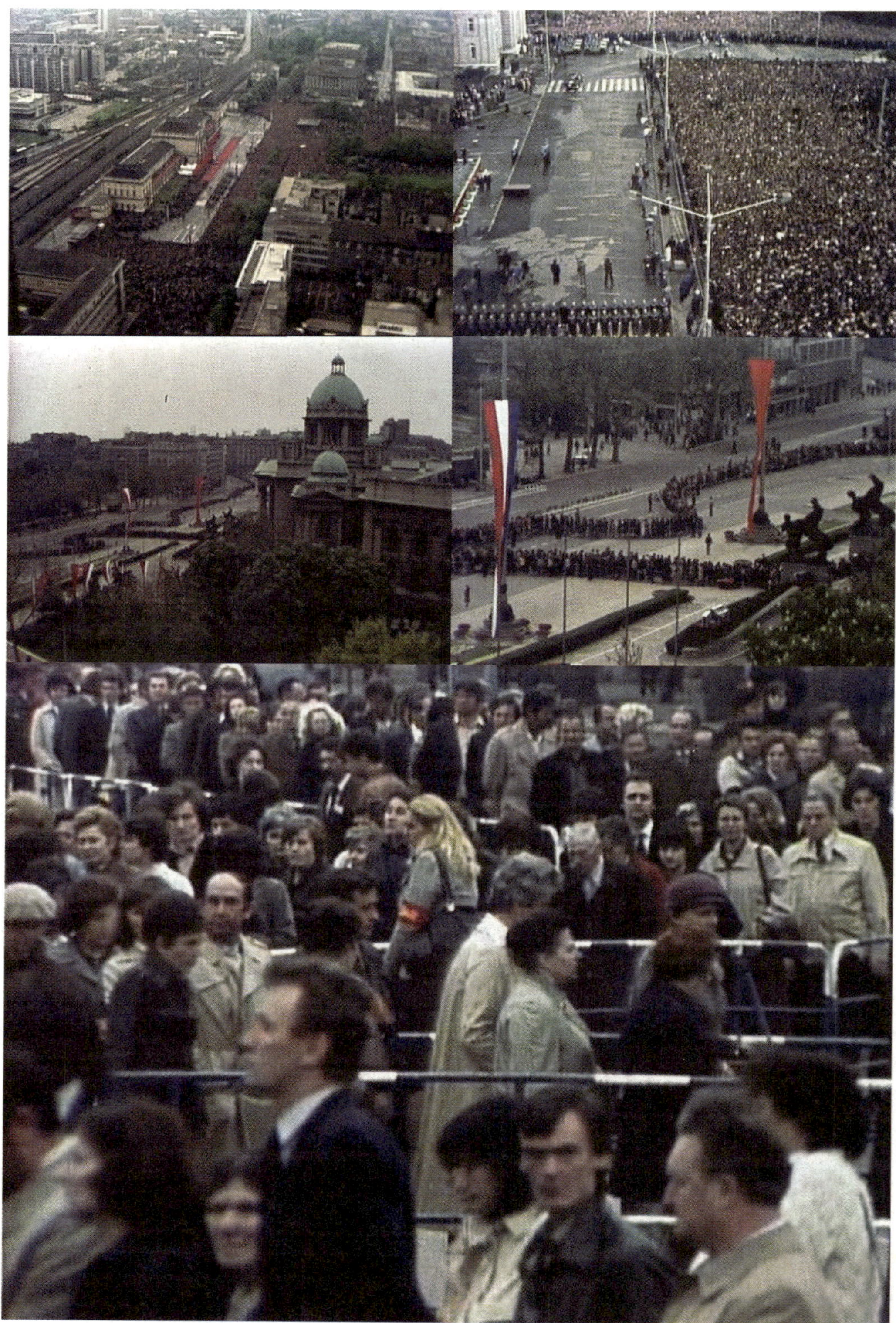

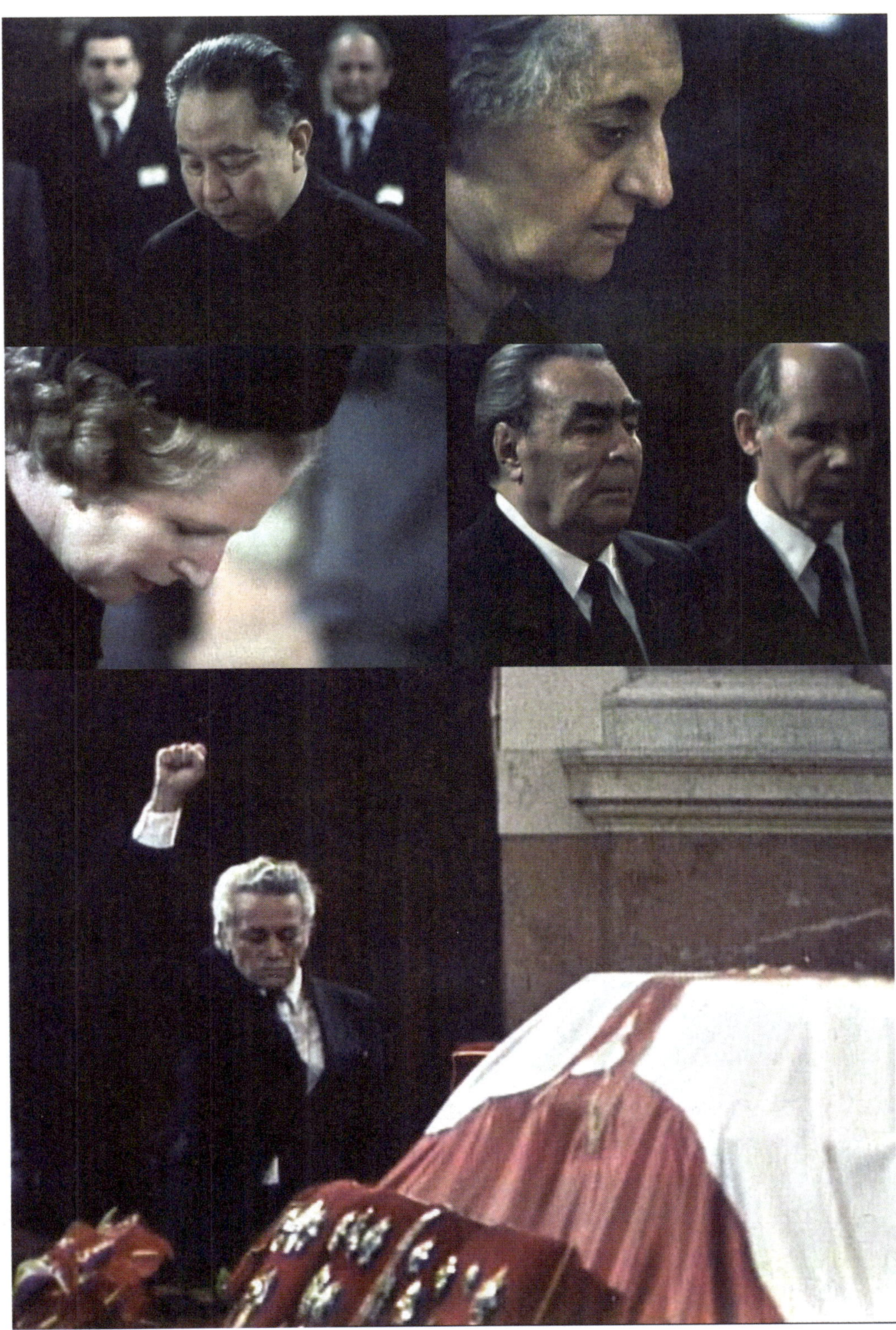

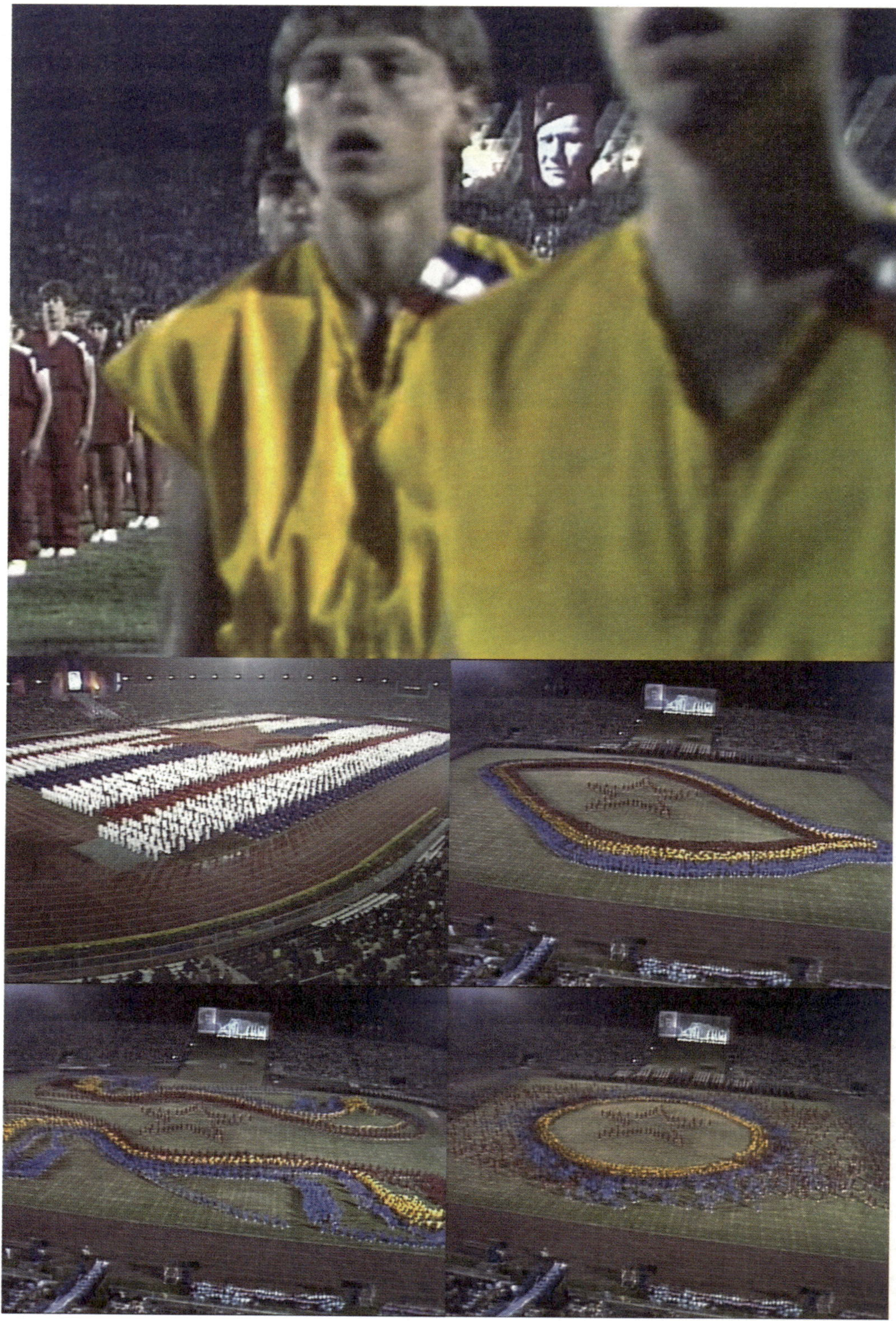

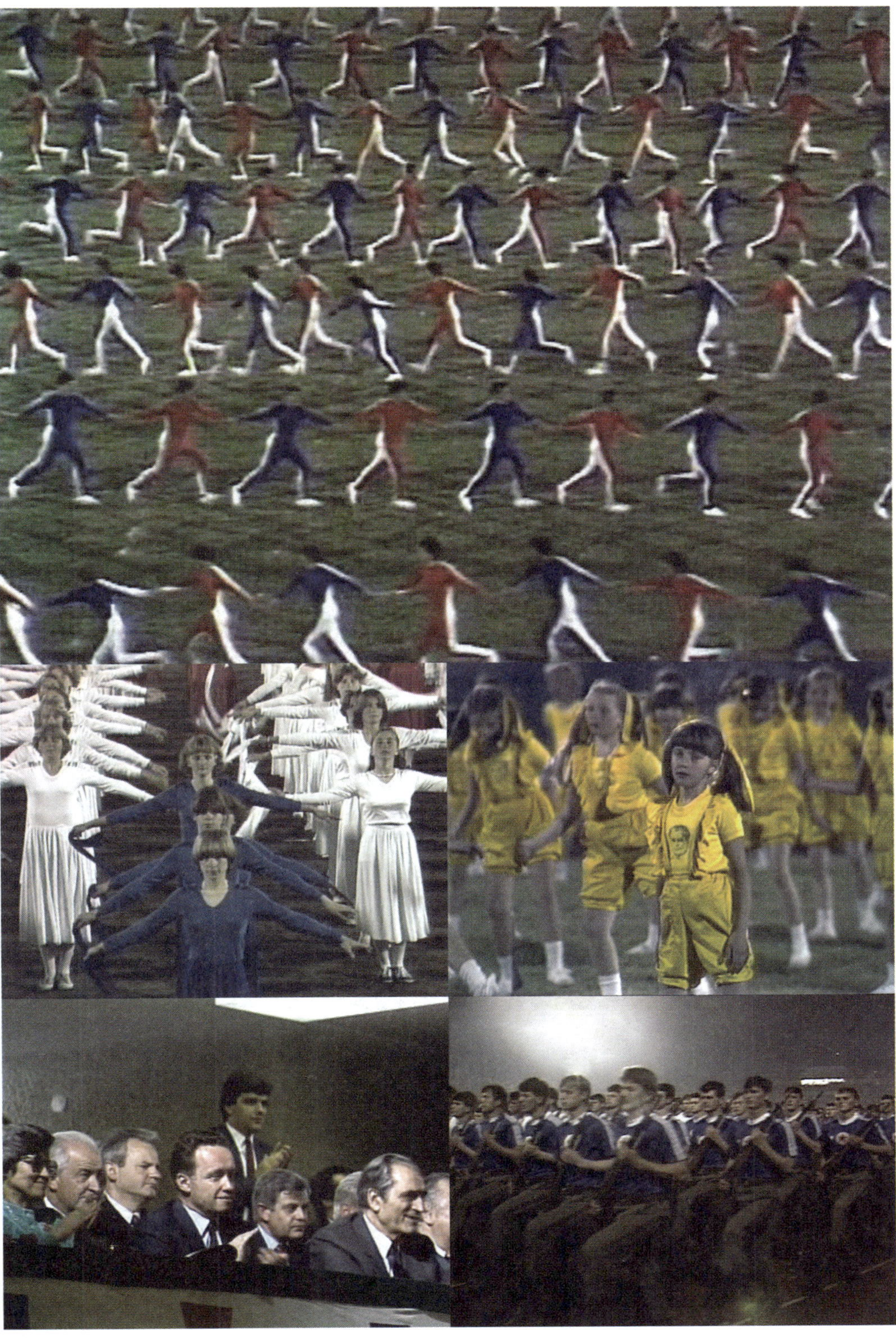

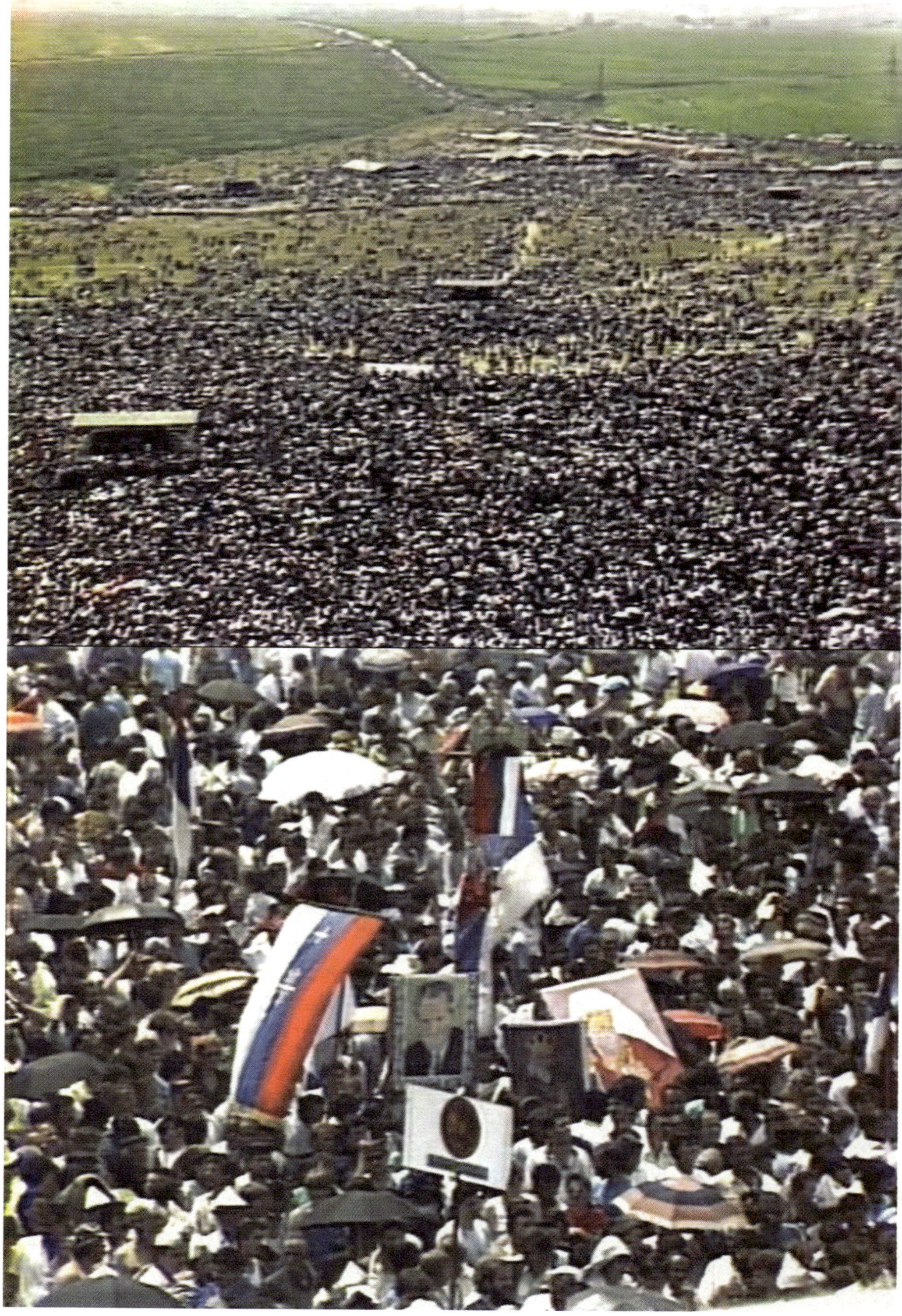

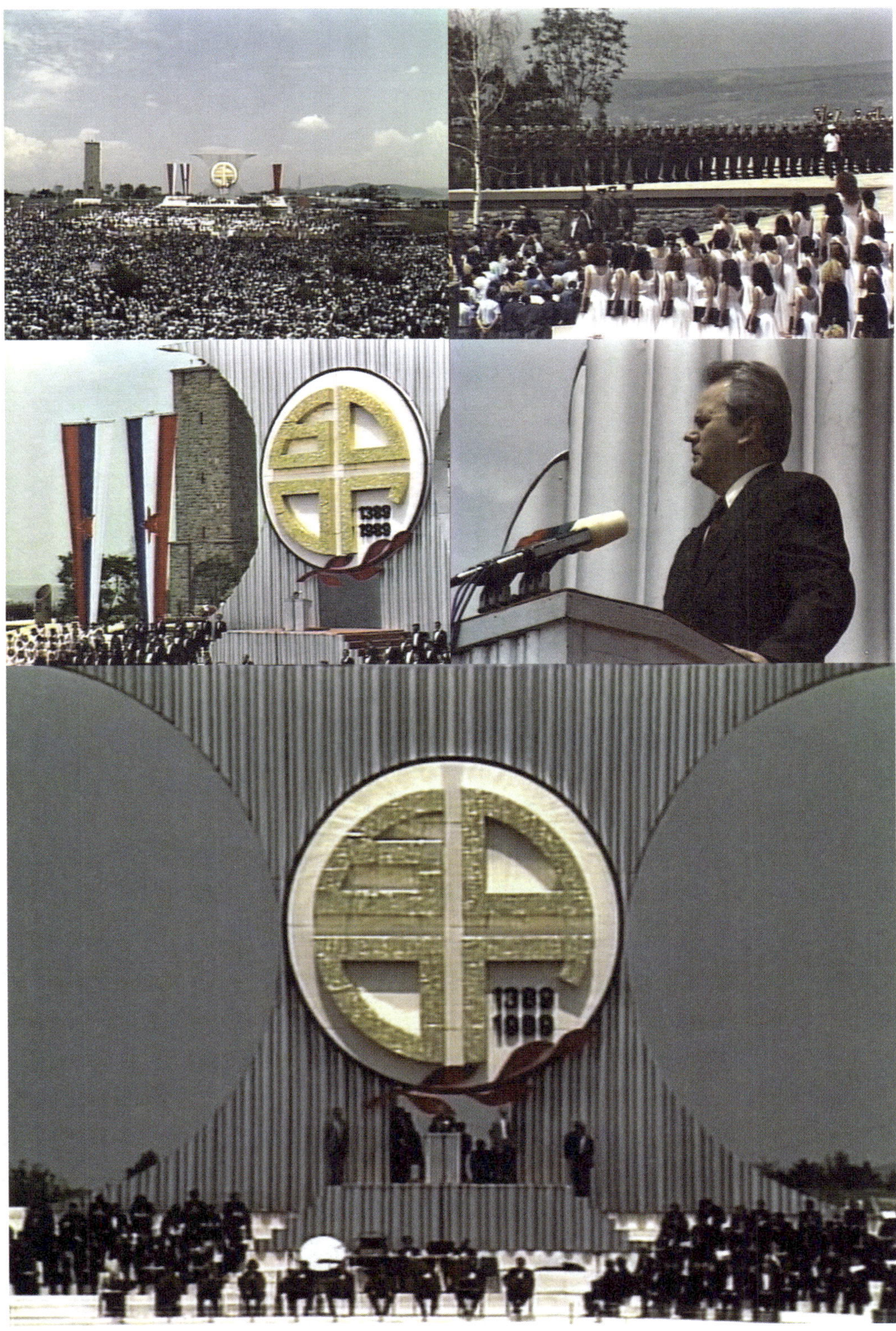

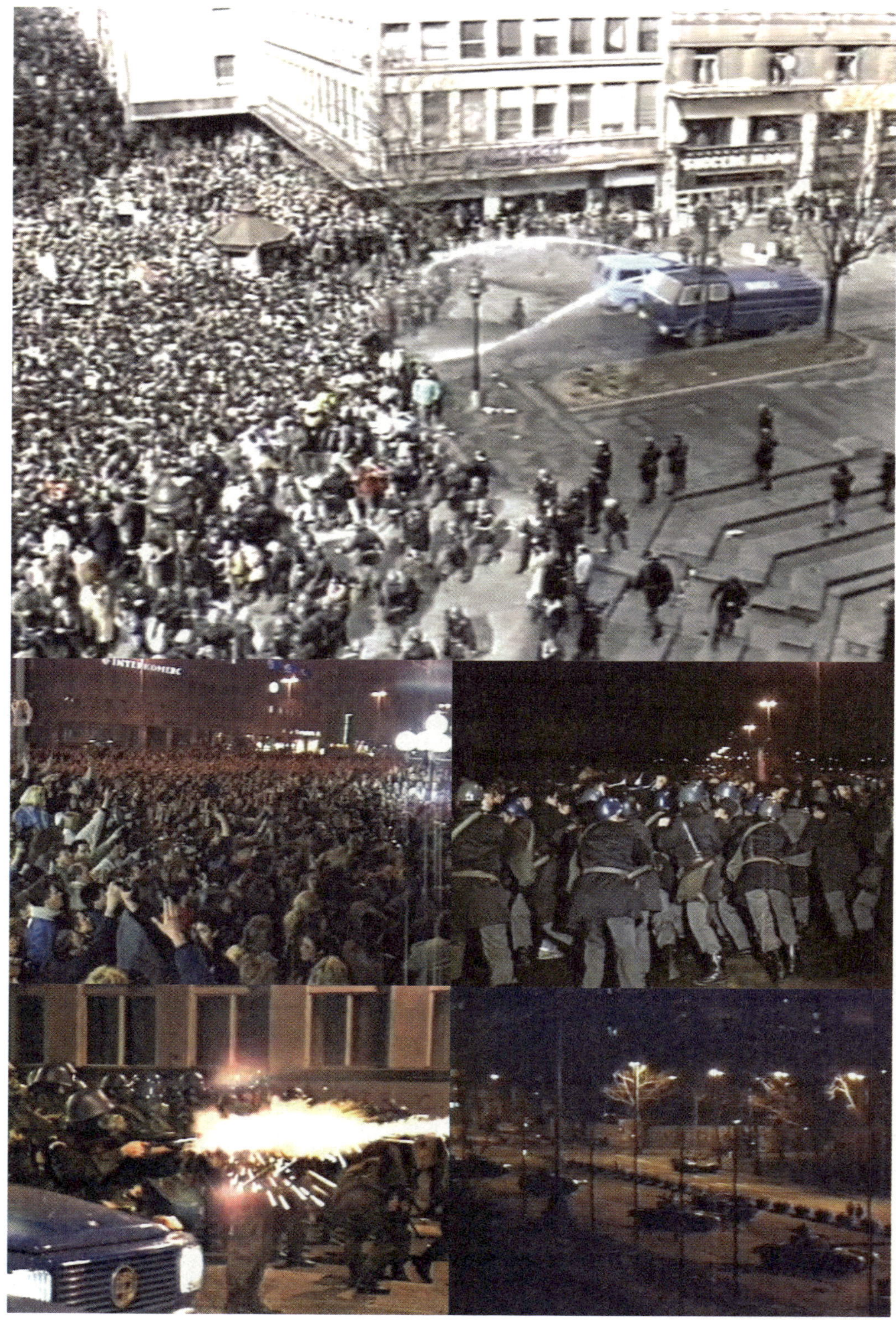

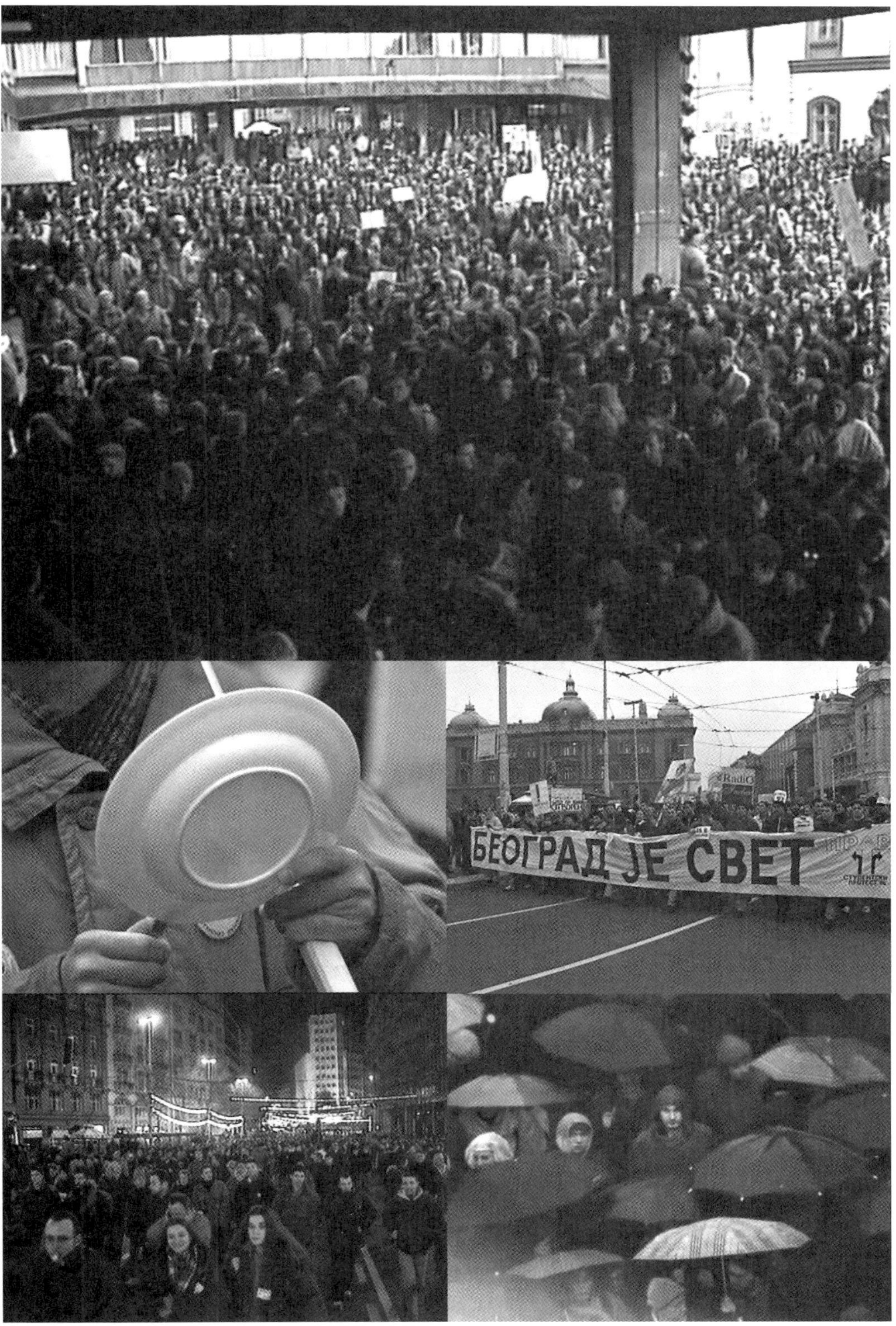
БЕОГРАД ЈЕ СВЕТ
RadiO

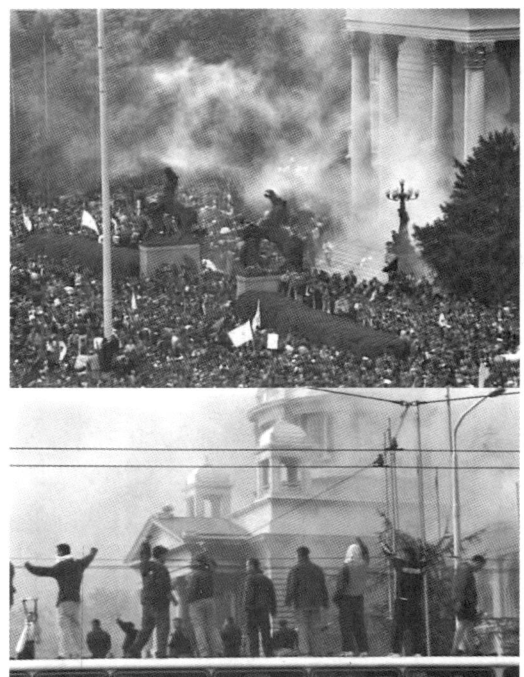

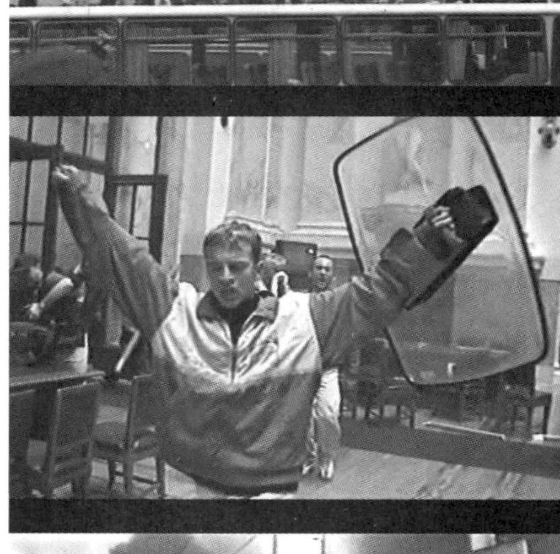

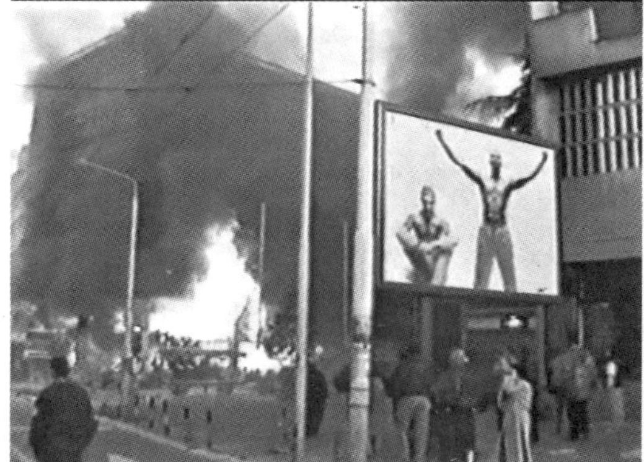

page 97
1947, MAYDAY PARADE, Belgrade
Federal People's Republic of Yugoslavia

pages 98–99
1946–1952, YOUTH WORK ACTIONS,
Federal People's Republic of Yugoslavia

pages 100–101
1960s, "YOUTH DAY," Belgrade
Socialist Federal Republic of Yugoslavia (FPRY)

pages 102–103
1968, PROTESTS OF 1968, Belgrade
Socialist Federal Republic of Yugoslavia

pages 104–105
1970s, "YOUTH DAY," Belgrade
Socialist Federal Republic of Yugoslavia

pages 106–107
1980, TITO'S FUNERAL
Socialist Federal Republic of Yugoslavia

pages 108–109
1980s, "YOUTH DAY," Belgrade
Socialist Federal Republic of Yugoslavia

pages 110–111
1989, GAZIMESTAN RALLY, Kosovo
Socialist Federal Republic of Yugoslavia

page 112
1991, MARCH 9 OPPOSITION PROTEST
Belgrade, Socialist Federal Republic of Yugoslavia

page 113
1996–1997, STUDENT AND CIVIL PROTESTS
Serbia, Federal Republic of Yugoslavia

page 114
2000, 5 OCTOBER OVERTHROW
Belgrade, Federal Republic of Yugoslavia

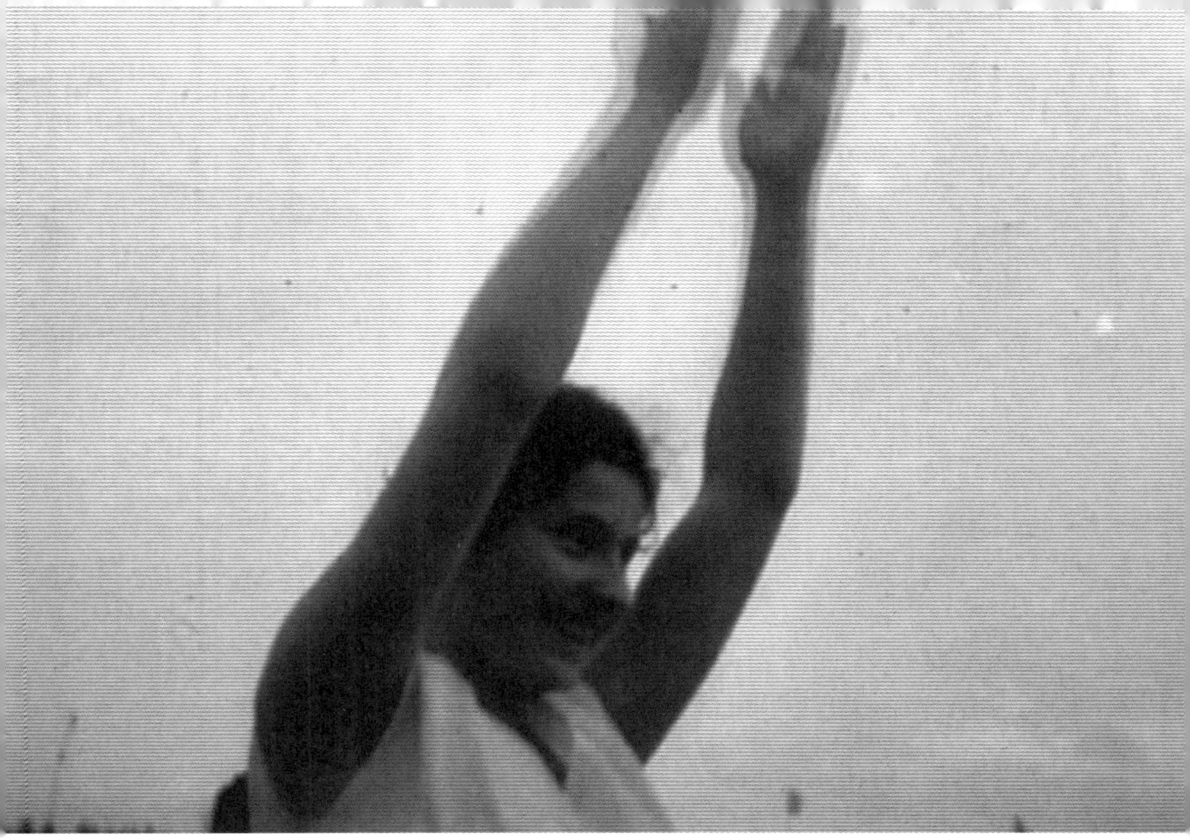

Part III

The Self and the Public

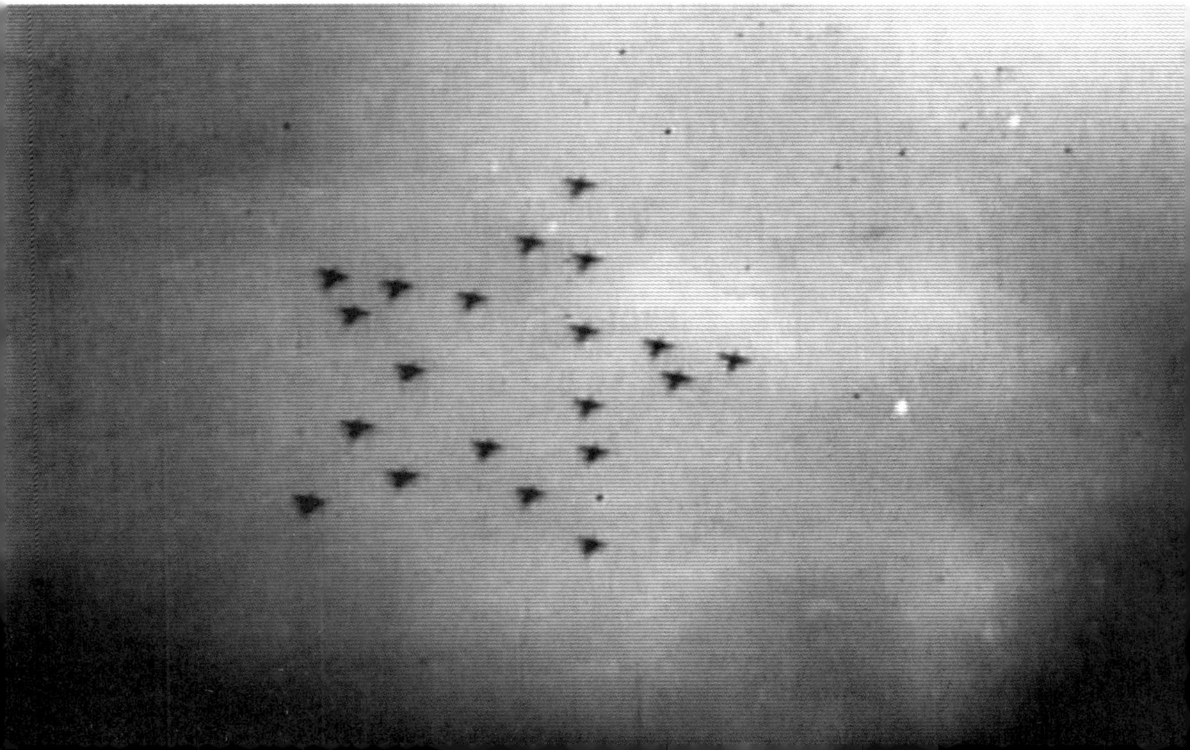

If the public as political sphere is constituted *in* ideology and *through* performance—the thesis we have hitherto been probing in public performances of state, communitas, or social movements—then a large part of this claim entails the question of how individuals inhabit, participate, or shape the public. Invoking them here as "individuals" rather than social subjects rests on the following observation: on our way to reaching the category of citizens, we constantly stumble upon human beings as individuals that plead their status prior to or beyond citizenship. This situation can be viewed as an imbalance along the axis of the public and the private that has been commented in a wide range of literature from Arendt's critique of the depoliticization and downfall of public life[210] to various sociological accounts, such as the American 1976 national bestseller, *The Culture of Narcissism: American Life in an Age of Diminishing Expectations*, by Christopher Lasch. Sennett describes it as the humanitarian spirit of an intimate society inherited from the nineteenth century, when political categories were transmuted into psychological categories and politics took an ethical turn, centralizing questions of identity, human rights, and the administration of good life.

210 | Hannah Arendt, *The Human Condition* (Chicago: University of Chicago Press, 1998); Arendt, *On Revolution* (New York: Viking, 1963), see esp. chapter 1, "The Eclipse of the Public."

Speaking in broader terms, while intimacy was certainly supported by the institutionalization of psychoanalysis in the twentieth century, creativity seems more characteristic for how the self is performed in the current form of capitalism. The narcissistic self needs an audience for its spectacle of self-affection, where producing, consuming, and trading experience is its significant mode. The social field is populated by diverse apparatuses today that offer individuals techniques for *indulging* their private selves in the public sphere with what Agamben calls apparatuses of *desubjectification* that capture, that is, control subjects by means of the very freedom they provide those subjects with. For Agamben, the promise of freedom lies in the discourse of technology, which in turn doesn't produce new subjects, but rather captures the "correct use" of apparatuses of the subject so as to subject her to an economic control.[211] Representative democracy enforces individualism as the ideology rooted in the liberal heritage of individual freedom, which has, through the realization of the self, proven to be the best driving force for the free-trade economy. This constitutes a paradox: the internalist orientation of the common understanding of the self is the very evidence of its external constitution in the social field. The crux of this claim is that the self is constituted externally, that is, in front of others, by or in performance. Several models inform the existing theoretical framework for considering the performance of the self. We will here examine a selection of a few key concepts developed in social theory throughout the twentieth century, concepts we find relevant for an analysis of the status of the self along the private-public axis. Hence the following sections will discuss habitus and the techniques of the body in the theories of Marcel Mauss and Pierre Bourdieu, the social roles and the performance of self as Erving Goffman has postulated it, man as actor and the fall of the public man in Richard Sennett's history of public life, the technologies of the self in Michel Foucault's late work, and the performing of identity in Judith Butler's theory of identity politics.

HABITUS

One of the earliest models that accounts for the performance of the self is the concept of habitus. The meaning of habitus is quite comprehensive and will introduce several problems we shall discuss later. Its terms in contemporary usage were first elaborated by the sociologists Marcel Mauss[212] and Norbert Elias,[213] further developed by Pierre Bourdieu,[214] and followed by many reinterpretations in social theory. Habitus could be described as the way an individual human is positioned in a social context, where the cognitive schemata and behavioral patterns operating in the context play a significant

---

211 | Giorgio Agamben, "What is an Apparatus?" in *What is An Apparatus and Other Essays*, trans. David Kishik and Stefan Pedatella (Palo Alto, CA: Stanford University Press, 2009).

212 | Marcel Mauss, "Techniques of the Body," *Economy and Society* 2, no. 1 (1973): 70–88; originally published as «Les techniques du corps», *Journal de Psychologie* 32, no. 3-4 (1934).

213 | Norbert Elias, *The Civilizing Process: Sociogenetic and Psychogenetic Investigations.* Vol. 1, *The History of Manners* (New York: Urizen Books, 1978); Vol. 2, *Power and Civility* (Oxford: Basil Blackwell, 1982); originally published as *Über den Prozeß der Zivilisation. Soziogenetische und psychogenetische Untersuchungen.* Band 1, *Wandlungen des Verhaltens in den weltlichen Oberschichten des Abendlandes.* Band 2: *Wandlungen der Gesellschaft: Entwurf zu einer Theorie der Zivilisation* (Basel: Verlag Haus zum Falken, 1939).

214 | Pierre Bourdieu, *Outline of a Theory of Practice* (Cambridge: Cambridge University Press, 1977).

role in the formation of the individual or groups of individuals as social subject. Therefore, we can speak about, for instance, the class, national, or professional habitus that the members of a class, nationality, or profession inherit and share. On the other side, some cognitive patterns and forms of conduct, e.g. table manners or bodily postures, can lose their origin in individuals and groups and shift to a wider and longer-lasting social register, thereby assuming the characteristics of habitus, as Andrew Pickel remarks:

> Thus from a macrosociological point of view it does not make sense to conceptualize habitus as the property of an individual. Instead, habitus should be seen as the property of a social system. The habitus of a social system is *reflected* in different ways in the *personalities* and "behaviours" of the individuals comprising the system (i.e. in their unique "personalized habiti"). But a habitus is *generated* by the system, i.e. it emerges from the joint activities and interactions of the individuals making up a system, not from the characteristics of its individual components.[215]

It is important to clarify that the habitus is close but not equal to ideology, for it is considered to be a set of cognitive and somatic dispositions, skills, and practices operating beneath any elaborated ideology. Since according to this its crucial aspect is embodiment, the habitus can be seen as an early biopolitical concept. Among the central notions explaining it, we would single out "body techniques" and "doxa."

Marcel Mauss defines the techniques of the body as the ways humans use their bodies in different societies, starting his analysis with the explanation of how the technique of swimming changed in the last few generations and how he, although he finds the old technique he learned in his childhood stupid, cannot get rid of it since it became his habit. However, Mauss' usage of the Latin *habitus* does not correspond entirely with the habit, which he saw as individual and soul related, a "metaphysical" category. He associates it instead with Aristotle's *hexis* (active condition or disposition, usually acquired) from the *Nichomachean Ethics*—which Mauss understands as "acquired ability" or "faculty." The reason is that they are socially determined:

> These "habits" [habitus] do not just vary with individuals and their imitations, they vary especially between societies, educations, proprieties and fashions, prestiges. In them we should see the techniques and work of collective and individual practical reason rather than, in the ordinary way, merely the soul and its repetitive faculties.[216]

In the distinction above between "habitus" and the ordinary notion of "habit," Mauss emphasizes the social dimension of habitus, involving education and the following imitative actions containing both psychological and biological elements. This allowed him to move from ceremonies and ritual formulas for hunting and running in non-European societies to an inference, namely, that there isn't at all a "natural way" to walk, eat, lecture, or position the hands at rest. All those are body techniques, actions both effective and traditional, which are "assembled by and for social authority,"[217] thus constituting the corporeality of our social lives and embodying the culture we live in.[218]

---

215 | Andreas Pickel, "The Habitus Process: A Biopsychosocial Conception" (Petersborough, ON: Centre for the Critical Study of Global Power and Politics, Trent University, 2005), 6. http://www.trentu.ca/globalpolitics/documents/Pickel051.pdf.

216 | Marcel Mauss, "Techniques of the Body," 73.

217 | Ibid., 85.

218 | In *The Civilizing Process*, Elias brought the problematics into a concrete social context, analyzing and historicizing the creation of the European habitus of sexual behavior, violence, eating manners, etc. His main focus—an ambivalent

In Pierre Bourdieu's definition, habitus is a system of durable, transposable dispositions that pertain to a social structure and that also structure practices ranging from the bodily hexis, through linguistic practices, to collective social actions. Habitus generates practice without conscious intention: It is what regulates it and makes it regular. On the other hand, it is what wouldn't exist without being practiced. In that way, the patterns of body postures, for instance, pass from practice to practice through learning, or more precisely, imitating and embodying the social process, which occurs without a conscious discursive elaboration. However, contesting free will with the fact that people are not necessarily conscious of the habitus doesn't make their practices mechanical. For Bourdieu, they are both individual and systematic; hence habitus functions neither fully voluntarily nor fully involuntarily, but as a dialectic between the will and the structure over time. The most important relation which arises here is the one between history and practice, where habitus appears in practice as "history turned into nature" and where unconsciousness is nothing other than "the forgetting of history."[219] This *genesis amnesia* is what makes habitus natural, that is, "the second nature" of both the human's practice and the experience, perception, and interpretation of the practice in the social realm.

The main outcome of the process is the creation of a commonsense world, predicated on a consensus on the meaning or sense of practices and the world in which they take place. Within that framework, Bourdieu defines *doxa* as the beliefs and values that are self-evident and taken for granted, functioning as an unconscious modus operandi for thinking, expressing, acting, experiencing, and perceiving. For that reason he opposes doxa to the (orthodox or heterodox) opinion which belongs to the "universe of discourse (or argument)," whereas doxa is located in the "universe of the undiscussed (undisputed)." A common sense, or truism, generated by doxa operates by means of a circular logic wherein it is never questioned because it hasn't come from any questioning or, even farther, "*it goes without saying because it comes without saying.*"[220]

> The adherence expressed in the doxic relation to the social world is the absolute form of recognition of legitimacy through misrecognition of arbitrariness, since it is unaware of the very question of legitimacy, which arises from competition for legitimacy, and hence from conflict between groups claiming to possess it.[221]

Bourdieu concludes from here that what doxa excludes or conceals is precisely the recognition of other, antagonistic beliefs and values. And thanks to the circular mechanism of securing misrecognition and being misrecognized, it engenders the dominant social structure that tends to naturalize its arbitrariness as universal, thereby reproducing and reaffirming the power relations that produce it.

explanation of the process of "civilizing" as well—is how this creation relates to the gradual increase of the threshold of shame and repugnance, the policing of human conducts, and how the constraints got internalized to the point that they shaped modern Europeans' conduct as natural.

219 | Bourdieu, *Outline of a Theory of Practice*, 78–9.
220 | Ibid., *Outline of a Theory of Practice*, 167.
221 | Ibid., 168.

SOCIAL ROLE

Another significant sociological model of performance of the self is offered by the concept of social role in Erving Goffman's book *The Presentation of Self in Everyday Life*.[222] It is considered the first twentieth-century analysis of the theatricality of social life. The author uses the model of theater performance—not in a metaphorical sense but through elaborate dramaturgical principles of theater—in order to theorize human interaction and the social construction of the self in diverse social realms. His point of departure is the premise that human actions are social and relational, or, more specifically, that they are "social performances" because, in parallel with being oriented toward their inherent purposes, they aim to give certain impressions to others in order to control their response and conduct. In addition, social roles are not what an individual creates; rather, they are socially defined (like the role of an experienced doctor or a credible politician) then chosen by individuals and adapted to their particular activities. Therefore, Goffman's notion questions the idea that there is a pre-existing inner self that is to be expressed; much more, what characterizes human conduct is first and foremost a learning of aspects and patterns of expression that we subsequently enact in order to construct "our selves" under particular socio-historical conditions. However, his study is not a constructivist manifesto about the self, but rather a sociological analysis of human conduct in Western, primarily Anglo-American, society in the mid twentieth century. So we shall briefly present some of its crucial theses and then consider their epistemic and socio-political legacy.

Goffman positions all human doing inside social situations that cannot be defined in only one way, thus the participants need to achieve a "working consensus" in order to define particular situations they find themselves in. Furthermore, since the consensus gains an imperative character, they are compelled to adjust their conduct to the accepted definition. Apart from that, the author distinguishes between two general modes of communication: "the expressions we give," which mostly refers to verbal and intentional communication, and "the expressions we give off," those that are non-verbal and often unintentional, but which people are sometimes aware of and capable of manipulating.[223] In social performances, there is either symmetry or asymmetry between the two, depending on the extent to which they agree with or contradict one another. Within that framework, Goffman identifies and analyzes several crucial aspects of performing social roles: "belief in the part one is playing," ranging from a full assumption of the role to cynicism; "front," that is, the collective representation functioning as the standardized and standardizing aspect of the individual's performance, including the setting and the personal front (the expressive equipment, such as appearance and manners, whose pertinence to individuals is perceived as natural); "dramatic realization," which indicates that since human actions are relational, in every action there is an intrinsic negotiation between doing and presenting the doing to others; "idealization," which modifies performance to fit into the values and expectations of the society in which it takes place, thereby regenerating them, and which is achieved by hiding inappropriate details, exaggerating the importance of one's actions, relationships to others, etc.; "maintenance of expressive control," which requires the whole "art of impression management" necessitated by the existence of

---

222 | Erving Goffman, *The Presentation of Self in Everyday Life* (Edinburgh: University of Edinburgh Social Sciences Research Centre, 1956).

223 | These two terms first appeared explicitly in the first American edition, Erving Goffman, *The Presentation of Self in Everyday Life* (New York: Doubleday, 1959), 2. All subsequent references refer to the previously cited British edition; see n222.

the fragility of social roles caused by the discrepancy between "all-too-human selves," with their changing moods and energies, as well as by more bureaucratized "socialized selves"; "misrepresentation," which, instead of addressing the false presentation of real self, addresses the facts regarding the performer's status, competence, etc.—which in turn authorizes her to give a certain performance; and "mystification," which is concerned with generating awe by keeping social distance, regardless of whether the secret behind the mystery exists or not, with the aim of protecting the performer and allowing her to act as she sees appropriate.

In general, Goffman's study is grouped within the branch of social constructivism, which considers performance constitutive of the individual as a social subject. However, such a definition usually trips over a few points in his book, such as the asymmetry between the expressions we give and those we give off, misrepresentation, and the discrepancy between all-too-human selves and socialized selves. For instance, the last point mentioned might indicate that Goffman believes in a pre-social self that expresses itself though social roles—or—the asymmetry between two types of expressions seems to open the issue of the real self. However, even when it is about the misrepresentation or the asymmetry between the expressions we give and those we give off, Goffman never concludes that it is a slip that reveals the real, natural, and authentic self that lies behind its performance. He rather speaks about degrees of socialization, and the only distinction he maintains is the one between the individual and the character she performs, solo or in a team, while playing one of the many social roles in her social life. In fact, the issue of the real and true remains outside of Goffman's interest throughout the book. Instead he keeps his focus on a sociological analysis of how human actions are performed as well as how, on the one hand, the asymmetry impacts our performance and, on the other hand, "what kind of impression of reality can shatter the fostered impression of reality."[224] Here is where we find Goffman's study comprehensive, since here the issue of production and reproduction of social values by means of performances of the self is opened by locating both the individual and the character in the domain of the social. Goffman explicitly claims that "when the individual presents himself before others, his performance will tend to incorporate and exemplify the officially accredited values of the society, more so, in fact, than does his behavior as a whole."[225] Consequently, the study doesn't speak about the existence or nonexistence of the true, natural self in absolute categories; instead, by way of meticulous analyses it offers an insight into how highly valued the natural, spontaneous, or authentic is in twentieth-century Western society and how difficult it is to achieve, so much so that the whole artificial theatrical apparatus needs to be engaged in its realization.[226] For this reason, Goffman's study is an analysis of social constructivism rather than a socio-constructivist analysis, because it unravels why we in our society cannot understand what the self is without understanding performance—which, in turn, implies the construction of social roles and conduct. Thus the performance of the self

---

224 | Erving Goffman, *The Presentation of Self in Everyday Life*, 44. He clearly explains his approach to this issue: "While we could retain the common-sense notion that fostered appearances can be discredited by a discrepant reality, there is often no reason for claiming that the facts discrepant with the fostered impression are any more the real reality than is the fostered reality they have the power of embarrassing" (ibid., 43–4).

225 | Ibid., 23.

226 | Cf. Ibid., 150–51. "Behind many masks and many characters, each performer tends to wear a single look, a naked unsocialized look, a look of concentration, a look of one who is privately engaged in a difficult treacherous task" (ibid.).

paves the way to a wider dialectical analysis of society, the values of which are embedded in human conduct through social roles and their more or less preferable aspects while in turn being created by the social roles that become patterns of human behavior.

MAN AS ACTOR

In a comment on the limits of Goffmann's "theoretical system, " the sociologist Richard Sennett situates his history of public culture and public space as having evolved from the mid eighteenth century to the end of the nineteenth century: although Goffman acutely observes a variety of social situations within the paradigm of performance and role-playing, his analysis is static, fails to account for historical changes, and gives "a picture of society in which there are scenes but no plot."[227] The relevance of Sennett's study for our discussion here lies less in its theoretical feat, subdued to a pragmatist sociological approach concerned with how society represents itself within the intellectual history of its key texts, and more in the strength of his thesis as formulated in the title of his book *The Fall of the Public Man* (1977). Sennett foregrounds the eighteenth century in which the public life of the city was conceived upon a clear divide between the private realm of natural yet impersonal order and the public realm of conventional performance, or in other words, on theatrical acting where public behavior was a matter of detachment from the personal self. The firmly maintained boundary between the public and the private is reflected in the fact that "the public was a human creation; the private was the human condition."[228] The nineteenth century witnessed one of the consequences of the French Revolution in its idea of liberty as joined to a "belief in individual character as a social principle,"[229] an idea that confuses public behavior with personality and intimacy. Here a culture of personality replaces the eighteenth-century ideal of civility, of public rhetorical gestures as expressions made at a distance to oneself. The man who inhabited the public realm of the eighteenth century was an actor whose freedom rested on the separation of the character from the act, which, paradoxically, entangled spontaneity of expression with impersonality of convention and enabled a greater mixture of classes:

> Can it be that the freedom to feel is greater when one's personality and one's identity in society are quite clearly separated? Can spontaneity and what we have learned to call "artificiality" have some hidden and necessary relationship? They do; that relationship is embodied in the principle of speech as a matter of signs rather than symbols.[230]

Thus, Sennett confirms the view of the artificiality of public performance, like Goffman, but limits it to the description of a particular historical figure: the man as actor in the *ancien régime* of the eighteenth century. The body of the public actor was regarded as "mannequin" who wears the mask of the social role and whose speech is coded in signs rather than symbols. While the mask and the clothing reveal his social rank, the talk is a "free flow" to the extent that it can suspend the social rank, as was the case in the first public places of anonymous gathering, such as coffeehouses and pubs.

227 | Sennett, *The Fall of Public Man*, 36.
228 | Ibid., 98.
229 | Ibid., 99.
230 | Ibid., 73.

Sennett accounts for three distinctive conceptions of "man as actor." The first, summarized by the idea of *theatrum mundi* or "the world is a stage," reflects the common sense view of "man as actor," where ordinary life and dramatic performance, the street and the stage, mingle and even literally translate into one another. It is best described in one of Montesquieu's *Persian Letters*, where the hero, upon walking into Comédie Française one night, can't distinguish between actors and spectators. *Theatrum mundi* denotes the morality of divorcing human nature from man's acts, which then characterized the social conduct of the everyday notion of man as an actor by the tones of amusement, cynical toleration, and pleasure. The second register, Sennet remarks, is conceived in Diderot's *Paradox of the Actor* (written in 1778, but published in 1830), the first view of acting as a secular activity, which is best summed up in the following: "Do not people talk in society of a man being a great actor? They do not mean by that that he feels, but that he excels in simulating, though he feels nothing."[231] Diderot considered artifice superior to nature in expressing an emotion. Through the artifice, the actor studies the emotion in its essence so as to become master of its effectiveness and thus arouse the same emotion in the spectator. Diderot's presentation of emotion as a rhetorical expression is fundamentally different from the representation of emotion, because in the latter, the recipient is supposed to empathize and identify with the true person suggested by the actor, rather than be moved by the act of the emotion. Social acts are expressible only when they are repeatable and not unique, according to Diderot. The third conception in Sennett invokes Rousseau's views on cosmopolitan life. Sennet studies the third term standing between the actor and the city—*mœurs*—best defined as the complete manner, the style a person possesses as well as her moral conduct. Sennett paraphrases Rousseau's critique in the following:

> The great city is a theater. Its scenario is principally the search for reputations. All city men become artists of a particular kind—actors. In acting out a public life, they lose contact with natural virtue. The artist and the great city are in harmony and the result is a moral disaster.[232]

Rousseau sees a corruption of *mœurs* in both abundance and play when they occur in social interaction, for they are beyond the principle of necessity that the Calvinist order of functional survival commands. Social interaction leads to dependence on others for a sense of self and, eventually, to a loss of an internal sense of the self. He thus anticipates what will become the norm in less than hundred years—the culture of personality—yet his prophecy didn't exactly play itself out as he imagined it would, namely, by invoking the virtuous, intimate life in the small town where more leisure time would allow the citizen to search for her true self, the honesty of her soul. To conclude, Sennett's study is a critique of the new paradigm of the intimate society that is settled from the nineteenth century to this day. He supports this critique by the image of theatrical social conduct in the eighteenth century in which the value of "civility" is strongly upheld as "the activity which protects people from each other and yet allows them to enjoy each other's company." Wearing a mask is, for Sennett, "the essence of civility, but the masks must be created by those who will wear them, through trial and error."[233]

---

231 | Sennett, *The Fall of Public Man*, 110.
232 | Ibid., 11.
233 | Ibid., 264.

TECHNOLOGIES
OF THE SELF

In his later work, most notably the three-volume work, *The History of Sexuality*, and in various lectures, interviews, and essays from the end of the 1970s and the early 1980s, the French philosopher Michel Foucault developed a new conceptual framework for his study of the subject and the production of subjectivity which he discussed using the term "technologies of the self."[234] Technologies of the self form the fourth level in the system of technologies that describe production, sign systems, power, and fourthly, self. They define a mode of action that an individual exercises upon herself and uses to produce her subjectivity. In a more comprehensive definition, Foucault contends that the technologies of the self "permit individuals to effect by their own means, or with the help of others, a certain number of operations on their own bodies and souls, thoughts, conduct, and way of being, so as to transform themselves in order to attain a certain state of happiness, purity, wisdom, perfection, or immortality."[235] This quote should be read together with what Foucault proposes with regard to the self in a lecture from the same period (1980), which seems contradictory to the earlier antihumanist, antisubjective claim of the "end of man" that he made in his archeological method of discourse analysis. Foucault doesn't retreat to a positive foundation of the self here, but instead suggests that the self should be studied as capable of critical self-transformation through the history of technologies, because "maybe the problem is to change those technologies. And in this case, one of the main political problems would be nowadays, in the strict sense of the word, the politics of ourselves."[236] By the "politics of ourselves," a concept that anticipated, through its own influence on humanities, debates on identity politics that would arise over the two following two decades, Foucault indicates ethics as his area of study: "the considered form that freedom takes when it is informed by reflection,"[237] or, in a brief formulation, the "practice of freedom." Freedom and power relations are mutually conditioning and not mutually exclusive terms here, since Foucault argues that power relations are mobile, reversible, and unstable, thus allowing the possibility of a resistance whereby subjects practice freedom. Foucault's preference of the *practice* of freedom over *acts* of liberation is tailored to Western democratic society, in which he develops his theory; for he admits that there exist states of domination where the relations of power are fixed and asymmetrical to the extent that freedom exists in an extremely limited margin. "Governmentality" is then a concept proposed for the Western genealogy of power relations.

> [It covers] the whole range of practices that constitute, define, organize, and instrumentalize the strategies that individuals in their freedom can use in dealing with each other. Those who

234 | *The History of Sexuality.* Vol. 3, *The Care of the Self*, trans. Robert Hurley (New York, NY: Pantheon Books, 1986); originally published as *Histoire de la sexualité.* Vol. 3, *Le souci de soi* (Paris: Gallimard, 1984). Apart from the third volume, which is our primary focus here and which, together with volume two, was published posthumously, we will refer to Foucault's following essays, lectures, and interviews: "About the Beginnings of the Hermeneutics of the Self: Two Lectures at Dartmouth," *Political Theory* 21, no. 2 (1993): 198–227; "Technologies of the Self," from the final lecture of a faculty seminar on "Technologies of the Self" at the University of Vermont, Autumn 1982; Foucault, *Essential Works of Foucault 1954–1984*, ed. Paul Rabinow and Nikolas Rose (London: Penguin, 2000), see esp. Vol.1, "Subjectivity and Truth," "The Hermeneutic of the Subject," "Sexuality and Solitude," "Self Writing," "On the Genealogy of Ethics: An Overview of Work in Progress," and "The Ethics of the Concern for Self as a Practice of Freedom."
235 | Foucault, *Ethics*, 177.
236 | Foucault, "About the Beginnings of the Hermeneutics of the Self," 223.
237 | Foucault, *Ethics*, 284.

> try to control, determine, and limit the freedom of others are themselves free individuals who have at their disposal certain instruments they can use to govern others. Thus, the basis for all this is freedom, the relationship of the self to itself and the relationship to the other.[238]

Three questions about Foucault's technologies of the self interest us here. Firstly, how does the notion of technology enable Foucault to give precedence to the individualist mode of subjectivation beyond the collective dimension of practice? Secondly, what sort of performance of the self can we infer from the techniques of the self if these are primarily contained in the private domain of the care of the self by oneself? Thirdly, and by consequence, when do the techniques of the self coincide with civic and political activity? Does the study of technologies of the self only serve to inform us about the changing boundaries between the private and the public spheres of the social field? Let's answer these questions in succession.

Having discovered the discursive relation between the truth about sexuality and the constitution of the subject in the eighteenth and nineteenth centuries, Foucault comes to the notion of "truth games" as specific techniques, guided by a set of rules that human beings use to understand themselves and produce truth. In comparison to ideology, technology is a rather neutral term, as it designates a set of procedures that lead to a certain result. For Foucault, the term serves to explain philosophical discourse about the living praxis in antiquity, wherein the self is cultivated by the imperative to take care of oneself. In the Greco-Roman age, this practice is defined as an art of living, an aesthetics of existence, where the "care" involves a sort of work, an activity, an attention to and concern with something, a knowledge and a technique. Unlike later Christianity, which instilled a religious system of prohibitions upon the self-renouncing subject who prepared for the afterlife, the Greco-Roman "problem" could be formulated thus: which *tekhne* do I have to use in order to live well and live as I ought to live?[239] The answer to why this *tekhne* pertains to the individual is that in the times of Socrates and Athenian democracy, taking care of one's own life (*tekhne tou biou*)—for the free citizens who participate in direct democracy—was to take care of the city, of his (not her) companions, all of whom rule the city. Thus, in one of the three arguments of his defense in *Apology*, Socrates says that when teaching people how to preoccupy themselves with themselves, meaning when he teaches them wisdom, truth, and the perfection of the soul, he also teaches them to occupy themselves with the city, how to be useful for the *polis*. Foucault stresses that various practices of reading, writing, speaking, corresponding, counselling, walking in the city, and so on, weren't exercises in solitude, but a true social practice. Hence, technologies of the self aim, first and foremost, to shape the subject as both a private and a political

---

238 | Foucault, *Ethics*, 300. According to some of Foucault's commentators, Foucault's turn to biopolitics here seems inconsistent with his earlier antihumanist critique of the autonomous subject: it discloses a quasi-liberal Foucault who presupposes a partially autonomous and reflexive subject. Cf. Eric Paras, *Foucault 2.0: Beyond Power and Knowledge* (New York: Other Press, 2006); Paul Patton, "Foucault's Subject of Power," in *The Later Foucault: Politics and Philosophy*, ed. Jeremy Moss (London: Sage, 1998), 64–77. Amy Allen seeks to resolve the apparent paradox from the position of critical theory and the post-Kantian legacy of the Enlightenment in which she situates Foucault by claiming that in the ethical project of self-transformation by technologies of the self, Foucault retains the critique of the transcendental and phenomenological subject but amends his critique with the power of self-constitution beyond the limits of the contingent forms of constraint imposed by the power-knowledge relations that structure the social. Amy Allen, "Foucault and the politics of our selves," *History of the Human Sciences* 24, no. 4 (2001): 43–58.
239 | Foucault, *Ethics*, 260.

person in one, a citizen in whom the distinction between the private and the political is overcome by participation in the public as a civic activity. The idea that the care of the self centralizes the self beyond the city, in withdrawal from political life and in movement toward a concern with the self alone, only begins with the Epicureans and then culminates in Seneca, himself a fine example from the Roman period. Foucault explains it as a kind of "individualism" that, owing to an increasing detachment from the city and the political life on the part of Roman citizens who lived isolated from one another and more reliant on themselves, accords more importance to the private sphere of life and to the values of personal conduct.

In what sense could these past technologies of the self be accounted for as "performances" of the self? Foucault avoids qualifying them as performances, although when he examines the Christian technique of "exomologesis," whereby one is obliged to disclose oneself either to God or to the community, he describes the penitential rite as a theatrical self-presentation involving a dramatic recognition of the sinner's status as penitent whose public confession of sins bears witness against herself. Although practiced in the private domain where one's care of the body includes physical exercise or food regimes, or meditation, the Greco-Roman technologies of the self involve communication with others, an obligation to reciprocally exchange "soul service." Yet, the reason for considering them as performances of the self lies elsewhere, in the very act of observance, in the reflection of showing that one is doing to oneself, in devising externally, through thought, the principles of action according to which the actions are then evaluated. Thus, Foucault's metaphor of the money changer in Epictetus brings to mind the proceduralist logic: "as soon as an idea comes to mind you have to think of the rules you must apply to evaluate it."[240] What makes techniques of the self difficult to discern is their invisibility, conditioned by their lack of material apparatus, Foucault argues; but this doesn't make them less an issue of performance. The sense and function of the technology of the self as a performance of the self has changed over history, from the aestheticization of life in the ancient Greco-Roman cultivation of the self to self-mastery, self-renunciation, and self-sacrifice in Christianity, to the modern (nonascetic) subject of knowledge who accesses truth by way of direct evidence, or common sense (according to which she is the autonomous founder of knowledge), all the way to the psychoanalytic techniques of the twentieth century. However, a major shift is noted from the Greek care of the self as the city to the Roman concern with the self only, which prompted Foucault's interlocutors to ask him if the latter is just an "early version of self-absorption, which many consider a central problem in our society." Foucault denies this:

> In the Californian cult of the self, one is supposed to discover one's true self, to separate it from that which might obscure or alienate it, to decipher its truth thanks to psychological or psychoanalytic science, which is supposed to be able to tell you what your true self is. Therefore, not only do I not identify this ancient culture of the self with what you might call Californian cult of the self, I think they are diametrically opposed.[241]

In response to this charge, Foucault classifies three kinds of individualism, which return in different epochs:[242] 1) the individualistic attitude, which values the individual in her singularity and independence vis-à-vis the structures to which she belongs, 2) the

---

240 | Foucault, *Ethics*, 238.
241 | Ibid., 271.
242 | Foucault, *History of Sexuality.* Vol. 3, *The Care of the Self*, 41.

appraisal of private life, advocating the values of family relationships, domestic activity, and patrimonial interests, and 3) the intensity of the relations to self as an object of knowledge and a field of action qua transformation, purification, or salvation of the self. While the first could be compared to a heroic, *übermenschliche* individualism or a radical isolationist individualism—the maverick—, as in Ralph Waldo Emerson' s notion of "self-reliance" and Henry David Thoreau's life experiments,[243] the second is given a historical coordinate only at the emergence of the bourgeoisie in Western Europe and North America in the nineteenth century. The third kind remains somewhat vague: on the one hand, it conforms with the ancient cultivation of the self, and on the other, it also entertains the narcissistic self with its (often psychologized) cult of personality. We can infer from his dismissal of the second type—made by saying that an individualism in societies that cultivate the private, domestic, and patrimonial sphere is weak because the relations of oneself to one's self remain undeveloped—that he gives precedence to the third kind. The intensification of the relation of oneself to one's self best corresponds to the technologies invested in the aestheticization of one's own life—to "the idea of the bios as a material for an aesthetic piece of art," and "the idea that ethics can be a very strong structure of existence, without any relation with the juridical per se, with an authoritarian system, with a disciplinary structure." These aestheticizing technologies, Foucault admits, fascinate him.[244] Thus, Foucault's late notion of ethics as a practice of freedom guided by technologies of self-transformation is criticized for an overly individualized and aestheticized notion of resistance.[245] Although we have pointed out that Foucault's practice of the self isn't entirely individualistic, but always developed in the context of, and through relations with, others (which is sufficiently explained by the concept of governmentality), an account of what the technologies of the group or collective, as it were, are or have been (which might explain the politics of collective action) is missing from his ethics. Perhaps this significant omission or silence on the collective dimension of politics would no longer imply a technology, but rather an ideology, the notion of which Foucault, as we have seen, avoids by any and all means.

PERFORMING IDENTITY

What remains latent in Foucault's enthusiastic remarks from his last interviews about the technologies of the self, namely, that the constitution of the self through its proper techniques doesn't only imply regulation but can effectuate resistance and transformation, is made explicit in the performative constitution of identity in Judith Butler. Butler developed the concept of performing identity in the early 1990s. Her theory of identity politics, drawing on Foucault's analyses of the institutional and historical constitution of the subject as well as the theory of speech acts, is situated in poststructuralist queer studies and made a remarkable contribution to the destabilization of the notion

---

243 | Cf. Ralph Waldo Emerson, Essays (New York: Thomas Y. Crowell Company, 1926), see esp. "Self Reliance," pp. 31–66; "Heroism," pp. 173–87; and "The Over-Soul," pp. 188–211; Emerson, *The Conduct of Life* (Boston: 1860), http://www. emersoncentral.com/conduct.htm; Henry David Thoreau, *Walden and Civil Disobedience* (Harmondsworth, UK: Penguin, 1983).

244 | Foucault, *Ethics*, 260.

245 | Cf. Thomas McCarthy, *Ideals and Illusions: On Reconstruction and Deconstruction in Contemporary Critical Theory* (Cambridge, MA: MIT Press, 1991); Lois McNay, *Foucault and Feminism: Power, Gender, and the Self* (Cambridge: Polity, 1992).

of "identity," thus disputing identitarian postulates of feminist theory.[246] Butler's basic premise is that gender, as well as sex, are social constructions. In her argument, which relies on the concepts of interpellation and the performative, she advances the then highly provocative thesis: "There is no gender identity behind the expressions of gender; . . . identity is performatively constituted by the very 'expressions' that are said to be its results."[247] Butler considers gender and sex to be aspects of the identity of the social subject and therefore locates the whole problematic inside the broader process of social subjectivation. According to her, the subject, in order to exist in the domain of the social, in order to be recognized by the law, in order, at bottom, for her life to be qualified as human, is produced by the process of normative regulation, which involves the ritualistic, embodied repetition of conventions. A part of that process is exclusion, and in the "uninhabitable" social zone, the zone of unthinkable and unlivable life, Butler seeks out numerous "abject beings." The norm does not normativize them according to heterosexual categories, hence they never achieve the status of the subject, although they are produced by that norm.[248] The inclusion of those beings as subjects in the social community is the crucial political question Butler is concerned with. On the one hand, the exclusion through which they apparently do not cease to exist exposes them to the oppression and injuries of the norm-governed community while denying them the possibility to politically partake therein; and on the other hand, they become the negativity of the subject, its "constitutive outside."

In *Gender Trouble* (1990) Butler adopts the Foucauldian thesis that nothing precedes the process of regulation; regulation produces subjects as well as that which it excludes at the same time. This calls into question the possibility of the political action that strives to intervene in the norm-governed context. For Butler, however, the constructive production of the subject does not entail determinism:

> The subject is not *determined* by the rules through which it is generated because signification *is not a founding act, but rather a regulated process of repetition* that both conceals itself and enforces its rules precisely through the production of substantializing effects.[249]

She takes this further through elaborations of the performativity of gender and sex, where the perspective of the performative allows us to see that the norm, the subject, and the failure are produced simultaneously and, even more importantly, that they are constitutive of each other.[250] Let us give a brief overview of her argument. Her key intervention in the theory of the performative, as expounded in *Bodies That Matter* and developed further in *Undoing Gender*, articulates not only that the subject of the performative constitutes the discursive position in the structure of the speech act, but also that the thing at stake in the performative production of the subject is the law's investment in the body. According to Butler, the regulatory norms instill the body with materiality; that is to say, they materialize the body's subjective attributes. Apart from that, the initial premise—with Austin,

246 | Here we mostly refer to Butler's following works: *Gender Trouble: Feminism and the Subversion of Identity* (London: Routledge, 1990); *Bodies That Matter: On the Discursive Limits of "Sex"* (London: Routledge, 1993); *Undoing Gender* (London: Routledge, 2004).
247 | Butler, *Gender Trouble*, 25.
248 | Ibid., 77.
249 | Ibid., 145.
250 | "Performativity" doesn't arrive in Butler's theory directly from Austin, but through Derrida's deconstructivist reading emphasizing its iterability. See Jacques Derrida, "Event, Signature, Context," in *Limited INC* (Evanston, IL: Northwestern University Press, 1988), 1–25.

as well as with Butler—claims that the subject of the performative does not exist before the speech act. The act can be performed either felicitously or infelicitously, depending on the context in which it takes place, where the former brings about the subject of the performative and the latter doesn't produce anything. Yet, the failure has the constitutive role, and Austin already infers that the performative that cannot be performed infelicitously is not performative at all. He doesn't advance the failure, while Butler makes it a central issue. For her, the constitutive nothing is a "stain" on the procedure, which tends to be hidden in order for the performative to be assigned a supposedly inherent juridical power. The exclusion plays the role of naturalization. In that sense, performativity is a larger concept than performance, for it involves its negativity and contests the performance's right to the whole truth of the subject. "What is 'performed,'" Butler asserts, "works to conceal, if not to disavow, what remains opaque, unconscious, unperformable. The reduction of performativity to performance would be a mistake."[251] What she proposes as one way of resisting normativization is the parody as a "critical mimesis"—her example is drag performance—which displays an awareness of the substantializing effects of the repetition of the norm and thus discloses the process of naturalization.

But it's still not clear how the awareness and disclosure lead to the subversion and rearticulation of hegemonic norms.[252] In order to achieve that, the excluded site of the failure needs to be activated and transformed into a social agency. Butler here introduces Althusser's scene of interpellation, insisting that the act with which the law hails and at the same time forms the subject is *per*-formative:

> The reprimand [by the policemen, with Althusser] does not merely repress or control the subject, but forms a crucial part of the juridical and social *formation* of the subject. The call is formative, if not performative, precisely because it initiates the individual into the subjected status of the subject.[253]

Thereby the subject needs to recognize and appreciate the law in order to put it to work, from which Butler infers that the unhappy performative opens the space for the disobedience of "bad subjects." Her thesis—misrecognition of the interpellation can parody and in that way subvert the law—is grounded on a Žižekian-Lacanian insight: the law, since it is not only formative but also performative, is not immune to its subjects, to its embodiments, to the bodies that bear it. Still, the performance as a "bounded act" is not sufficient, and what is in question here is a long-term process of subjectivation as repetition of the performative. At this point, it becomes clear that the necessity of iteration is exactly what makes the performative imperative fragile and dependent upon performances that, while citing it, twist, remake, and change it.

The other issue that concerns us here relates to the structural place held by the motivation to change the norm within the process of subjectivation. In other words, who is the one who changes it? Butler's early answer is that the attempt to change comes from affectivity, a pre-subjective existential narcissism that characterizes the body as the main bearer of

---

251 | Butler, *Bodies That Matter*, 234.
252 | For instance, Martha Nussbaum stresses that Butler's discourse on a "gender as performance" that extends an invitation to parody norms is also a discourse of passivization that doesn't lead to breaking the norms. Nussbaum, "The Professor of Parody," *The New Republic Online*, February 1999, http://www.akad.se/Nussbaum.pdf.
253 | Butler, *Bodies That Matter*, 121.

the law. Whether it is an individualist perspective on the subject or not, the framework apparently centers the individual subject and, in the last instance, concerns itself with how to emancipate the individual from the social institution. In such framework the method of how to make the subversive activity a more comprehensive social practice—except by a mechanical proliferation of the activity—remains undeveloped. But in her later work,[254] Butler developed and changed this perspective somewhat, moving toward ethical problems and the relation, the encounter with the Other. Affectivity and embodiment remained in her focus, but she has transitioned toward a broader social register of the precarity and the precarious, emphasizing more and more a need for collective formations and actions. In political terms, in the course of that transition the performing identity concept shifted from a liberal stance of Cultural Studies toward a clearer New-Leftist position.[255]

***

The brief overview above singles out from the history of theoretical concepts those which elaborate the external construction of the self and its identity in the *performative* mode. It provides us with notions that we will draw on in the last two chapters, both of which focus on how individuals are performed in an individualistic manner. We will observe strikingly similar genres and techniques of self-performance in the arts and everyday life. Privileging art doesn't imply a familiar approach by which art is considered the model for how the individualistic subject is economically and politically constituted today, as some studies have recently suggested.[256] Although many of the concepts of self-performance above have had an impact on practices of theater, dance, and performance—such as Mauss's body techniques in the physical theater of Jerzy Grotowski or Eugenio Barba, or Foucault's and Butler's theses of self/identity construction in performance art since the 1980s—we will deliberately avoid this transference from social theory to art. Our claim is slightly different: the peculiarities of the performative production of subjectivity in art can shed light on the intensive form of individualism also found in every domain of social life. Through art we can observe how individualism operates as an ideology and which notions and manners of performance it exercises.

---

254 | Judith Butler, *Precarious Life: The Powers of Mourning and Violence* (London: Verso, 2004); Butler, *Giving an Account of Oneself* (New York: Fordham University Press, 2005).

255 | This could be traced to her observations of Occupy in "Bodies in alliance and the Politics of the Street." See also our applications of the theses on the political power of aligned bodies in Chapter 6 of this book.

256 | Lazzarato critiques the recent work of sociologists and economists—such as Luc Boltanski and Eve Chiapello in *Le nouvel esprit du Capitalisme* [The New Spirit of Capitalism] (Paris: Gallimard, 1999) and Pierre-Michel Menger in *Portrait de l'artiste en travailleur. Metamorphoses du capitalism* [Portrait of the Artist as Worker: Metamorphoses of Capitalism] (Paris: La République des Idées / Seuil, 2002)—who use artistic activity as a model from which neoliberal economics draws its inspiration. He shows how dangerously ambiguous this discourse is because it fails to recognize how contemporary forms of labor in the arts act against neoliberal styles of production. Lazzarato, "The Misfortunes of the 'Artistic Critique' and of Cultural Employment."

In this chapter we would like to analyze how art intensifies the personal and the personality as notions that significantly shape the individual human as social subject in neoliberal capitalist society. Since one of the points where the process operates most prominently can be found in the figure of the author—including the related formation and recognition of artistic authorship—in the following pages we shall examine the conjunction of authorship and the personal, which constitutes what is considered art. The analysis refers mostly to the performing arts, where the problematic is directly transported to the terrain of performance as a public activity, thereby enabling us to construct a triangle between the personal, the author, and the performance, which deeply condition one another but whose conditioning is the subject of social and epistemic change.[257]

Excluding or not including the personal in art straightforwardly raises the following questions: Why don't I, an author, involve the personal in my artistic work? Do I resist it?

257 | The point of departure for this discussion lies in *Four Choreographic Portraits*, a performance project made by Christine De Smedt, since it crucially addresses our problem here: the relation between artistic authorship and the artist's self-understanding of the role of the personal therein.

Or do I hide it? Why?[258] Expanding on this, the following questions arise: What does this avoidance result in? In an artwork which is less authentic, less sincere, less credible, less my own? Which is more general, more indifferent, more technical, more a cold speculative construction? What intrigues us in this reasoning is how these concerns are constructed in the epistemic and socio-political senses, namely, how the paradigm of art predicated on the expression, manifestation, or actualization of a person's individuality, her will and creative force, has been silently naturalized to the extent that these questions seem a reasonable concern of an author herself. Indeed, this paradigm is one of the strongest paradigms for art today, and it looks as if the personal and authorship are inseparably connected in an organic bind, rendering what we call art. The bind directly leads to the ultimate question: what is art if not an expression of individual will and creative force? Apart from the last instance, it appears in many variations, and today—when the artist's name functions as brand, and when she with her individuality and personality is the art product *par excellence*—it is gaining momentum. In our attempt to open the topic up, we will begin with the Foucauldian premise that the tie between the personal and authorship, however "solid" it looks, in fact "came into being" at a particular moment in Western history, and it may "pass out of being" in some other social context or historical moment. Thus our concern here is not "What is the problem with me, an author, not including the personal in my artwork" but rather "What is the problem with the art for which the personal is an essential condition for it to be art?"

But, first of all, what does the personal mean? In ordinary speech as well as in dictionaries, it signifies individual, unique, distinctive, particular, authentic, private, intimate, one's own, etc., from which we can hardly induce a coherent definition; as the term obviously carries some very different denotations. Apart from that, the notion of the "person" is close to concepts of individual, self, and identity, which, from a theoretical viewpoint, deserve serious definition. Still, the way they operate in the Artworld doesn't presuppose a clear demarcation line, and the terms often overlap, which would lead us to assume that the overlapping is an important aspect of how the personal functions in this context. And while we will discuss its foundational status in a moment, at this point we would like to introduce a basic systematization of the ways in which the term "personal" is employed in art, wherein it addresses:

• unique and associated qualifications, like particular, distinctive, one's own, etc., which refer to the particular and distinctive identity and individuality of the artist, expressed in art by her specific "signature," by the artwork that only she can do;
• the private and the intimate, which address the life-story and related experiences, thoughts, feelings, and self of an author as individual human, which serves as a repository of her inspiration or even forces her to make art;
• the authentic and the original, which refer to the proximity of a work of art to the model-image shaped in the mind of its author, then materialized in the unique work of art, whose aura of authenticity provides the audience with a ritualistic, artistic, or aesthetic experience.

258 | This is the case in *Four Choreographic Portraits*: "I realized that in my work there was a hidden premise not to involve biographical and personal elements. But what do I mean by *personal*? What is the relationship between how I think *the personal* and the work I make?," Christine De Smedt, "4 Choreographic Portraits," in companion booklet to *4 Choreographic Portraits* (Ghent: les ballets C de la B, 2012), 3.

Although we would refrain from hasty conclusions, we cannot but remark that the systematization given above already demonstrates that the personal again addresses at least three different concepts as well as different registers in the realm of art, hence amounting to a rather elusive object of analysis, critique, or questioning. In view of all this, we would regard it as a habitus of thinking—a doxic commonsense in Bourdieu's sense—and try to challenge its self-evidence by pointing to and discussing the constructive seams of the seemingly smooth and natural bind between art and the personal.

THE BIRTH OF THE ARTIST'S PERSONALITY: A CRITICAL HISTORICAL PERSPECTIVE

If we look into history, we face quite a surprising trajectory for the construction of the conjunction between authorship and the personal, along with contextually conditioned changes of the notion of "art" itself. According to the traditional Western division of human activities into labor, work/production, and action/practice, which can be traced back to ancient Greece, labor responds to the general cyclical human metabolism with nature, while production and practice distinguish the human being as specific and unique on Earth. According to Aristotle's *Nicomachean Ethics*, the distinction between the two was fairly sharp in his time, where production (*poiesis*) was the act of shaping, of "coming into being" in a particular shape, and practice (*praxis*) implied a performed action, intervention—a voluntary activity in public. As a consequence, poiesis claims a value, a goal beyond itself: it results in a product, a piece of work that invests in the civilization, whereas praxis results in the public action itself and, accordingly, focuses on organization of actual social relations. Craft and art are paradigmatic instances of production, and political action is a paradigmatic instance of practice. At this point, the central concept concerning art is poiesis. In classical Greece, from Plato to Aristotle, the understanding of it changed. For Plato (in *Symposium*), poiesis means each cause for the creation of something previously *nonexistent*. It may relate to nature or man (Plato doesn't make a distinction) and he conceives poiesis as the unique activity of creating. The difference came with Aristotle, who distinguished (in *Physics*) what exists by nature and claims a cause and origin in itself from what exists by other causes—the principle of its creation being the productive activity of man. Art was, consequently, related to the latter form of poiesis and distinguished from natural creation; and, as such, for a long time it made no reference to the personal, the individual, the self, or related categories. In classical Greece, such a view was very explicit and was confirmed in Aristotle's *Poetics*, where poetics refers to poiesis and designates art as a paradigmatic form of the human capacity to make, to create, to produce.

Later in modern Western society, the definition and social position of art as well as its relation to the personal changed remarkably. The changes relate to the circumstances of production in industrial and then post-industrial capitalist society and its liberal and individually oriented epistemology, which feature divisions of production, a transformation of the concept of practice, and a reconfiguration of the public and the private.

The division of poiesis that we would single out as key to understanding the increased interest in the figure of the author lies in the division of aesthetic and industrial production. According to Giorgio Agamben,[259] the division and the related distinction of human products into works of art and products in the strictest sense (industrial, technical) corresponds with the development of modern technology and the first industrial revolution in the second half of the eighteenth century. At that time, the following characterization was introduced: the aesthetic products are characterized by authenticity, and technical products, by reproducibility. And at this point the artist as a person entered the art sphere. The notions of authenticity and originality, which Agamben considers synonymous, have been widely embraced by Western art since the nineteenth century, with different connotations. Apart from their connection with the ideology of individualism, which promotes the figure of the individual throughout modern Western society, all these connotations share a common production basis, i.e. their nineteenth-century interpretation. Here, the principle of originality, according to Agamben, implies the proximity of an artwork to the origin, the "image-model" in the artist herself, which is lost in technical products due to their mass reproduction. As a consequence, unique, unrepeatable, credible, and similar modern features of the artwork all derive from the basic principle of originality, made possible by the permanent proximity of an artistic product to its origin in the artist's particular mind, in her mental image, which functions as model for the product. Once introduced, this principle provided artworks with an aura of authenticity and, in the long run, distinguished art from other, reproductive forms of poiesis, like industrial production and technics. However, in the early twentieth century, according to Walter Benjamin, the aura was endangered by new art forms—photography and film—that involved reproducibility, depriving the audience of the unique aesthetic and ritualistic experience of art.[260] This caused a shift in the discourse on authenticity during the twentieth century from artworks to artists, which we will look at later.

One more historical process that should be explained here is the gradual change in the relations between poiesis and praxis, as well as the transformation of the notion of praxis. In his essay "Poiesis and Praxis,"[261] Agamben demonstrates how, throughout Western history after the classical age in Greece, these changes have happened on a conceptual level. According to him, the process of the convergence of poiesis and praxis can be traced back to the Roman era, and it is already manifest in the translation of the Greek term *poiesis*, which designates human "productivity," into the Latin *agere/actum*, to act, to do, which means "the manifestation of a will that produces a concrete effect."[262] Later, Christian theology proclaimed the Supreme Being as an *actus purus* and firmly tied the interpretation of being as actualization and act to Western metaphysics. However, the process of convergence wouldn't be possible without a radical change in the notion of practice. Agamben made an important point in this respect when he noticed that, in the modern Western world, all human doing began to be perceived as practice—but now conceived as a productive activity. In this process, the meaning of praxis was not only broadened to such an extent that it became a general term for all human activities; it went through a complete transformation to the point that it started to signify a manifestation of the human being's will and vital impulse, along with the concrete effects thereof.

259 | Giorgio Agamben, "Privation Is Like a Face," in *The Man Without Content* (Palo Alto, CA: Stanford University Press, 1999).
260 | Walter Benjamin, "The Work of Art in the Age of Mechanical Reproduction," in *Illuminations: Essays and Reflections*, trans. and ed. Hannah Arendt (New York: Schocken Books, 1968).
261 | Giorgio Agamben, "Poiesis and Praxis," in *The Man Without Content* (Palo Alto, CA: Stanford University Press, 1999).
262 | Ibid., 42.

In these epistemic and social processes, the conception of art changed accordingly. During the nineteenth and even the twentieth century, art was also predominantly seen as practice; but practice is now seen as an expression, manifestation, and actualization of the artist's will and creative force. As instances of this reinterpretation, Agamben cites Novalis' definition of poetry as a "willful, active, and productive use of our organs," also citing Nietzsche's identification of art with the will to power; Artaud's aspiration to a theatrical liberation of the will; and situationist efforts, based on human creative impulses, at crossing the borders of art. As Agamben underlines, "The metaphysics of will has penetrated our conception of art to such an extent that even the most radical critiques of aesthetics have not questioned its founding principle, that is, the idea that art is the expression of the artist's creative will."[263] This is another path through which the importance of the personal has been promoted in art, where it was identified as the essence of the unique creative will of the artist—now seen as "the creative genius"— that forced her to do art. In this paradigm, the personal mostly refers to her biography, experience, private life, inner self; or, in more picturesque words, her traumas, failures, loves, dreams, fears, adventures, and miseries, which, in a stereotypical vision, function as the strongest of the creative forces.

Besides understanding art practice in terms of the metaphysics of creative will and allying art with authenticity or originality, the social process that influenced the promotion of the personal in art, especially connoting the private, was the reorganization of public and private life, which began in the second half of the eighteenth century. Richard Sennett, who described the process meticulously, named the change sharply as "the fall of public man."[264] Since we already discussed this thesis in the previous chapter, we would here only stress that the change addresses the new configuration of bourgeois society, where public life was conceived in the eighteenth century as being based on artificial social roles and relations while the private was the domain of the authenticity of the human being, the domain where we are the closest to our selves. Giving preference from the nineteenth century onward to the private as authentic resulted in its mystification and an escalation of curiosity about it, as it provoked the suspicion that the public subject is only a mask that hides the real person and her motives and reasons. And, even more importantly here, it resulted in a privatization of the public sphere, which has gradually replaced political practice with activities based on intimacy and similar personal and private categories.

As a consequence of these processes, in the art field the "monograph" became the crucial text in art history, starting in the nineteenth century in its presentation of certain artistic opuses as intertwined with the life story of the author, which is supposedly deeply embedded in her work and hence can explain it. Apart from not being very believable—we probably all know boring people who make very exciting art and those who are quite extravagant yet make kitsch—one of the most serious problems with such a conception is that it largely deprives art of social concerns it might possess as a practice, reorienting it toward the individual and her private matters. And if we return to the Greek conception, practice is basically something quite different—public activity, free citizens' action carried out in a social situation. The political implications of the rejection of such a conception of practice are wide-ranging. First of all, it redirects art as practice from the citizen's public action for and with the social community to the individual's public action against the communal background, or in other words, her personal accomplishment in the public domain.

263 | Agamben, "Poiesis and Praxis," 72. See also *Critique of Creativity: Precarity, Subjectivity and Resistance in the 'Creative Industries,'* ed. Gerald Raunig, Gene Ray, and Ulf Wuggenig (London: MayFly Books, 2011).
264 | See Richard Sennett, *The Fall of Public Man.*

MAKING AND DOING ART
IN *THE CENTURY OF THE*
SELF

After the historical construction of the conceptions of art explained above, what we encounter in the twentieth century as common sense is a personalization of art sustained by the consensus of creative will. Agamben's list of nineteenth- and early twentieth-century art practices, where we may come across such a conception, might be broadened by many more or less recent inputs such as abstract expressionism and action painting, the majority of emancipatory and ludic neo-avant-garde theater, humanistic theater anthropology, expressionist dance, postmodern autobiographical and identity-based literature, and performance, graffiti, and similar forms of street art, not to mention numerous open and processual formats of contemporary work, including the widespread notions of energy, creativity, liberation, expression, impulse, and so forth. From a critical standpoint, it may be claimed that these artistic forms and concepts tend toward an atrophy of the political potential of art practice. This criticism rests upon the inference that, in these cases—which are many as well as paradigmatic of the twentieth-century Western Artworld—the aspect of free human action within the social realm is, in principle, replaced by a creativity that strives for the humanistic emancipation of the artist as an individual: her personal realization, affirmation, and liberation.

This trend was fostered additionally by the emancipatory politics of the 1960s, condensed into such slogans as "be individual," "be unique," "be different," "be yourself," and so forth. There was an explosion of intimacy in the public sphere, which Sennett traced back to the early nineteenth century, though now it was accompanied by warmth, friendship, personal liberation and accomplishment, and private happiness as publicly relevant issues and requests. This kind of celebration of the individual, invested in resistance to the mass society developed after World War II, gradually led to the cult of personality in many social spheres. Accordingly, in the art field, the artistic aura has shifted from artworks—which since then have been produced both as unique objects and reproduced copies—toward artists themselves, who are assigned the social role of being authentic, different, outstanding, and above all, non-conformist personalities.

Today, we can observe how this trend is gaining momentum in the course of a continued blurring of the borders between practice and production, understood, by post-Operaist and bio-political theorists such as Antonio Negri, Michael Hardt, Paolo Virno, and Maurizio Lazzarato as the general human condition of contemporary Western capitalist society, the production of which is based on the post-industrial fostering of immaterial labor and the post-Taylorist and post-Fordist organization of work. The theorists mentioned above claim that post-industrial production is more concerned with the cultural-informational content of material products than the products themselves: the production of images, tastes, opinions—and subjectivity. Likewise, as Lazzarato warns, in the work process, management is based on the slogan "become a subject (of communication)" and tends to become more totalitarian than the old divisions of poiesis due to its attempt at engaging the whole worker's personality and subjectivity in the production of value. Thus the expression of a supposedly unique individuality becomes a social imperative in the capital-ist world. An employee is no longer obliged merely to "get the job done"; in Lazzarato's words, "one *has to* express oneself, one *has to* speak, communicate, cooperate."[265] Therefore, "Actually, subjectivity is capitalism's biggest output. It's the single largest commodity we produce, because it goes into the production of all other commodities."[266] The same is true for the Artworld, where the imperative is visible, for instance, in the recent proliferation of artistic events organized as "encounters" between artists whose primary task is to be present, in person. The imperative has resulted in the glorification of the artist's signature, in establishing the artist's name as a brand, and in promoting the artist's personality as the art product *par excellence.* Thereby, the principles of work in (economic) production and in art overlap, and artists are becoming the paradigm of immaterial workers—but in a very opportunistic sense. In saying this we are trying to focus attention on the fact that, apart from being romantic and metaphysical, the exaggerated role of the personal in art is also very profitable for the capitalist art system.

And if, in spite of this criticism, it still seems difficult to speculate on an art practice that is extricated from the ties between the personal and authorship, we would like to give some concrete twentieth-century examples of different or even opposite conceptions of art.

Firstly, we should depart from the idea of the Western Artworld as the only possible horizon for thinking about art. And the paradigm of art in real socialist states—excepting Yugoslavia—already faces us with quite a different perspective: socialist realism. It can be traced back to the post-revolutionary Soviet Union, where it was officially adopted by the Congress of Soviet Writers in 1934, and then it became prevalent throughout the entire postwar Eastern Bloc, where it affirmed the socialist social order, also functioning as a counterpoint to abstract expressionism, which was promoted in the US as a paradigm for art as an expression and actualization of the artist's unique creative impulse. A telling testament to how the conception of the artist expressing personal freedom contributed to a political cause is situated in the late 1960s, when the US government recognized in abstract expressionist art, especially the actionist painting of Jackson Pollock, a propaganda tool during the Cold War. The Congress for Cultural Freedom was founded in order to promote the idea of individual liberty and autonomy as a defense against the threat of totalitarian communism, and its members included the art critic Clement Greenberg, Pollock, and the artists Robert Motherwell and Alexander Calder. The institution was financed by the Ford Foundation, as well as the US government. The Museum of Modern Art issued a program of traveling exhibitions which sent American art abroad with the message of personal, individual freedom, and *Life* magazine joined with a spread titled "Arms for Europe," where the "arms" would be cultural rather than military. This elicited a reaction on the part of the Communist Party in the USSR and Eastern Bloc countries in Europe against American abstraction as "decadent" and "reactionary."[267] In the socialist realist conception of art, instead of being regarded as a creative genius, the artist is rather seen as "a social engineer." That is to say, she is a cultural worker who works

265 | Maurizio Lazzarato, "Immaterial Labour," in *Radical Thought in Italy*, ed. Paolo Virno and Michael Hardt (Minneapolis: Minnesota University Press, 1996), www.generation-online.org/c/fcimmateriallabour3.htm.

266 | Maurizio Lazzarato, "Conversation with Maurizio Lazzarato," in "Exhausting Immaterial Labour in Performance," joint issue of *Le Journal des Laboratoires* and *TkH*, no. 17 (2010): 14.

267 | Matthias Hannemann, "Kalter Kulturkrieg in Norwegen?: Zum Wirken des 'Kongreß für kulturelle Freiheit' in Skandinavien," NORDEUROPA*forum*, no. 2 (1999): 15–41; Michael Hochgeschwender, "Freiheit in der Offensive? Der Kongreß für kulturelle Freiheit und die Deutschen, (München: Oldenbourg Wissenschaftsverlag, 1998).

in the domain of the social superstructure and who—like all other workers—deals with and works for society in her own domain and by her own means, instead of expressing her unique personality against the community. Moreover, focusing on the individuality of the artist is seen as a "bourgeois luxury," quite inappropriate in the situation where the new social order, based on collectivity and equality as a radical critique of Western capitalism and individualism, was meant to have been established. Although this approach provides us with an example of the real, existing twentieth-century conception of art wherein the personal is an irrelevant or even forbidden aspect of making or doing art, it has its widely discussed shortcomings. First of all, since it developed in the states that tended toward totalitarianism, the approach often resulted in a replacement of the Western pressure put on artists to be unique and invest their unique personality in art with the even bigger pressure to exclude any particular, individual, or personal elements from art. This way, socialist realism finally affirmed the figure of the "artist as party member," an impersonal maker who was subsumed under and thus more or less merely promoted (by artistic means) the party's politics and its vision of society.

The other case we would like to mention here is the famous theoretical debate on the relation of the author to the artwork, which—within the poststructuralist theoretical platform of the 1960s–70s—was opened by Roland Barthes's "death of the author," followed by Michel Foucault's rethinking of the discursive position of the author subject. We are recalling this debate, since Barthes[268] here breached the common-sense thinking of the work of art in its connections to the author as the person who lies behind it—he mostly refers to the writer—by claiming that the author is "dead," since she neither controls the meaning of the artwork regarded as text (or signifiers' weave) nor, accordingly, holds the key to reading it. Put differently, in the complex cultures of signifying practice, meaning is determined only intertextually, whereby artworks interact freely among themselves and are closer to each other than to their authors. From this perspective, the author as an individual human is completely irrelevant to the functioning of artworks in society, and the writer, or in a broader sense the artist, is more a "scriptor," an operator of the surrounding texts, than a lone genius from which the artworks spring. Foucault[269] will agree that the author's personality is not essential for an artwork, and the notion of the "author function" which he affirmed shouldn't be confused with the person of the author, nor does it refer to the real individual. However, according to him, the author as an artistic/textual subject is still needed in order for readers or audience to reconstruct a genealogy of a discourse, to link it, and to understand it in its linkage. And while the author's name here has a primarily classificatory role, the "author function" is instead a "narrator" who is part of a larger social and discursive system of beliefs and assumptions that determine and even limit meaning. This determination is associated with Foucault's great resistance to the vision of the artist as an individual isolated from the rest of society, and it further implies that even that which is seen as the individual personality of an author is always already a socially conditioned subjectivity. And seeing the author as constitutively involved in social contexts and discursive frames instead of as an isolated, unique individual might be a direction that overcomes its withdrawal as implied in Barthes' proposition. Keeping this remark in mind, at this point we would leave the Barthes/Foucault debate and once again change the terrain of discussion.

268 | Roland Barthes, "The Death of the Author," in *Image, Music, Text* (New York: Hill and Wang, 1977).

269 | Michel Foucault, "What is an Author?," in *Aesthetics, Method, and Epistemology*, ed. James Faubion (London: Penguin, 2000).

RETHINKING THE PERSON OF THE AUTHOR: TO BE A PERSON, I NEED THE MASK

The last topic that we would open here is how various and different performances of a self and its multiple social roles relate to the supposedly unique, coherent, and relatively long-lasting entity we call a "person," and furthermore, how the multiplicity, incoherence, and difference may be seen as its integral elements instead of as that which undermines it.[270] In some aspects, these issues resonate with postmodern thought, where the theses about multiple, dispersed, socially constructed identities have been articulated. We will now skip them and start by recalling Goffman's conception of social roles and the conclusion to which his study leads: without understanding performance, we cannot understand what the person as social category is, since it is nothing other than social roles or, in other words, its own performances. As we explained, Goffman's theses from the late 1950s not only interfered radically in the prevalent Western understanding of the person as formulated over the last few centuries, but at the same time showed how social constructivism in regard to the authentic self as the core of the person operated in Western society in the mid-twentieth century. The historical genesis of that understanding is traced precisely by Sennett when he claims that the fall of public man that has taken place in European bourgeois society from the late eighteenth century onward is caused by the view that while the public is the sphere of artificial social roles, the private is the domain of the human being's authenticity, the realm where we are closest to ourselves. This historical and geopolitical sharpening is crucial for the issues we are opening here; because only thanks to this sort of interpretation, it stands to reason that the authentic, private person needs to wear a costume or a mask to go public, and that public social performances are exactly what "de-personalize" us. That it is not an essential condition of the self but a contextually based and hence quasi self-evident common sense is visible already in the fact that only a few decades earlier, the "man as actor" had quite a different—and equally "self-evident"—connotation. As Sennett describes,[271] the early bourgeois public sphere at the time of the *ancien régime* was formed in the theater during and after performances, while conventions of social relations, conduct, and behavior in the theater passed into the street by way of the conceptions of body as mannequin and speech as sign (instead of symbol). What we can conclude is that, from the point of view of the early eighteenth century, what a person did in the social situation had a founding role; it was real and not what masked the real.

The etymology of the term "person" signals the same reversal of our habitual thinking about its uniqueness and essential coherence. The "person" and "personal" come from the Latin *persona*, from the Greek *prosopon*, which actually means "mask" and derived from Greek theater; then migrated to theatrical vocabulary as *dramatis persona*, meaning "theatrical character"; and then "persona" in current everyday speech. So originally, "person" was used to refer to someone other than oneself, someone other than we "are," and obviously other than what we today consider "person" to be. In a word, the person is a persona, not its opposite. This brings us in medias res of the ambivalent title of this chapter, which oscillates between theatrical and legal denotations, suggesting that the

270 | This could require a broad rethinking of the notion of the person, but we will again narrow the discussion down to a framework of the performing arts.
271 | Sennett, "Public Roles," in *The Fall of Public Man*, 64–89.

person of the author is what emerges from being in the person of the author. In other words, the author as person and especially as personality is a social role with quite clear social and historical coordinates. For this reason, we would claim that the person is a persona rather than its opposite since there is no individual human who is not a social being from the start, constituting herself with and before others. Seen in this way, the seemingly complicated question of the multiplicity of social roles and differences in performances of a self indicates that the personal is basically about founding self-performances in their own right. This constellation was almost lost in the later history of Western thought—theater discourse included—partly due to the influence of the Christian understanding of the person in terms of hypostases as different appearances of the same, of the essence of being, and later also due to the aforementioned historical process in the eighteenth century, a process which turned this understanding into a doxic common sense that reproduced the social order that created it.

Therefore, the reasoning that came out of these changes still reverberates in the dilemma we have today when speaking about the person and the performance, be it in art or in the wider social sphere: is there such a thing as the person who performs different personas, or is the person an outcome of these performances? Although postmodern multiple identities and Barthes' dead author can give us clear answers while contesting the traces of both Christian and bourgeois postulates in this matter, we would take the problematics further; because these answers cannot resolve the problem which latently resides in this dilemma, the problem, namely, of responsibility in the doing of art. We will introduce this problem as the final point of the discussion. Foucault's and Barthes' conceptions point precisely to and relieve us from the pseudo-essential constitution of the author by the personal. We find it their most significant achievement for the argument we have interwoven throughout this chapter: the essentialization of the author by the personal, that is, her personalization, means a privatization of the author subject and ultimately leads to its depoliticization. However, in order to repoliticize the author, de-essentialization is not enough. And at this point we meet the limit of the Barthesian and postmodern theses which void the locus of responsibility, either as a result of the author's loss of control over meaning, playing freely in intertextual space, or by a dispersion of the author subject into multiple, socially, and arbitrarily constructed identities. This is why we found Foucault's remark about the contextual conditioning of the author-function worth keeping in mind, as it implies that although the author as an individual human does not control the artwork and its functioning in public, as a part of larger social and discursive systems the author does determine it—or at least takes part in determining it, thereby assuming a portion of the responsibility for it as well. Therefore, what seems to us politically more radical than the withdrawal of the author is to reassign her the responsibility for what she does in art as a public matter. Not, in this case, due to a preexisting personality expressed or actualized in her doing, but because one *is* what one *does* in a certain context. However, one should be reduced neither to the preexisting inner self nor to the arbitrary external readings of the deed. Instead, in doing, the "self-construction work" is accomplished as a joint effort between self-awareness, bodily existence, and external social agencies. And how these three different and possibly incoherent and divergent, yet nevertheless intertwined, forces correlate is changeable and depends precisely on the predominant ideology or, more often, the prevailing doxa that operates in a certain context, defining the social subject and role of the doer. Furthering this thesis, in closing, we would reverse the entire problem of art and the personal by concluding that no author can indeed escape the responsibility for doing art, and "the person" is too weak an alibi to mask it for long.

However, we would like to add that we are aware of how our analysis—which contributes to theoretical efforts to contest the essentialization and depoliticization, at the hands of the personal, of the author as a social subject—can only explain the ways in which this paradigm for art is constructed and cannot really destabilize it. It cannot because the cult of personality in art as well as in all other spheres of contemporary society is a doxa that has to do neither with its own conceptual strength, nor with a humanistic concern for the fragile human terrified of false public life. This doxa is only one aspect of an ongoing, overall privatization of the social which can be traced to social relations and relations of production in neoliberal capitalism, a privatization that musters any and all means necessary to promote individualism and personal rights, thereby legitimizing the public relevance of private interests and property.

If there is one performance genre that has retained a privileged status since its emergence in the beginning of the twentieth century, it is solo, first and foremost in dance.[272] Solo dance performance is the format in which the pioneers of modern dance, such as Isadora Duncan or Mary Wigman, acted out not only a historical rupture with ballet, but also their own emancipation as women who choreographed and interpreted their own dance in the first person. The coincidence of the body that is both the source, the material, and the instrument of movement determines a conflation between that body and the self, binding the subject to her sense of self-identity through physical, emotional, spiritual, etc., experience. Solo is probably the most abundant format in dance performance, a mandatory test of artistry in education, as well as a fetish item in a choreographer's oeuvre. It is often the most inexpensive commodity traded in the performance world nowadays, too. But it is also the form in which many bodily systems and techniques are instructed and exercised in the everyday, ideologically framing the present-day practice of the care of the self through embodiment.

272 | The precedent of solo dance is the solo virtuoso performance in music, which dates back to the nineteenth century and is commonly understood as the expression of Romantic subjectivity, as in Franz Liszt or Nicolo Paganini.

This chapter will examine solo dance as a technique of the self and the related practices of improvisation and body systems from two symmetrical points of interest. Firstly, we will take a naïve departure by asking ourselves why solo has been a privileged form of dance and performance since the beginning of the twentieth century. Why are configurations of two or more bodies or group choreographies in modern and contemporary dance throughout the last century until today less prominent than before? How does this relate to the disposition of the public and private spheres of the social field? Answering this question will unpack what historically and politically underlies the emergence of the solo, its characteristic association with democracy in America, to paraphrase Alexis De Tocqueville's seminal work as well as the exclamatory title of Duncan's essay "I See America Dancing."[273] Not only does solo owe its stable prevalence to an individualism that ideologically frames capitalist relations of production and to the rise of bourgeois society since around 1800; moreover, it is strengthened in the current form of post-Fordist capitalism to the extent that it could be claimed as *the performative mode* of production, dominant even when it includes collaboration and teamwork. The other side of our inquiry is social: What can we observe *through* solo about subject-formation and social self-performance? In which space do the solo-dance and body-system techniques in improvisation and techniques of the private self overlap toward indiscernability? What role can these techniques have in politically structuring the private/public disposition today?

EMOTIONALISM IN
SELF-EXPRESSION

The history of solo dance traces various operations in which the self is constituted corporeally. The distinction of these historical operations yields to the techniques which no longer belong exclusively to dance, but which are nowadays largely available and implemented as techniques in subject-formation, reflecting the aesthetic mode of individualism qua ideology. The first and most ingrained one concerns self-expression in dance, which we will briefly examine here together with the operation that is closely related to it: empathy as self-expression's intended effect.

Self-expression is bound up with the view that dance arises from an expression of an inner compulsion of the dancer and choreographer whose movement is the index of their interior psychic life. The "expressionistic" dance of Mary Wigman and her American counterpart, Martha Graham, was advocated on the basis of the connection between movement and personal feeling. The peculiarity of John Martin's conception of modern dance[274] as linked with self-expression lay in foregrounding emotion as the cause, meaning, and effect of movement in its aesthetic form, which he defined with the term of his own coinage, "metakinesis." In movement, or kinesis, lies a necessary correlation between the physical and the psychical as "two aspects of a single underlying reality." In Martin's theory,

273 | Isadora Duncan, "I See America Dancing," in *What is Dance? Readings in Theory and Criticism*, ed. Roger Copeland and Marshall Cohen (Oxford: Oxford University Press, 1983), 264–5; written in 1927.
274 | John Martin is an American dance critic and historian as well as the most—but not only—instrumental person in defining and categorizing modern dance in America. John Martin, *The Modern Dance* (New York: A. S. Barnes, 1933) and *Introduction to Modern Dance* (New York: W. W. Norton, 1939).

metakinesis explains how "authentic movements" are produced through the intuition of the choreographer, who externalizes her individual experience, her process of "feeling through with a sensitive body" in an aesthetic form that must provoke a reaction in the beholder. Self-expression is not solipsistic, but communicable since it invokes kinaesthetic empathy in the beholder, or "metakinesis." The causal relation between the performer's feeling, her movement, and the feeling it arouses in the recipient of the movement is founded upon a speculation about the muscular isomorphism in the body of the performer and the spectator, a kind of "inner mimicry":

> We shall cease to be mere spectators and become participants in the movement that is pre-sented to us, and though to all outward appearances we shall be sitting quietly in our chairs, we shall nevertheless be dancing synthetically with all our musculature. Naturally these motor re-sponses are registered by our movement-sense receptors, and awaken appropriate emotional associations akin to those which have animated the dancer in the first place. It is the dancer's whole function to lead us into imitating his actions with our faculty for inner mimicry in order that we may experience his feelings.[275]

The ideological fallacy of emotionalism is that it instills a unilateral determination of cause and effect in the genesis and the reception of dance: One moves out of feeling. And because one is moved by a certain feeling when one watches dance, the movement must be expressing that feeling. Movement is predicated of the body that feels. And because it arouses the feeling in its beholder, it is believed to be a medium for the transference of an aesthetic and emotional concept from the consciousness of one individual to that of another. Such a belief is the very essence of an aesthetic ideology, as Hewitt argues in *Social Choreography: Ideology as Performance in Dance and Everyday Life* (2005), because it idealizes the body as a locus of truth, which is succinctly articulated in Graham's motto: the body doesn't lie.

If we isolate this belief from its originary historical context of modern dance, we observe how it epitomizes an act of private communication under the spell of intimacy. Out of the dark place of the stage looms a figure under the spotlight whose dancing and speaking will always be in the first person because her performance is, as a matter of intuition, thought to reveal her true self or indicate her personal, emotional life. Solo dance thus functions as a truth-game in the Foucauldian sense, by which the body is understood as the means for expression of individual freedom. It is deemed to offer a physical experience of transcendental subjectivity, which, on one side, suppresses the contingencies that structure experience, and on the other, reduces the expression of movement to the individual self, or to the form that reassures its identity. Thanks to the legacy of modern dance established by the choreographer-dancer's dancing solo in the twentieth century, solo dance today still raises the expectation that it will serve the dancer to present her "art" of dance, where art bears a sense of craftsmanship, original invention of movements, bodily expression, and even, to a varying extent, a conviction or statement of faith in one's own kind of "art-religion," founded on one's inner compulsion to move. Dance education pedagogically legitimates and reinforces solo as the truth game: solo is a standard format through which dancers and choreographers are trained to use their own body as an instrument of expression referring to their individual self and their inner motivation

---

275 | John Martin, *Introduction to the Dance* (New York: Dance Horizons, 1965), 53.

to move. The focus of expression may shift to formal, stylistic, technical, or to any other concerns besides the supposedly inherent emotional nature of movement, but the bottom line of this doxa demands that all these concerns be understood as belonging to the individual self of the dancer.[276] The intimate and private act of communication in a solo consists of the situation in which the dancer seems to reveal her art primarily to herself and with herself, whereas the others are allowed to observe this as an emergence of discovery.

At the core of solo's intimism lies something which Jacques Derrida has analyzed under the terms "auto-affection" and "metaphysics of presence," often invoking a genre that is close to solo, as solo is often interspersed with its elements—autobiography—as the perfect instance of auto-affection as self-relation.[277] Auto-affection occurs when one affects oneself, when the affecting is the same as the affected. It has also been described in the late writing of Maurice Merleau-Ponty as the chiasm in the intertwinement of the subject-object positions in the body: the hand that touches is touched.[278] If modern dance has a special affinity with the phenomenological notion of lived experience (as in Edmund Husserl), or even, as in the later phenomenology of Merleau-Ponty, with embodied experience in the living present of the performance, solo is the form that best entertains this illusion of self-proximity, of there being no external detour between moving one's body and sensing one's body move, seeing oneself in the mirror, hearing oneself speak. Derrida's deconstruction of auto-affection in phonocentrism, or in self-image in the mirror, highlights the hiatus that detaches the subject from the self, a gap which spaces out the difference between the I-eye and the self as an other. Here we invoke Derrida's critique of the self-identity which is constituted in one's own immediate experience of self-presence because the production of solo in contemporary dance, but also many other bodily techniques of the self, rests on the essentialist phenomenological postulates of consciousness as the embodied experience of one's living present. Derrida's deconstruction critically unfolds the consitution of the modern subject in self-presence and logos, which situates his critique in the Western history of metaphysics. But for an account of the persistence of solo today, Derrida's critique won't suffice. An explanation must be sought elsewhere, as the next section will convey: in the materialist critique of the relations of production that sustain and perpetuate the fantasy and success of this format.

276 | An explicit illustration of this point can be found in the title and profile of the Master of Arts program in dance at the Universität der Künste in Berlin, called, in its abbreviated form, SODA: Solo/Dance/Authorship. See the website of the Universität der Künste, http://www.hzt-berlin.de/?z=2&p=11&lan=en&PHPSES SID=c22d3300218cc4830a1a40bac99869f0.

277 | While it abounds in many of his works, Derrida's deconstruction of auto-affection is most instructive in *Voice and Phenomenon: Introduction to the Problem of the Sign in Husserl's Phenomenology* (Evanston, IL: Northwestern University Press, 2010), originally written in 1967.

278 | Maurice Merleau-Ponty, "The Intertwining – The Chiasm," in *The Visible and the Invisible*, trans. Alphonso Lingis, ed. Claude Lefort (Evanston, IL: Northwestern University Press, 1968), 130–55.

**A WHEEL THAT TURNS
ON ITSELF IN A ROOM OF
ITS OWN**

Taking her cue from Badiou's famous essay "Dance as a Metaphor for Thought," where the French philosopher describes dance as a figure of a wheel that turns on itself, "like a circle in space, but a circle that is its own principle, a circle that is not drawn from the outside, but rather draws itself,"[279] the Slovene philosopher Bojana Kunst argues that contemporary dance is still mired in the modern notion of the autonomous, self-determined subject, where "bodily autonomy" recurs as an aesthetic utopia time and again. She writes:

> Autonomy thus became the key strategy employed by the body to enter the stage of modernity and disclose its own contemporary flow: it is autonomous yet evasive, self-disclosing yet artificial, an eternally wanted but never touched self-rotating wheel.[280]

Kunst identifies the paradox that governs the autonomy of the subject in dance through the autonomy of the body. The more exclusivity it claims through self-reference expressed in the spontaneity of one's "authentic" movement, the more its autonomy is reduced to a fleeting moment. Thus it discloses its obsession with presence and being-in-the-present at the same time as it decries the historicity and context it rests upon.

Apart from being an aesthetic utopia, the quest for the autonomy of the solo-dancing body resurged as a political strategy in the performance of the particular, where the identity of the subject lies in alterity, in the difference of gender, sexuality, race, nationality, culture, HIV/AIDS, or even, in the 1980s and 1990s, as a constructed story of oneself. Although it particularizes the self, this usage of solo still maintains the regime of representing a certain identity. Only a few initiatives can be noted that utilized the format of solo to undo its representative function and destabilize the identity and subject position of the dancing body. Their strategies include composing monstrous bodies, making assemblages of part-bodies of opposite genders and of human and non-human, treating body as an object, and appropriating expressions of foreign bodies in lieu of original and authentic movement—all of which are strategies, as could be concluded, that revolve around otherness.[281]

In addition to Kunst's critique of bodily autonomy that tackles the temporal side of performing autonomy, we would like to address the spatial aspect of the problem, which can be usefully analyzed through two seemingly unrelated notions, Virginia Woolf's "room of one's own" and Deleuze and Guattari's "territory." The thesis of the English writer's eponymous essay famously marked the emancipatory feminist stance in 1929: "A woman

279 | Alain Badiou, "Dance as a Metaphor for Thought," In *Inaesthetics* (London: Verso, 2005), 58.
280 | Bojana Kunst, "Subversion and the Dancing Body: Autonomy on Display," *Performance Research* 8, no. 2 (2003): 62.
281 | These initiatives can be traced in a series of solos by Xavier Le Roy, *Narcisse Flip* (1994–1997), *Self Unfinished* (1998), *Product of Circumstances* (1999), *The Rite of Spring* (2007), and *Product of Other Circumstances* (2009); a series of solos by Maria La Ribot called *Distinguished Pieces* (1997–ongoing);Vera Mantero's three solos *one mysterious Thing, said e.e cummings* (1996), *Perhaps she could dance first and think afterwards* (1991), and *Olympia* (1999); Eszter Salamon's *What A Body You Have Honey* (2001); Mette Ingvartsen's *50/50* (2004); Antonia Baehr's *Rire* (2008).

must have money and a room of her own if she is to write fiction."[282] In our view, the condition of personal liberty for women to create art—having a place of isolation and a little bit of cash—can be taken as a parable that cynically describes a characteristic mode of biopolitical production in dance today: the artist's residency. The solo represents a typical format of a small-scale project that rejuvenates the labor force by a capital investment in youth as both a promise and cheap labor. The residency is then offered as a cautious and relatively cheap investment, because it substitutes working space and facilities for a budget to make the performance.

The solo dance that might result from a residency, but also any other working situation, is an inexpensive and efficient product, easy to tour and transport from one theater to another, making networking appear as a smooth space of artistic operation. However, the real commodity that the residency pays for isn't the solo: the space and the money amount to an allowance that supports the life of the artist, who is subsumed under labor that defers her achievement, which only later comes to fruition in the form of a product. Hence the production of the solo often turns into a work-in-(open-ended)-progress that supports itself through the artists' relaying from residency to residency. This is where the concept "territory" emerges in relation to "nomadology." In contrast to a sedentary place that protects its borders by power in a historical conception of time, Deleuze and Guattari's "territory" is, on the one hand, a soft site of passage, always connected with the "line of flight" and "becoming-other," a leaving of one territory for an entering of another, a "deterritorialization" for a new "reterritorialization."[283] Its extension is unstable, its borders loose, as in Deleuze and Guattari's images of the animal's marking of territory by an assemblage of postures, colors and sounds; or, more paradigmatically, the constituting of territory is compared with the "birth of an art," where the role of the artist's signature is like placing a flag on a piece of land.[284] Territory, with its movements of deterritorialization and reterritorialization, implies a mobile, shifting center, the agency of which rests in the nomadic subject of the artist. Proficiency in making a territory emerge, inhabiting it, leaving it, and entering another territory is equated with the ability to navigate opportunities in the market, where the artist as product is regarded as the ultimate object of exchange.

According to the dance artist Dragana Bulut's interpretation, where she cites the Slovene theorist Marina Gržinić by directly inscribing her signature on stage in a solo, the dancer establishes a brand of her art. The solo ties the author to the self "not in relation to itself, because there exists no interiority. The interiority is exteriority: it is my brand."[285] While the solo was historically introduced as an autographic act, or as that which the performance theorist Rebecca Schneider qualified as a "precise and human gesture" of "unrepeatable and unapproachable nature" that "rescues origin, originality, and authenticity,"[286] nowadays it more and more becomes a fragmented and dispersed practice of the self.

282 | Virginia Woolf, *A Room of One's Own*, 4th ed. (New York: Harcourt Brace, 1989); originally published in 1929.

283 | Gilles Deleuze and Félix Guattari, *A Thousand Plateaus: Capitalism and Schizophrenia*, trans. B. Massumi (London: Continuum, 1988), 380–82.

284 | Gilles Deleuze and Félix Guattari, *What is Philosophy?* trans. Hugh Tomlinson and Graham Burchell (New York: Columbia University Press, 1994), 68.

285 | Marina Gržinić, "Subjectivization, Biopolitics and Necropolitics," *REARTI-KULACIJA* no. 6 (2009), http://www.reartikulacija.org/?p=59&langswitch_lang=si; cited in Dragana Bulut, "Negotiating Solo Dance Authorship in Neoliberal Society," *Tkh* no. 18 (2010): 59.

286 | Rebecca Schneider, "Solo, Solo, Solo" in *After Criticism*, ed. Gavin Butt (Oxford: Blackwell, 2004), 33.

"The Portrait of the Artist as a Worker" by the Belgian philosopher Dieter Lesage gives a graphic account of it:

> You are an artist and that means: you don't do it for the money. That is what some people think. It is a great excuse not to pay you for all the things you do. So what happens is that you, as an artist, put money into projects that others will show in their museum, in their Kunsthalle, in their exhibition space, in their gallery. So you are an investor. You give loans nobody will repay you. You take financial risks. You speculate on yourself as an artistic asset. You are a trader. You cannot put all your money into one kind of artistic stocks. So you diversify your activities. You manage the risks you take. You would say it differently. I know. You say you suffer from a gentle schizophrenia. You are multiple personalities. You are a photographer, but also a DJ. You have a magazine, you are a publisher, but you also organize parties. You take photos from party people. You throw a party when you present a magazine, you make magazines with photographs of party people, you throw a party and you are the DJ.[287]

The notion of the artist as an entrepreneur of herself involves *désoeuvrement* through multiple activities and operations that propel the self of the artist through networking and circulation. The fragment above also points to how the artist's solo practice spills into life, making art and non-art, art and life, and work and non-work indistinguishable.

BETWEEN PRACTICE AND THERAPY

In common parlance, dancers and performance makers nowadays refer to their work not as art, but as practice. This corresponds to what we discussed in chapter seven as the transformation of the meaning of practice into the manifestation of the human will and vital impulse. In dance and performance it acquires the specific significance of training, exercise, repetition by which contemporary artists take a humble workerist position that considers their art as existing outside of masterpiece culture.[288] We might ask ourselves what is problematic about this denomination if it can only accurately describe the current post-Fordist subsumption of life under art and capital. It conveniently resolves the impasse of the earlier critique of the gap between process and product. The question could be posed differently by asking whether there is an aim to such a practice that could be tested, a problem that the practice poses, revolves around, and tries to solve; and what this practice enables or achieves, or if it is an end in itself.

These questions arise from a paradigmatic case of the conflation of solo dance with daily practice, Deborah Hay's *Solo Dance Commissioning Project* (SDCP), which we will briefly examine here. The project was initiated by the well-known choreographer, whose work carries the aura of experimentation with the everyday as practiced by the neo-avant-garde Judson Dance Theater in the 1960s. It starts as an eleven-day-long residency where dancers "commission" Hay to "guide and coach them" in making a solo performance. "At the conclusion of the residency each participant signs a contractual agreement to a

---

287 | Dieter Lesage, "The Portrait of the Artist as Worker," In *Vertoog over verzet. Politiek in tijden van globalisering* (Antwerp: Meulenhoff/Manteau, 2004).
288 | See Chrysa Parkinson. "On Practice," in *6M1L*, ed. Mette Ingvartsen (samizdat, 2008), 24–33.

daily solo practice of the new piece, for a minimum of three months before their first public performance."[289] Hay states her motive in the following: "I felt like I could promise artists a choreographed solo dance that would simply require *a daily practice, otherwise called learning without thinking*, for three months prior to their first public performance of the solo adaptation" (italics ours). The technology for the practice that she offers consists of "concepts through directives that each performer translates individually into movement in his/her unique way" and "meditation-like exercises" that bind the artist to "the material." The outline of the project underlines its uniqueness in that the artist is also obliged to raise funds for Hay's fee, and for her, the artist's, own income in her own community, where "family, friends, local, state, or national granting agencies, corporations, become the patrons for each dance."

Several points from the discussion above appear problematic here. The solo performance of the dance artist is authorized by the guru who transmits conceptual directives and exercises accumulated throughout her own lifelong practice. The contract doesn't only posit Hay's ownership, but financially instructs the artist how to sell this future brand-name product to a community in which it could belong. Apart from the tight grip of the hierarchical division of labor and profit implied by this contract, the dance artist submits to a process which explicitly rests on passing faith without critical reflection, as Hay succinctly defined her notion of practice as "learning without thinking." The lure of faith lies in consistency validated through a solitary labor-intensive process where the dancer binds her body to movement, under the auspices of the master. The question arises as to what motivates dancers to seek such guidance from a guru. The project gives insight into the motivations of individuals, one of which is particularly striking to us:

> Through her courageous choreographic and performance practice, remarkable language and immediate presence, Deborah has touched and stimulated the most essential places in my artistic expression, encouraging the integration of every aspect of my performing self with my dance. And here I remember the pleasure in dance. I experience an availability, a flexibility, a wholeness rarely evoked through any other form—touching on my child, adult, fool, craftsman, artist and essential nature—accessing a very alive and ready state from which to work.[290]

The process of creating the solo within Hay's project thus instills a technology of the self in which the artistic sense of self is reinvigorated through a vitalist commitment to physical work. The statement above would lose nothing of its specificity if the words "choreographic," "performance," "artistic," "with my dance," and "dance" were omitted. It would read as a report of successful psychotherapy whereby the patient regained confidence in her capacities as well as joy in work. The project displays a model of governmentality where the individual internalizes disciplinary mechanisms by investing desire and fantasy about self-actualization in work.

Solo Dance Commissioning Project is an intensive example of how dance provides a set of vitalist techniques of embodiment in which the self is performed at the boundary between individualistic artistic work and psychotherapy. But modern dance has a long history of engagement with the performance of the self in various body systems and movement practices since the 1950s. A more explicit example among many body system techniques

289 | All information about SDCP, including quotations, was obtained at the official website of the Deborah Hay Dance Company, http://www.deborahhay.com/about.html.

290 | Statement by Ross Warby, dancer/choreographer, website of the Deborah Hay Dance Company, http://www.deborahhay.com/about.html.

developed throughout the twentieth century is "Authentic Movement." It was originated by Mary Starks Whitehouse (1911–1979), who associated modern dance's practice of self-expression with Jungian psychotherapy in group processes where participants engage in spontaneous expressive movement exploration. Movement that arises from self-expression was termed "authentic" by Whitehouse's follower Janet Adler, who developed the discipline of Authentic Movement on the following premise: "When the movement was simple and inevitable, not to be changed no matter how limited or partial, it became what I called 'authentic'—it could be recognized as genuine, belonging to that person."[291]

Another widespread technology of the self in dance can be found in improvisation as a mode of performance. Here movement is spontaneously generated as it is performed before an audience. The improvisation which is based on the legacy of contact improvisation promotes a holistic approach to the body that celebrates the unconcious and a free flow of subjectivity manifested in a form of visceral thinking, as opposed to the rational control of mind and thought expressed in language. In the lingo of practitioners of improvisation, whose legacy is built on contact improvisation, one of the recurrent themes is a concern with the self expressed as "losing" and "getting in touch" with oneself. Loss of the self is specifically linked with a sensibility of time, *improvviso ex tempore,* which is perceived in the dancer's auto-affection as "unexpected" and "unknown." According to such practice, improvisation offers a technique of inducing the experience of the sublime within one's presence and being in the present.[292] Movement without a pregiven rhythm and time frame becomes open-ended and thus "unforeseen." This, according to Steve Paxton, whose role nowadays spans from pioneer experimentor to master of improvisation, calls for an interpretation of "out of time" (*ex tempore*) in two contradictory ways. The time of improvisation should be equated with human experience of duration, which he defines as the experiences accumulated in life. "'Out of time' means that, out of experience (conscious or not) there is material for making something," writes Paxton. Similarly, improvisation has served to void the body from the self, in the famous practice of "detraining" Paxton proposed with his *Small Dance.*[293] The process of detraining involves relaxation, which is, according to Paxton, a voluntary act of a certain kind:

> An act of "Won't." That is, I won't hold this tension any longer. It's not a negative. It's the opposite of insisting that you have to be what you are in terms of the tensions that have arrived within your body. That insistence is very much some part of the body that says "This is me, this is myself."[294]

291 | Janet Adler, *Offering from the Conscious Body: The Discipline of Authentic Movement* (Rochester, NY: Inner Traditions, 2002), xii.

292 | The Portuguese choreographer whose work is based on improvisation, Joao Fiadeiro, reports that "although the 'unexpected' is extremely rare to an experienced player, it is precisely for that moment that I work—to see a good player in suspense before an 'unexpected,' 'intriguing' and 'enigmatic' move from his opponent. I truly believe that it is exactly in that void, the time parentheses where life stays on hold for a brief moment, that art (like the game) becomes sublime." Fiadeiro, "If you don't know, why do you ask? An Introduction to the Method of Real-Time Composition," in *Knowledge in Motion: Perspectives of Artistic and Scientific Research in Dance*, ed. Sabine Gehm, Pirkko Husemann, and Katharina von Wilcke (Bielefeld: transcript, 2007), 108.

293 | See the interview with Steve Paxton, "In The Midst Of Standing Still Something Else Is Occurring And The Name For That Is The Small Dance," in Dir. P. Hulton, *Arts Archives: Theatre Papers, The First Series 1977–78* (Exeter, 2004), http://spa.exeter.ac.uk/drama/research/exeterdigitalarchives/theatre_papers/paxton.pdf.

294 | Ibid.

An exercise of the emancipation of the physical self, detraining has the purpose to reach what improvisers deem the deepest hidden ground of the body—its automatic unconscious movements and sensations. Or, in other words, detraining should enable a kind of existence which appears truer and more essential than the truth of the subjective experience of a particular self. Whether it aims for embodiment whereby the sense of self becomes organically bound up with body or, conversely, paves the way for desubjectivation through the immanence of the body, as we have observed in the various cases above, dance improvisation encapsulates both the individualist ideology and technique of the self in the biopolitical age. It underlies a large part of solo dance practice for the simple reason that it facilitates a free flow of expression in the first person, considered the truest, most intimate and personal experience of oneself. It favors the inner life of the self in the body, whose privacy is cultivated through imagination and metaphors in which movements, sensations, and emotional states are described. A common technology of dancers entails invoking images that correspond to movements while dancing.

The work of the imagination can be based on belief, like in the Body-Mind Centering system, which is founded on a dual claim: firstly, a movement can be initiated in places in the body, such as bodily organs and fluids, that elude any scientific verification of their host's ability to be aware of them; secondly, the nature of the place in which the movement is initiated will be reflected in the quality of the movement.[295] Or, the production of images can be equated with an intentional feigning, a pretending to know the cause of one's affection and movement for the sake of sustaining such experience. Regardless of being unconscious or voluntary and intentional, the production of images in the dancer who focuses on her own body (primarily in solo) resembles early psychiatric and pseudomedical practices of psychotherapy, such as the power of imagination and autosuggestion, developed from the end of the nineteenth into the early twentieth century, approximately during the same period as the solo dance emerged in early modernism. The method of the French pharmacologist and practitioner of hypnosis Emile Coué and autogenic training by the German psychiatrist Johannes Heinrich Schultz are exemplary here. While the Coué method centers on the routine repetition of an expression by eliminating the resistance of willpower and independent judgment, autogenic training involves exercises practiced daily in which a set of visualizations is repeated to induce a state of relaxation caused by its influence on the autonomic nervous system. The exercises read like a score in a manual or how-to of self-mastery. The tasks are to be executed in the imagination rather than in movement, yet the very form of writing in the imperative, in the direct address, and the call to occupy oneself with one's own body and consciousness makes any comparison with dance scores quite striking. An autogenic training session may include the following instructions:

> Sit in the meditative posture and scan the body
> "my right arm is heavy"
> "my arms and legs are heavy and warm" (repeat 3 or more times)
> "my heartbeat is calm and regular" (repeat 3 times)[296]

295 | Body-Mind Centering is a widely spread body practice, applied not only in dance, but in many kinds of bodywork, yoga, psychotherapy, child development, athletics, music, etc. It was developed by Bonnie Bainbridge Cohen in the 1970s as: "an experiential study based on the embodiment and application of anatomical, physiological, psychophysical and developmental principles, utilizing movement, touch, voice and mind." See the official website of Body-Mind Centering, http://www.bodymindcentering.com.

296 | Karl Hans Welz, "Autogenic Training: A Practical Guide in Six Easy Steps," (HSTCI, 1991), http://www.autoaura.com/autogenic.html.

The Swedish choreographer Efva Lilja begins her booklet *100 Exercises for a Choreographer and Other Survivors* with the following:

> Exercise I: Stand still. Close your eyes and think of the last three sentences you spoke. Seek movements that express what you meant. Take a step and formulate three sentences that express the experience of what you are now doing.
> Do it.
> Exercise II: Stand still. Close your eyes and let your hands scan your body's contours. Touch every part of the body, with particular attention to those parts you normally cannot see. Write down your experiences and save them as Portrait No I.
> Do it. (...)[297]

The mantra-like repetition of the imperative "do it" indicates submission to the task, an advice to refrain from any further thought and judgment, which is presented as necessary to attain the state or experience that the exercises promise. The concrete and simple nature of the task that resembles an everyday routine contrasts with a vague sense of purification to be reached, or perhaps livelihood in an intensified experience of one's own vitality. The sense closes upon the self, writing it—at least for a moment of this intensive experience of being in the present—out of history, geography, social and political context, relations with disturbing others, as well as away from any thought which problematizes itself.

***

The above analysis has not attempted to reduce solo dance or dance at large to its relation to self-identity; instead, its aim has been to observe how the tradition of dancing solo has produced an intensive model of performance of the self and what we can observe about the particular techniques of the self today through this model. Our conclusion rests on the image of the closing paragraph above: one of self-absorption.

If the intimate society from the end of the nineteenth century, as Sennett defines it, has yielded the narcissistic self that confuses the spheres of private and public, the question remains: what has twenty-first-century society in its various qualifications—the society of biopolitical control, Post-Fordism, the experience society, and so forth—changed with respect to the position and performance of the self in those spheres. What can be preliminarily inferred is that the change is of a degree and not of a kind: the performance of individuals demonstrates absorption in self-affection and the experience of oneself. This might not mean that the division between public and private is abolished due to the public sphere's overpopulation by individualistic interests and expressions, but that the divide persists in the disconnection of the techniques and performances of individuals from the public as a political sphere. The loss of the public sphere is attributable to the public

297 | Efva Lilja, *100 Exercises for a Choreographer and Other Survivors* (Stockholm: Ellerströms, 2012), 6–8. The book opens with a statement of intent: "These exercises are written down to remind me of what we need to stay alive, vivid and strong. . . . I wish to be supportive to you who want to train and develop your sensitivity towards that which carries meaning in human movement and the components that become wonderful tools in the choreographic work needed to reshape reality."

as it turns toward the individual, stimulating the individual's self-expression and auto-affection, its preoccupation with its own well-being, bolstered by a practice of techniques that intertwine or inhabit the border between art and therapy. One of the implications of this centralization of the self in society which we will pursue further is how self-absorption stands as an obstacle to the social imagination of group formations, collectivities, or movements that would reclaim the public sphere.

This book ends the first phase of our research, which will continue from the conclusions of the third part, dedicated to the performance of the self. One of the implications of the centralization of the self in today's society is how self-absorption stands as an obstacle to the social imagination of group formations, collectivities, or movements that would reclaim the public sphere.

Among the questions that arose here to be pursued further, we register the following: how are individualism and collectivism ideologically confronted today? One path to answering this is to search for the models of collectivity upon which the public sphere has been historically constituted. Another way is to examine how the performance of the self functions within group, collective, and mass *agencements* of the public. Yet another set of problems revolves around art and the public sphere, on the one side, and art and the public and common good, on the other side.

The status of art within many debates about the transformation of the public sphere and society today is volatile, and, as we remarked, in some cases controversial—when art is uncritically set as a model of revolutionary change or as a playground for exercising radically adverse developments of capitalism. The most difficult inquiry concerns the defense of art as a public and common good. This will necessitate its measurement against more unequivocal social demands and concerns, such as free education and healthcare. Lastly, for us to further explore the relations between self and group, collective, and mass configurations of the public, as well as the set of functions and places art can occupy in the public sphere today, we will have to revise our analytical framework, derived from performance, where, in addition to choreography, drama and performance, dramaturgy, and staging will resurface.

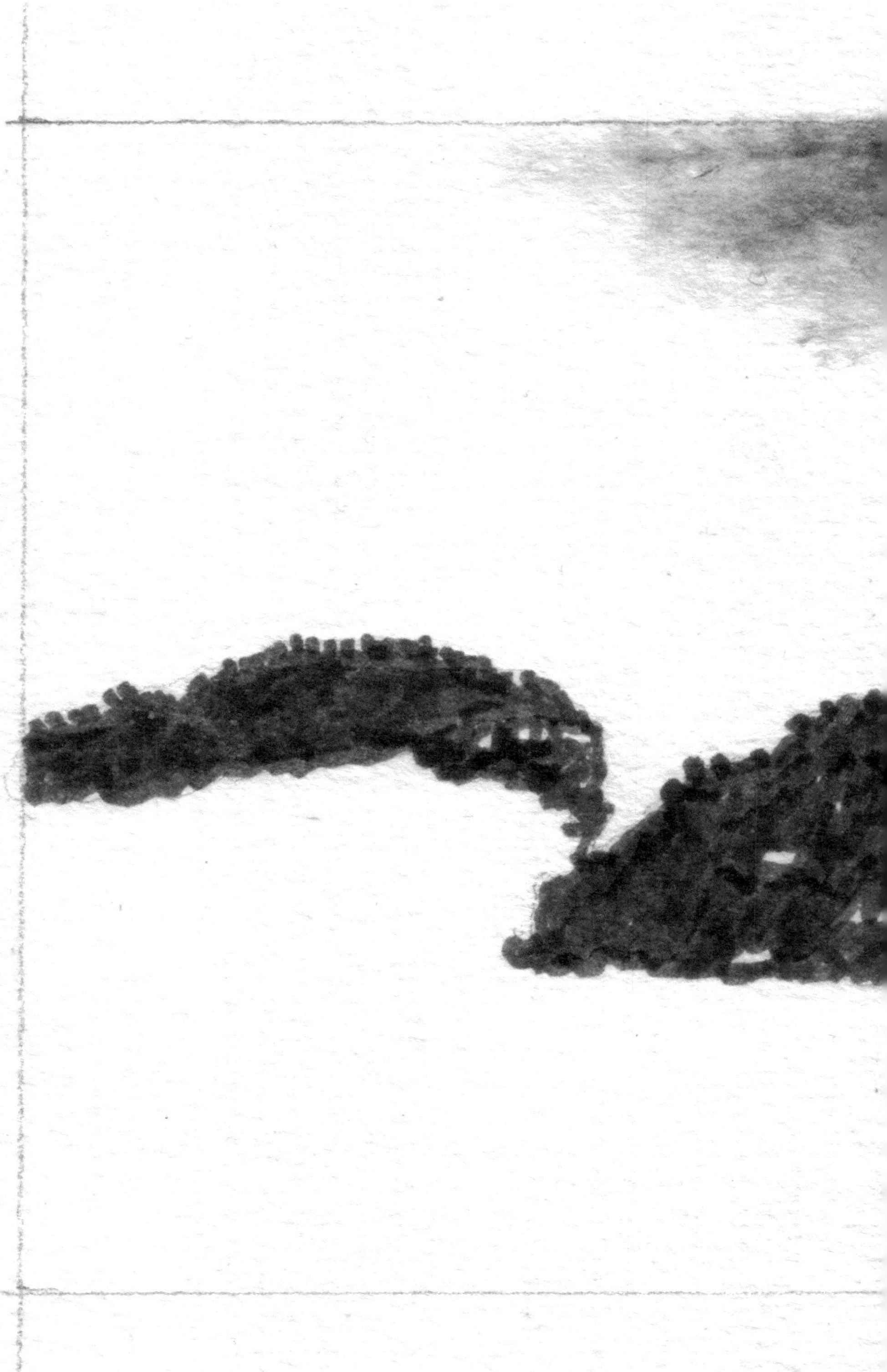

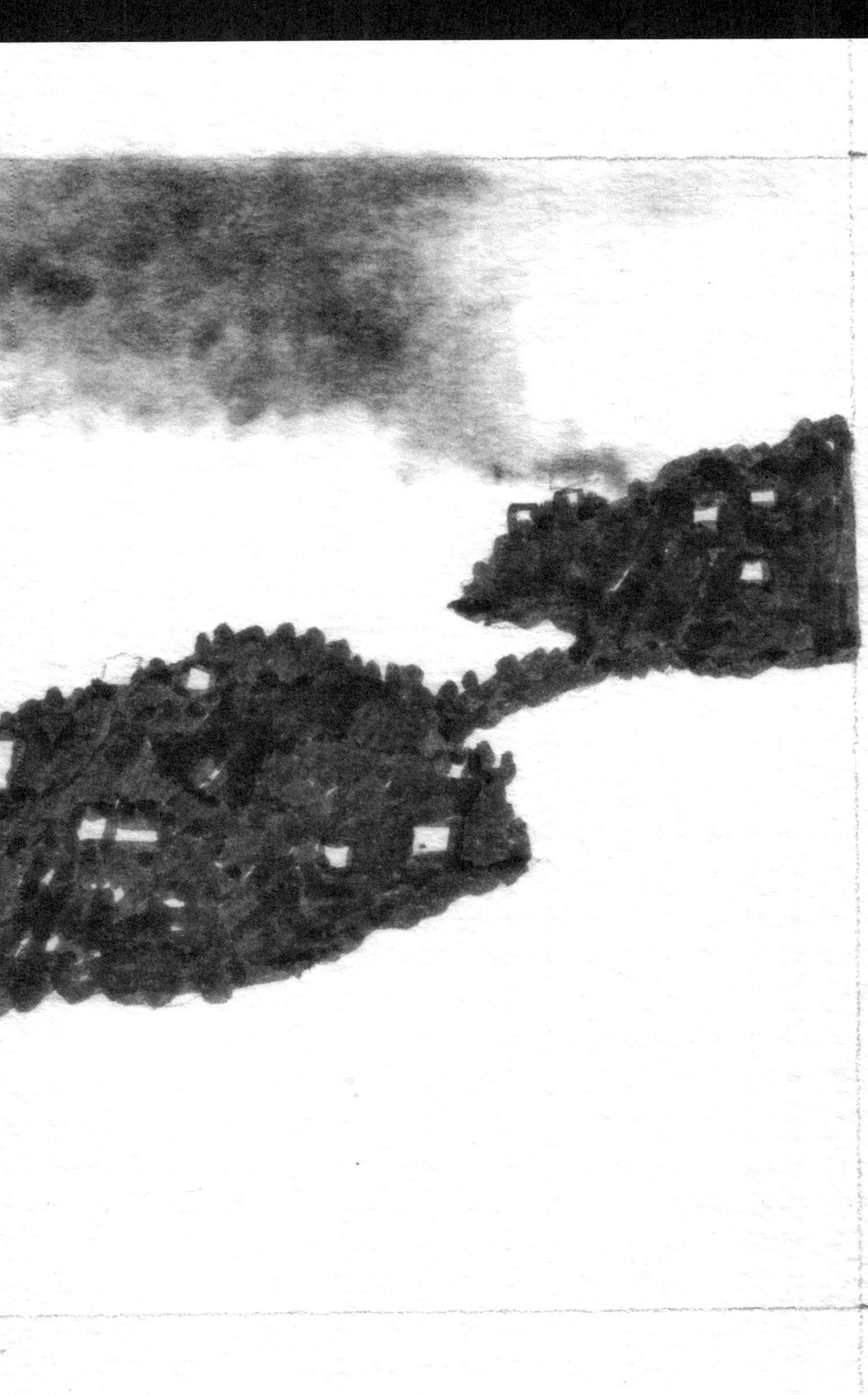

POLICEMEN HAVE JUST BEATEN UP A MORON. ...MORON'S SKIN
IS THIN AND FRAGILE. IT HAS TORN AND OPENED UNDER THE
BEATS, CEASING TO BE A FIRM BORDER BETWEEN HIS BODY AND
THE WORLD. MORON'S FLESH IS SEEING THE LIGHT OF DAY.
GOOD MORNING. A NICE DAY, ISN'T IT? WONDERFUL WEATHER
INDEED.

IT MUST HAVE BEEN A MISUNDERSTANDING HERE: THE POLICE-
MEN AND THE MORON HAVE QUITE DIFFERENT DEFINITIONS OF
THE WORD "BEAT" (NOT TO MENTION THE WORD "MORON").
THEY OVERLAP AT THE POINT OF CIVIL DISOBEDIENCE.
AND, IMMEDIATELY AFTER THE POLICEMEN HAD MADE THEIR
BEAT CLEAN, THEY REALIZED THAT 99% OF US WERE MORONS. (I
THINK THEY MISCOUNTED.) TENS... HUNDREDS... THOUSANDS...
OF THE MORONS HAVE APPEARED, SWARMING AND OCCUPYING
SLOWLY THE PUBLIC SPACE...
IT SEEMS NO ONE STAYS HOME TODAY. IT'S A VERY NICE DAY, I
TOLD YOU.

IT'S THE DAY WHEN THE MORONS OF THE MODERN WORLD
NAMED "CITIZENS" INFER THAT THEY LIVE IN THE MOMENT
"THAT JOINS IN A UNIQUE EPOCHAL KNOT THE FAILURE OF ALL
COMMUNISMS WITH THE MISERY OF NEW INDIVIDUALISM".

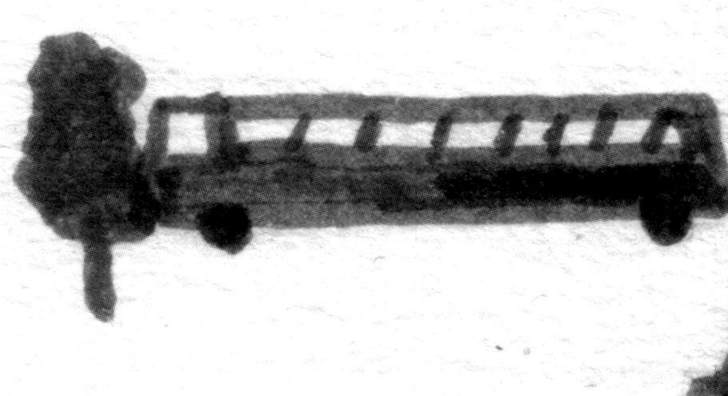

OMG! IT'S A GOOD PLOT FOR A BLOCKBUSTER.
FOR A STORY WE TELL OURSELVES ABOUT OURSELVES.
WE LIKE TO THINK ABOUT OUR MOMENT AS EPOCHAL. EVEN IF
FAILURE AND MISERY IS THAT WHAT MAKES IT SO UNIQUE.

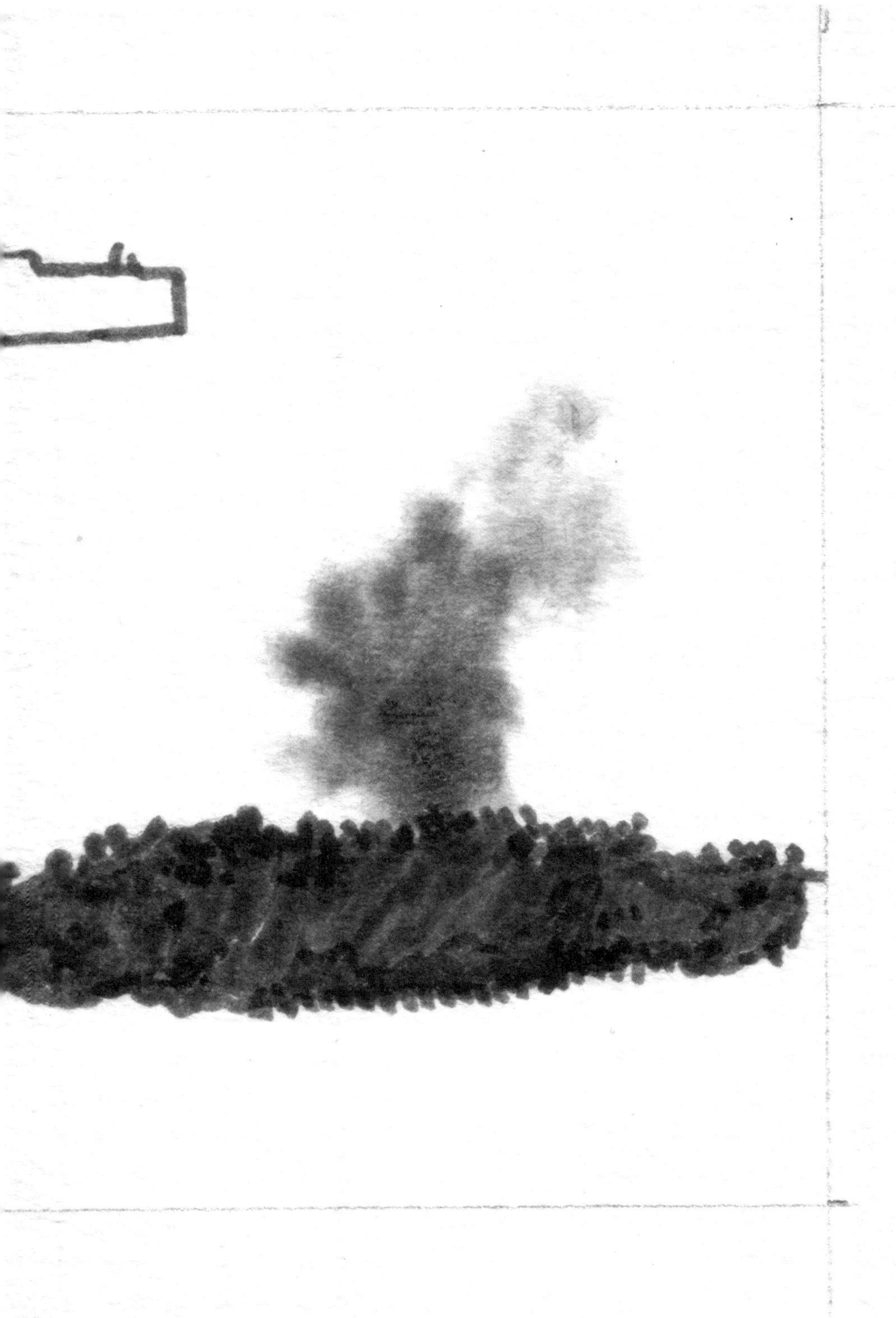

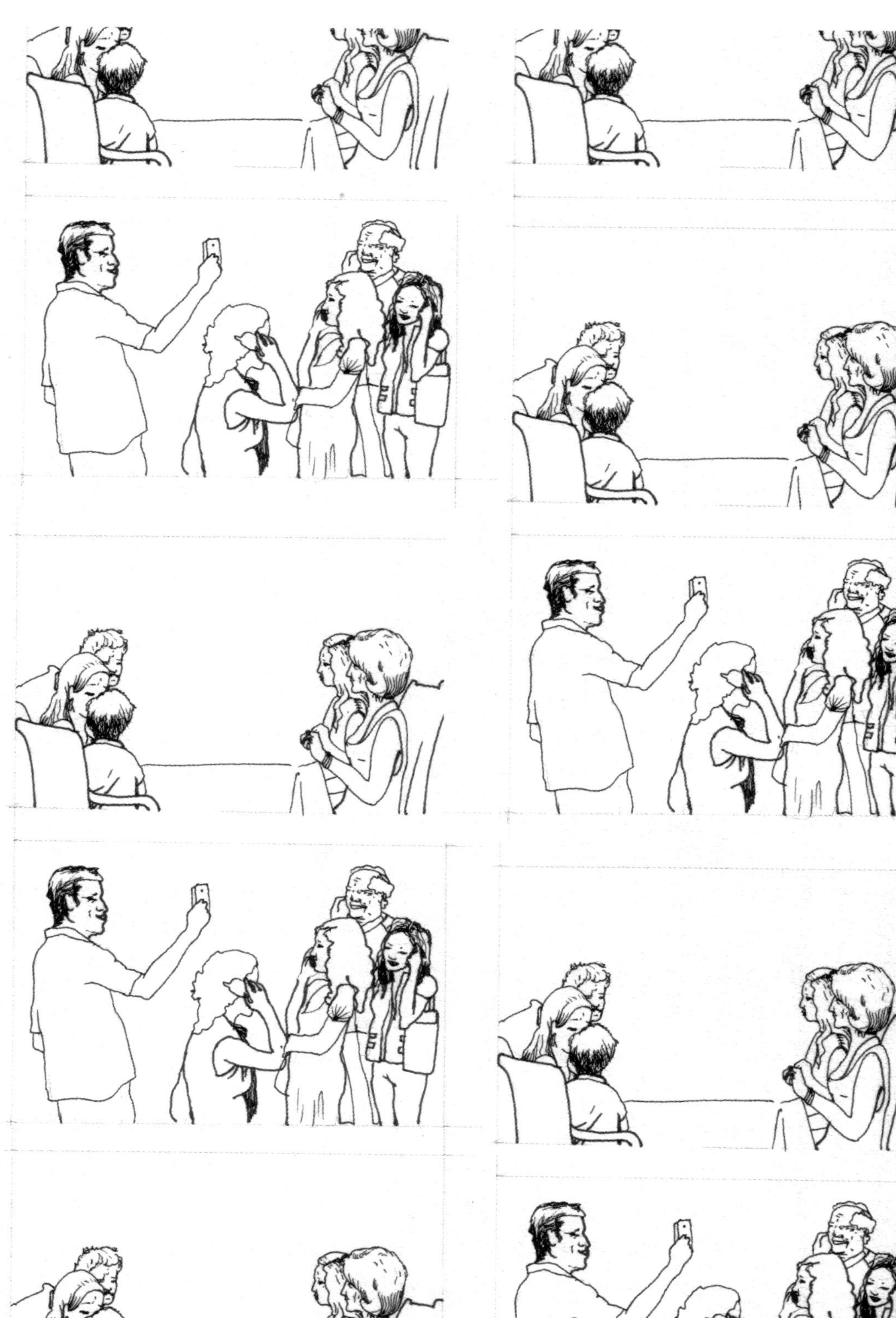

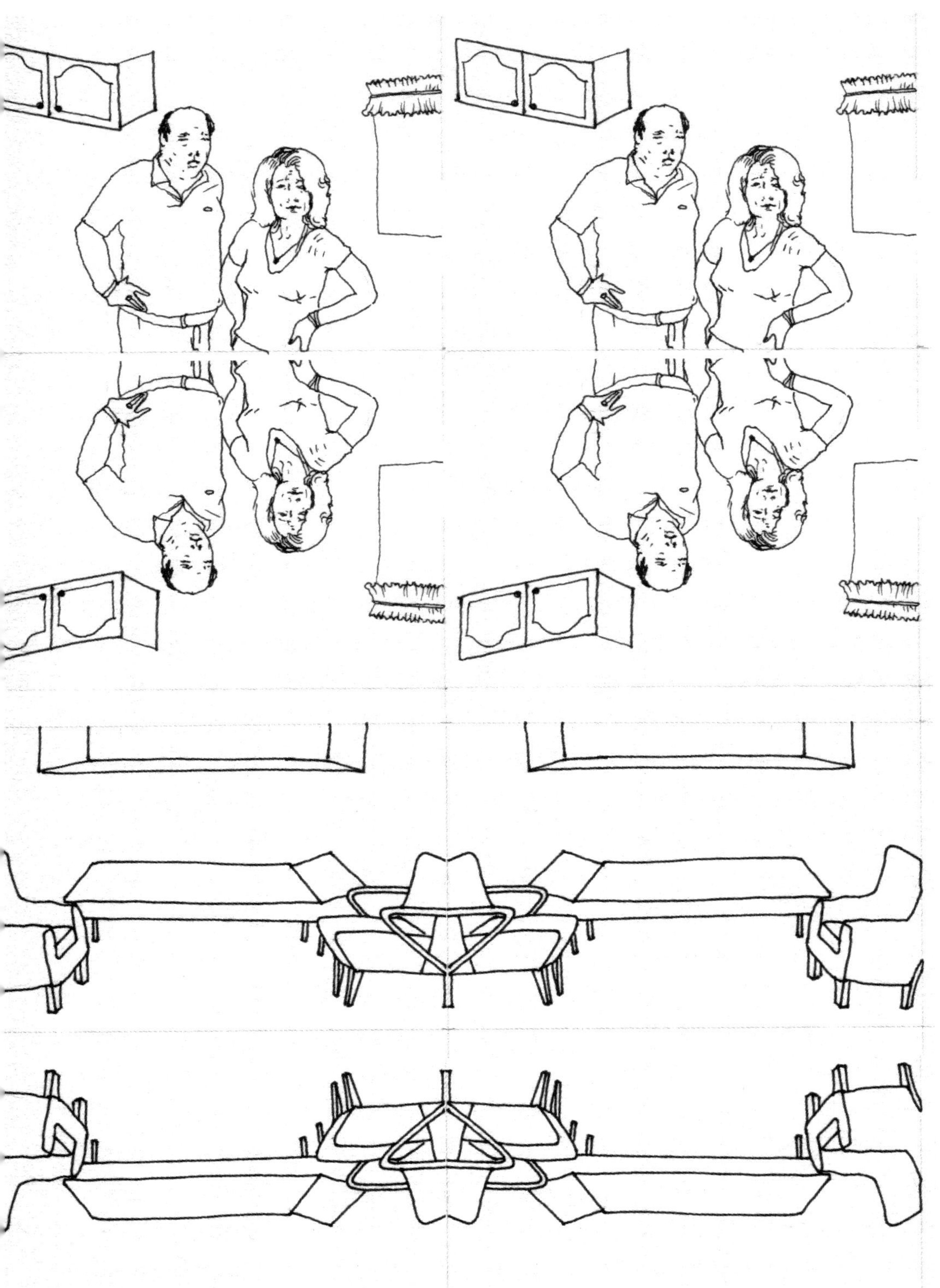

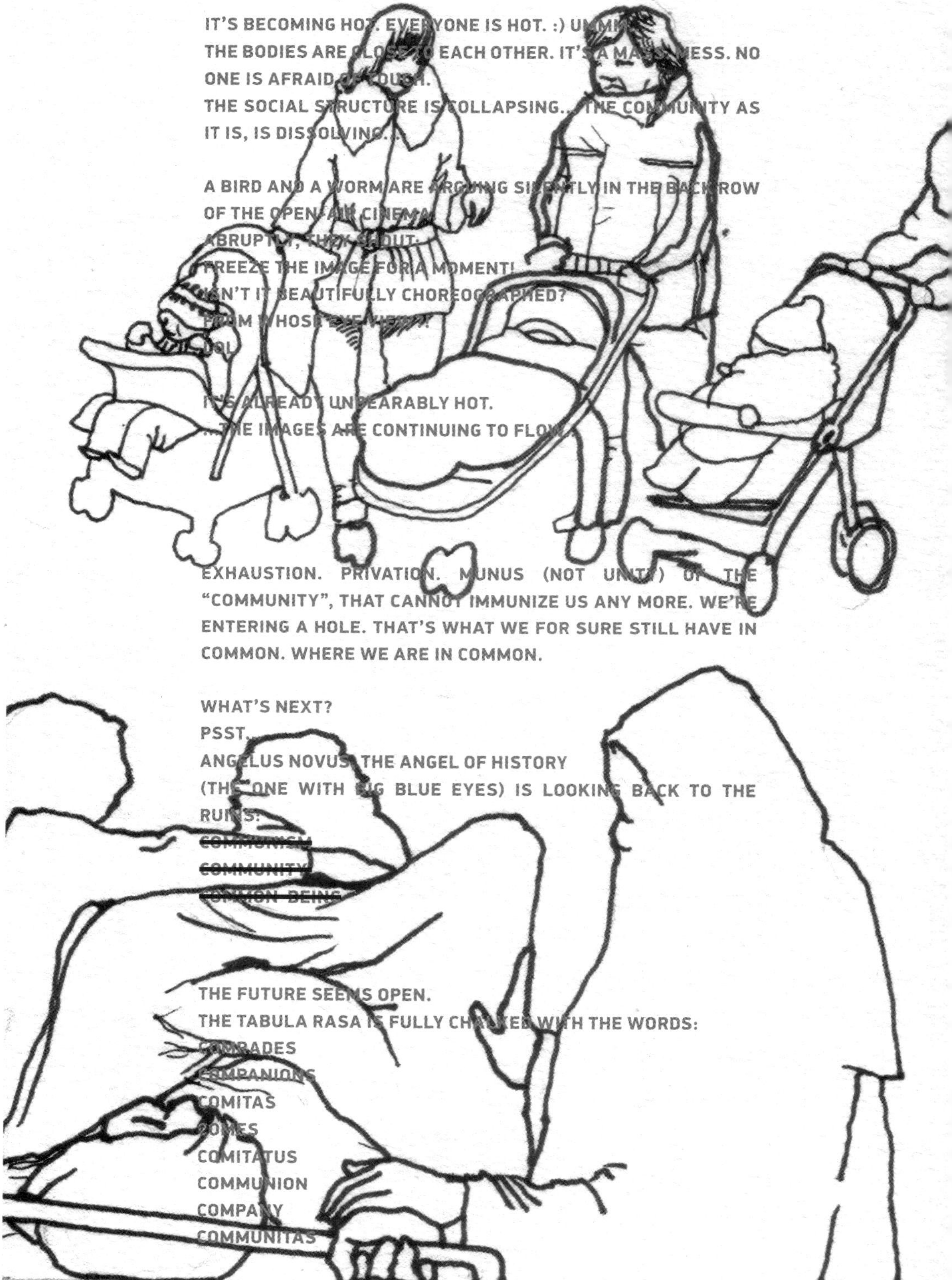

IT'S BECOMING HOT. EVERYONE IS HOT. :) UMMM
THE BODIES ARE CLOSE TO EACH OTHER. IT'S A MASS MESS. NO
ONE IS AFRAID, OF TOUGH.
THE SOCIAL STRUCTURE IS COLLAPSING… THE COMMUNITY AS
IT IS, IS DISSOLVING…

A BIRD AND A WORM ARE ARGUING SILENTLY IN THE BACK ROW
OF THE OPEN-AIR CINEMA.
ABRUPTLY, THEY SHOUT:
FREEZE THE IMAGE FOR A MOMENT!
ISN'T IT BEAUTIFULLY CHOREOGRAPHED?
FROM WHOSE EYE VIEW?
LOL

IT'S ALREADY UNBEARABLY HOT.
…THE IMAGES ARE CONTINUING TO FLOW.

EXHAUSTION. PRIVATION. MUNUS (NOT UNITY) OF THE
"COMMUNITY", THAT CANNOT IMMUNIZE US ANY MORE. WE'RE
ENTERING A HOLE. THAT'S WHAT WE FOR SURE STILL HAVE IN
COMMON. WHERE WE ARE IN COMMON.

WHAT'S NEXT?
PSST.
ANGELUS NOVUS, THE ANGEL OF HISTORY
(THE ONE WITH BIG BLUE EYES) IS LOOKING BACK TO THE
RUINS:
COMMUNISM
COMMUNITY
COMMON BEING

THE FUTURE SEEMS OPEN.
THE TABULA RASA IS FULLY CHALKED WITH THE WORDS:
COMRADES
COMPANIONS
COMITAS
GOMES
COMITATUS
COMMUNION
COMPANY
COMMUNITAS

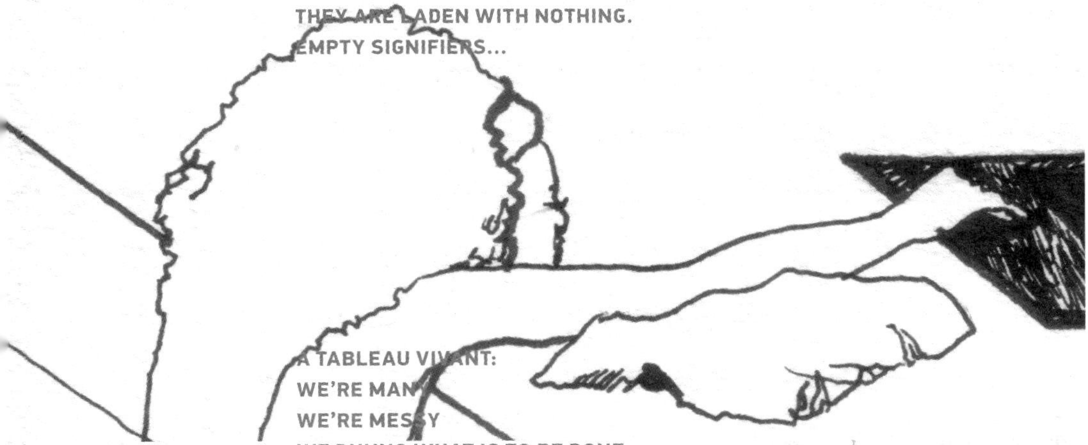

THEY ARE LADEN WITH NOTHING.
EMPTY SIGNIFIERS…

A TABLEAU VIVANT:
WE'RE MANY
WE'RE MESSY
WE DUNNO WHAT IS TO BE DONE
THE FUTURE BELONGS TO US

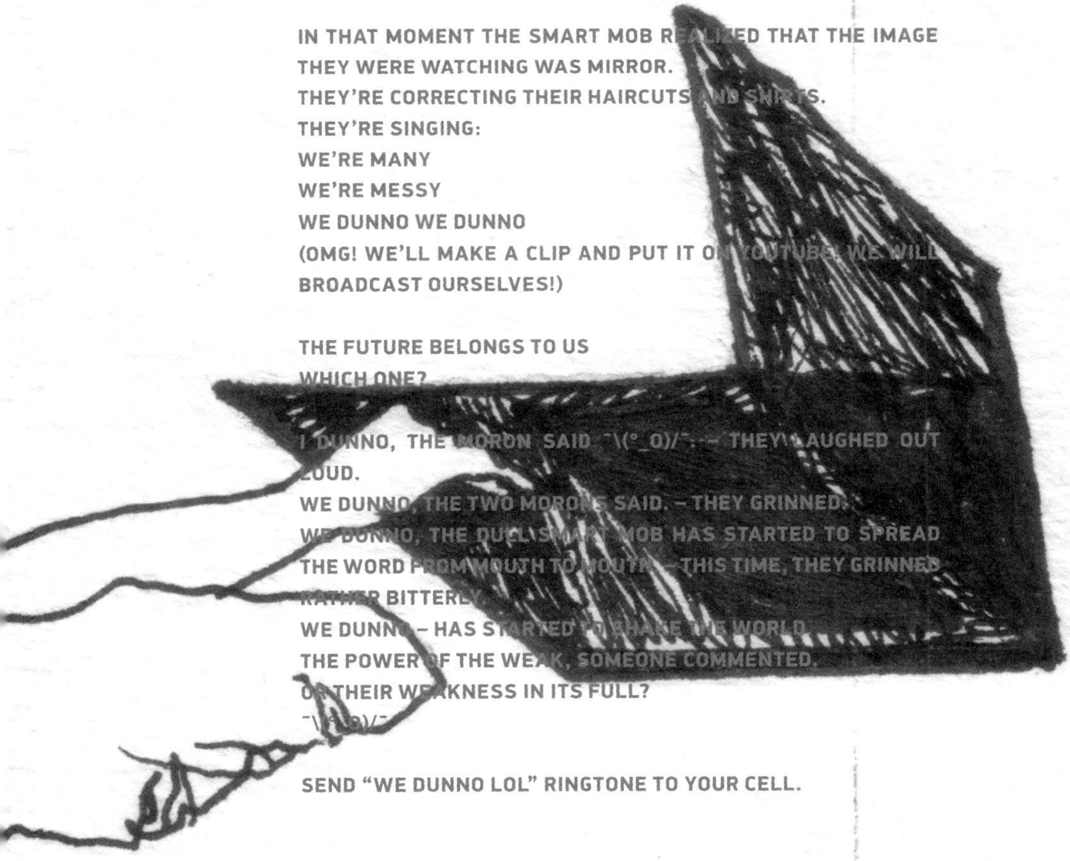

IN THAT MOMENT THE SMART MOB REALIZED THAT THE IMAGE
THEY WERE WATCHING WAS MIRROR.
THEY'RE CORRECTING THEIR HAIRCUTS AND SHIRTS.
THEY'RE SINGING:
WE'RE MANY
WE'RE MESSY
WE DUNNO WE DUNNO
(OMG! WE'LL MAKE A CLIP AND PUT IT ON YOUTUBE! WE WILL
BROADCAST OURSELVES!)

THE FUTURE BELONGS TO US
WHICH ONE?

I DUNNO, THE MORON SAID \(°_O)/¯. – THEY LAUGHED OUT
LOUD.
WE DUNNO, THE TWO MORONS SAID. – THEY GRINNED.
WE DUNNO, THE DUCLISM MAT MOB HAS STARTED TO SPREAD
THE WORD FROM MOUTH TO MOUTH. – THIS TIME, THEY GRINNED
RATHER BITTERLY.
WE DUNNO – HAS STARTED TO SHAKE THE WORLD.
THE POWER OF THE WEAK, SOMEONE COMMENTED.
OR THEIR WEAKNESS IN ITS FULL?
¯\(°_O)/¯

SEND "WE DUNNO LOL" RINGTONE TO YOUR CELL.

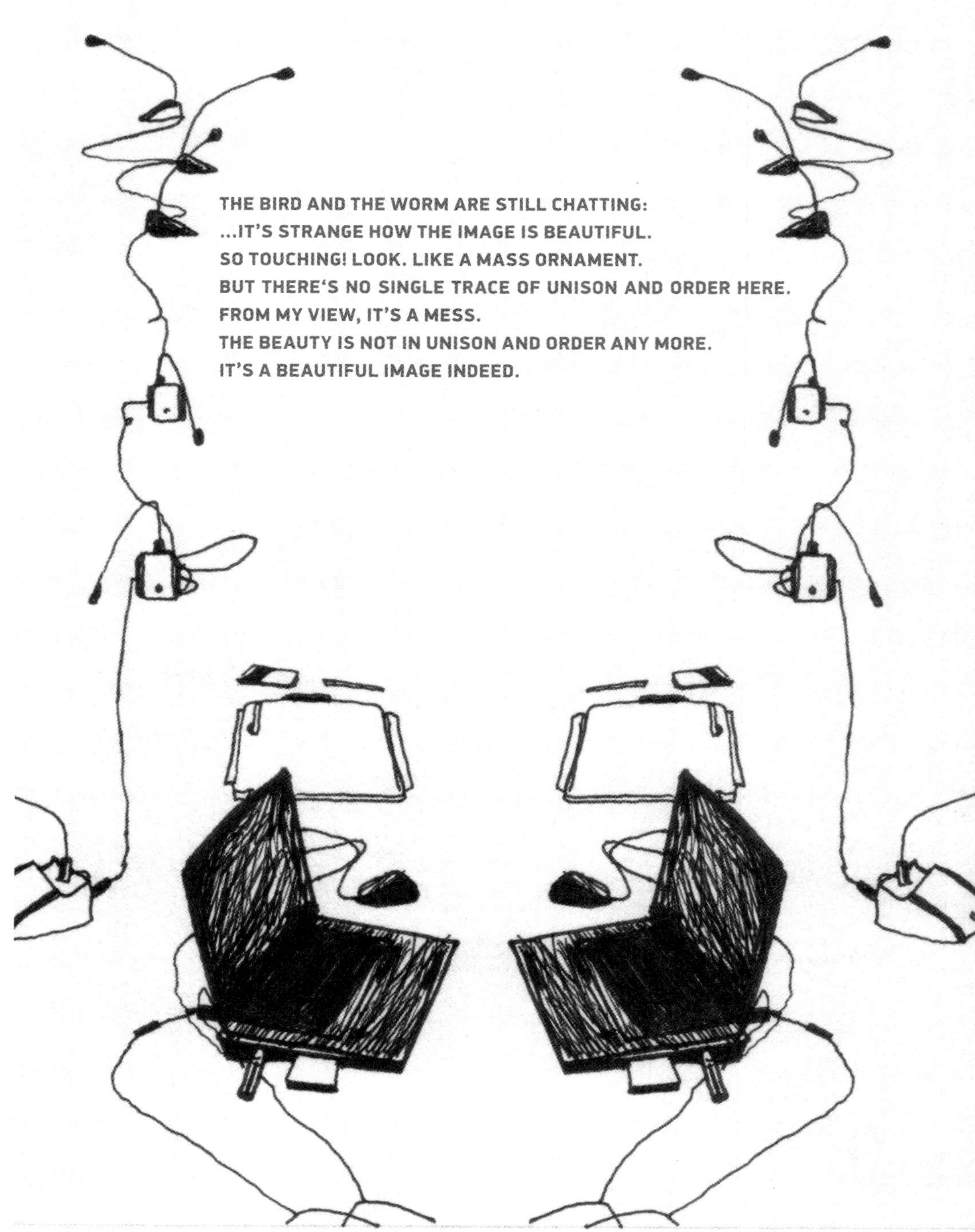
THE BIRD AND THE WORM ARE STILL CHATTING:
...IT'S STRANGE HOW THE IMAGE IS BEAUTIFUL.
SO TOUCHING! LOOK. LIKE A MASS ORNAMENT.
BUT THERE'S NO SINGLE TRACE OF UNISON AND ORDER HERE.
FROM MY VIEW, IT'S A MESS.
THE BEAUTY IS NOT IN UNISON AND ORDER ANY MORE.
IT'S A BEAUTIFUL IMAGE INDEED.

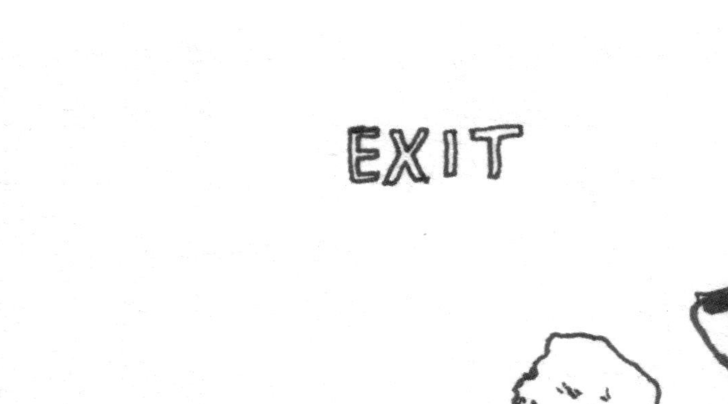

THEY'RE STARTING TO LIKE IT.

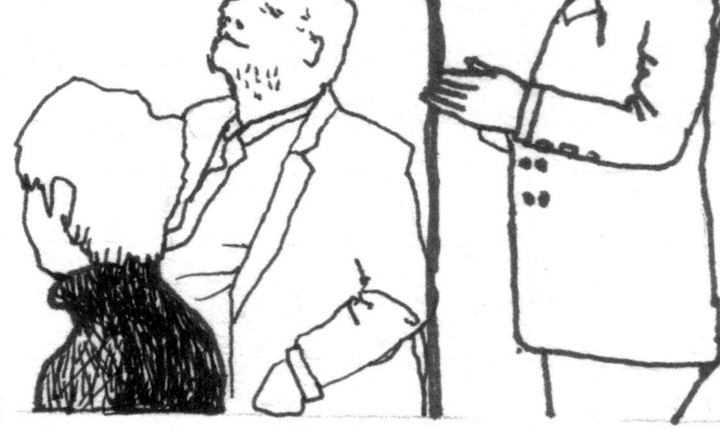

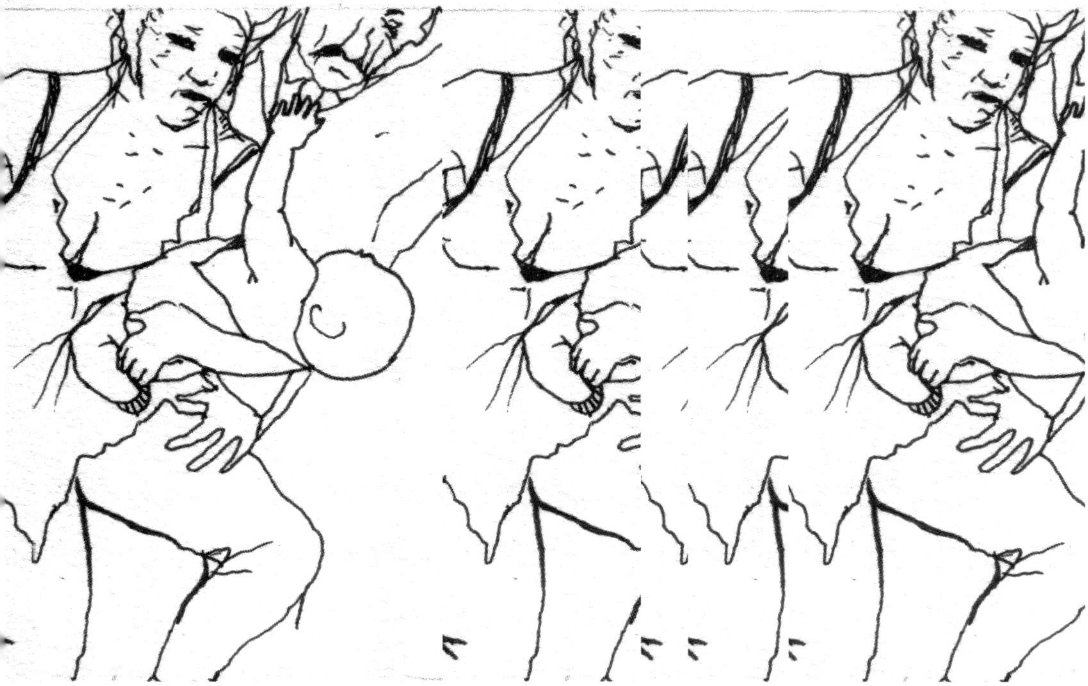

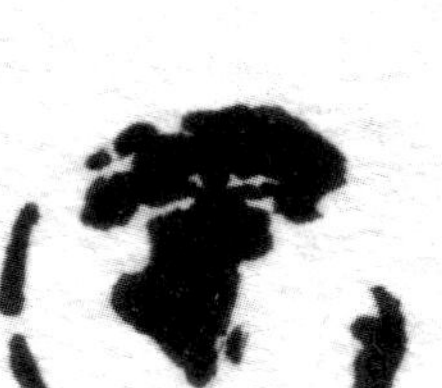

WE'RE CLOSING DOWN THE COMICS, VERY PROUD OF WHAT WE'VE DONE, AND JOINING THE MOB.

WE ALL ARE STARTING TO LIKE IT. TO LIKE IT VERY MUCH. WE'RE GETTING TO FEEL STRONGER AND STRONGER. WE'RE STARTING TO BROADCAST OURSELVES BETTER AND BETTER. WE'RE STARTING TO LOVE THE IMAGE. TO LOVE IT MORE AND MORE. TO LOVE IT VERY MUCH. WE ARE STARTING TO FORGET THAT WE'RE ALONE, IN THE HOLE... THAT WE'RE WEAK, AND MANY...

WE'RE STARTING TO LOL. THEN TO LOL. WE'RE LOLLING, LOLOLOLOL

SHALL WE LOL OUR EPOCHAL MOMENT OF FAILURE AND MISERY?

¯\(°_O)/¯

THE VELOCITY OF THE DAY IS DECREASING...

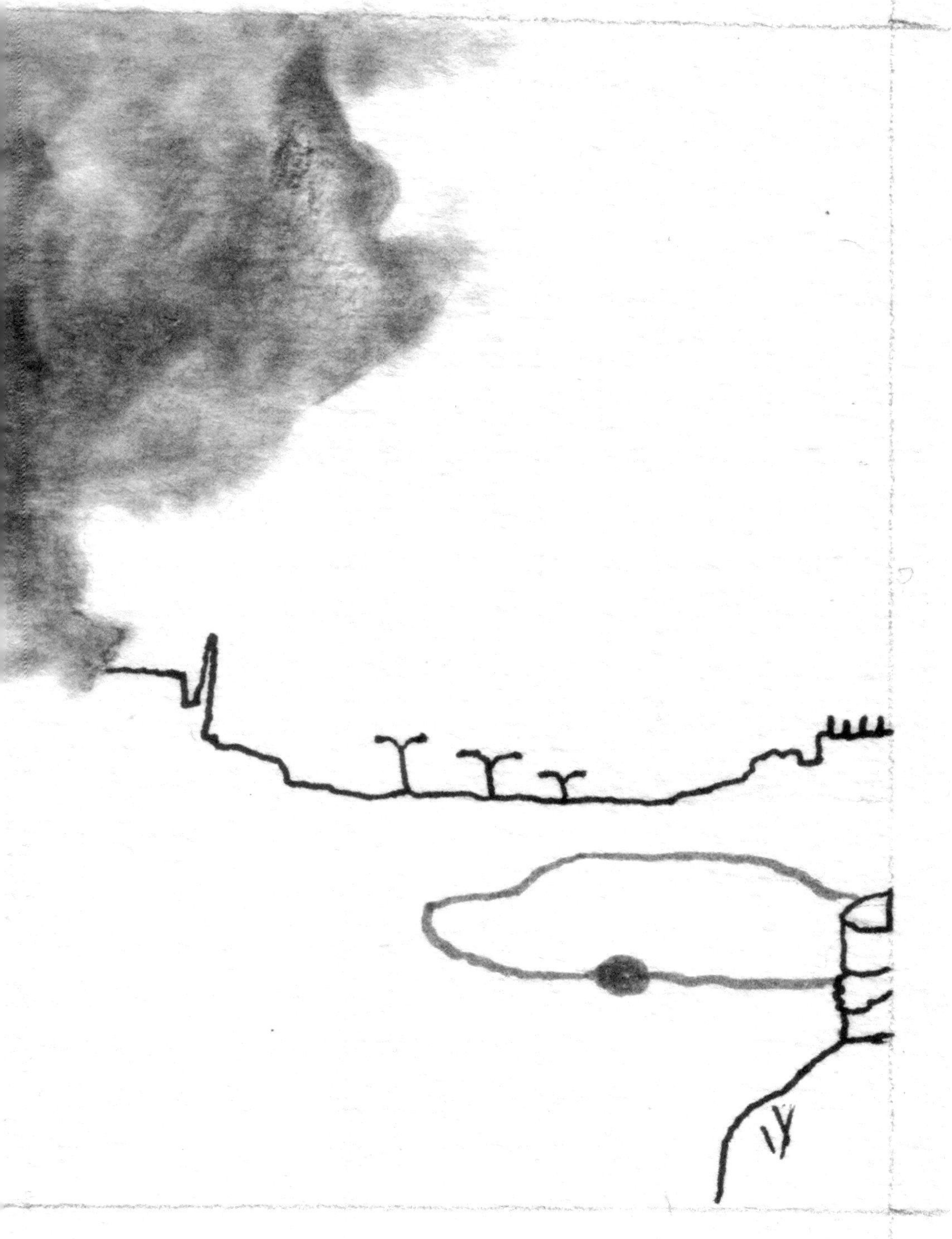

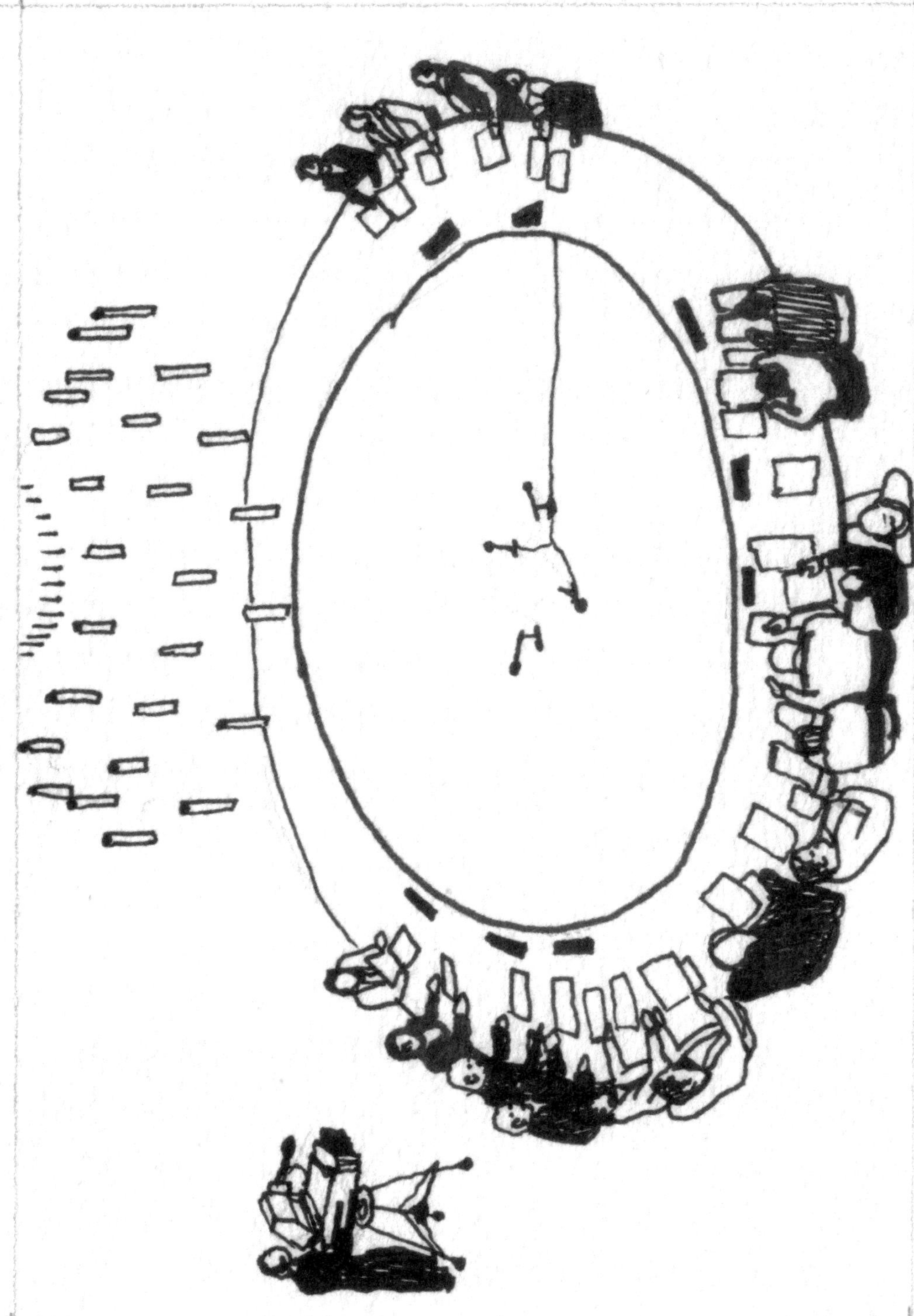

ZOOM OUT:
A DISPERSED PACK OF CITY DOGS SUNBATHING AT THE SQUARE
NEARBY IS TRYING TO ORGANIZE PLENUM... BUT THEY ARE
STUCK IN THE PRE-PLENARY DISCUSSION ON WHAT THE TOPIC
OF THE PLENARY SESSION SHOULD BE...
THEY NEED A CLEARER DECISION-MAKING PROCEDURE.
OTHERWISE, I'M AFRAID, THE NIGHT WILL COME AND FIND THEM
LIKE THIS...

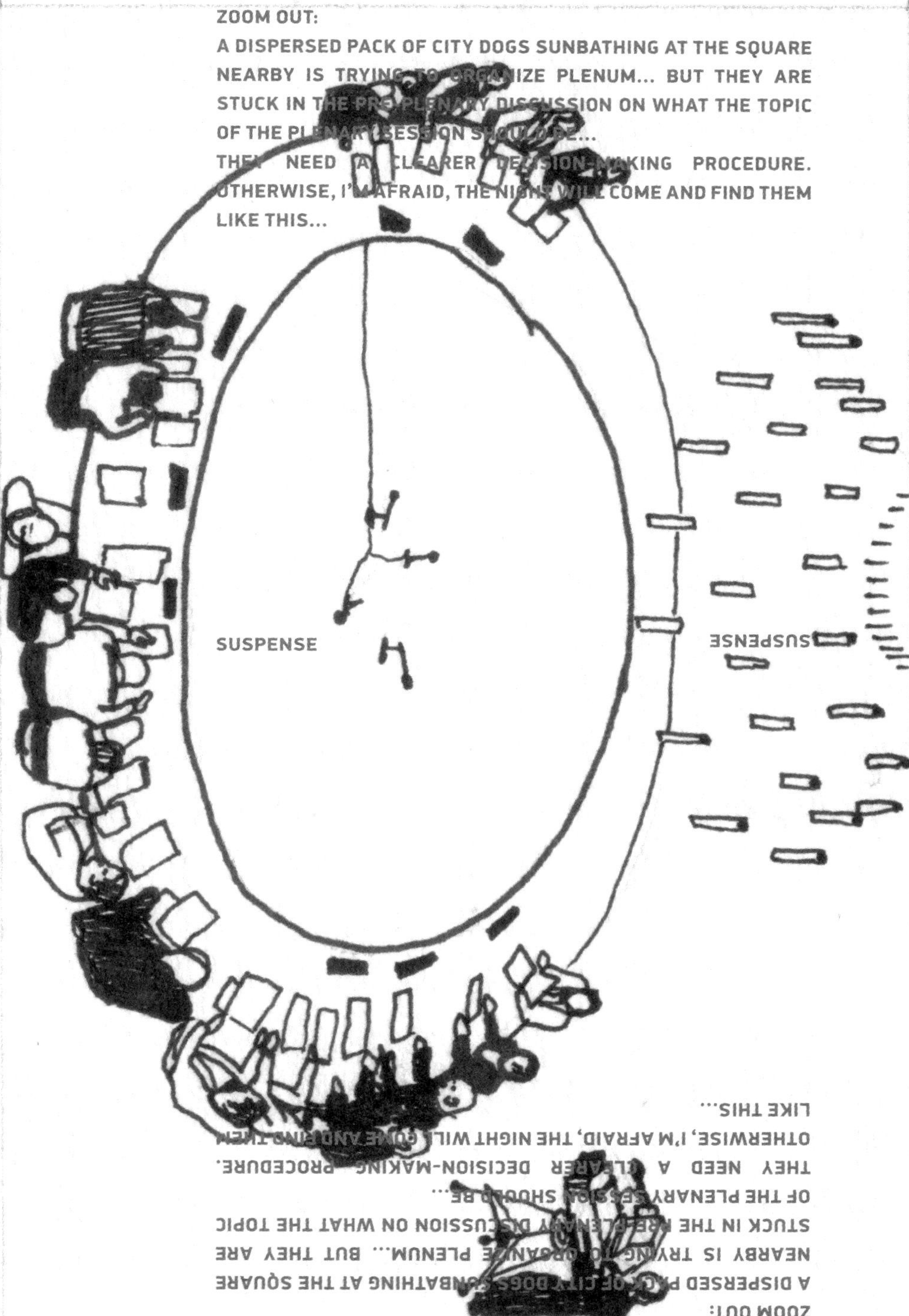

ZOOM OUT:
A DISPERSED PACK OF CITY DOGS SUNBATHING AT THE SQUARE
NEARBY IS TRYING TO ORGANIZE PLENUM... BUT THEY ARE
STUCK IN THE PRE-PLENARY DISCUSSION ON WHAT THE TOPIC
OF THE PLENARY SESSION SHOULD BE...
THEY NEED A CLEARER DECISION-MAKING PROCEDURE.
OTHERWISE, I'M AFRAID, THE NIGHT WILL COME AND FIND THEM
LIKE THIS...

Adler, Janet. *Offering from the Conscious Body: The Discipline of Authentic Movement*. Rochester, NY: Inner Traditions, 2002.

Agamben, Giorgio. *The Coming Community*. Minneapolis: University of Minnesota Press, 1993.

———. *The Man Without Content*. Palo Alto, CA: Stanford University Press, 1999.

———. *What is An Apparatus and Other Essays*. Translated by David Kishik and Stefan Pedatella. Palo Alto, CA: Stanford University Press, 2009.

Allen, Amy. "Foucault and the politics of our selves." *History of the Human Sciences* 24, no. 4 (2011): 43–58.

Arendt, Hannah. *Crises of the Republic*. New York: Harcourt Brace, 1972.

———. *The Human Condition*. Chicago: University of Chicago Press, 1998.

———. *On Revolution*. New York: Viking, 1963.

Asselberghs, Herman, and Dieter Lesage. "Homo politicus. Pim Fortuyn: A Case Study." *nettime.org, nettime-l* (mailing list), 2002. http://amsterdam.nettime.org/Lists-Archives/nettime-l-0207/msg00102.html.

Austin, J. L. *How to Do Things with Words*. Cambridge, MA: Harvard University Press, 1975.

Badiou, Alain. "Dance as a Metaphor for Thought." In *Inaesthetics*, 57–71. London: Verso, 2005.

Banes, Sally. *Democracy's Body: Judson Dance Theater 1962–1964*. Durham, NC: Duke University Press, 1995.

Barthes, Roland. "The Death of the Author." In *Image, Music, Text*, 142–9. New York: Hill and Wang, 1977.

Beissinger, Mark R. "How the Impossible Becomes Inevitable: The Public Sphere and the Collapse of Soviet Communism." In "20th Anniversary of the Fall of the Wall." Special issue in "Public Sphere Formation." Also special issue of the online journal *Transformations of the Public Sphere*. The website of the Social Science Research Council, November 2, 2009. http://publicsphere.ssrc.org/beissinger-the-public-sphere-and-the-collapse-of-soviet-communism/.

Benjamin, Walter. "The Work of Art in the Age of Mechanical Reproduction." In *Illuminations: Essays and Reflections*, translated and edited by Hannah Arendt, 217–51. New York: Schocken Books, 1968.

Berlin, Isaiah. "The Pursuit of the Ideal." In *The Crooked Timber of Humanity*, edited by Henry Hardy, Jr. Princeton, NJ: Princeton University Press, 1998.

Bennett, Melanie, Richard Gough, Laura Levin, and Marlis Schweitzer, eds. "Performing Publics." Special issue, *Performance Research* 16, no. 2 (2011).

Blanchot, Maurice. *The Unavowable Community*. Barrytown, NY: Barrytown, 2006.

Bogost, Ian. *Persuasive Games: The Expressive Power of Videogames*. Cambridge, MA: MIT Press, 2007.

Boltanski, Luc, and Eva Chiapiello, *Le nouvel esprit du capitalisme*. Paris: Gallimard, 1999.

Bourdieu, Pierre. *Outline of a Theory of Practice*. Cambridge: Cambridge University Press, 1977.

Bulut, Dragana. "Negotiating Solo Dance Authorship in Neoliberal Society." *Tkh* no. 18 (2010): 54–9.

Butler, Judith. "Bodies in alliance and the Politics of the Street." In "#occupy and assemble∞."
Special issue of the online journal *transversal* (October 2011).
http://eipcp.net/transversal/1011.

———. *Bodies That Matter: On the Discursive Limits of "Sex."* London: Routledge, 1993.

———, Ernesto Laclau, and Slavoj Žižek. *Contingency, Hegemony, Universality: Contemporary Dialogues on the Left*. New York: Verso, 2000.

———. *Frames of War: When is Life Grievable?* London: Verso, 2009.

———. *Gender Trouble: Feminism and the Subversion of Identity*. London: Routledge, 1990.

———. *Giving an Account of Oneself*. New York: Fordham University Press, 2005.

———. *Precarious Life: The Powers of Mourning and Violence*, London: Verso, 2004.

———. *Undoing Gender*. London: Routledge, 2004.

Bücher, Karl. *Arbeit und Rhythmus*. Leipzig: Raubner, 1902.

Carpentier, Nico, and Bart Cammaerts. "Hegemony, democracy, agonism and journalism: an interview with Chantal Mouffe." *Journalism studies* 7, no. 6 (2006): 964–75.

Cash, Arthur. *John Wilkes: The Scandalous Father of Liberty*. New Haven, CT: Yale University Press, 2007.

Castells, Manuel. *The Power of Identity*. Oxford: Blackwell Publishers, 1997.

Chilton, Stephen. "The Problem of Agreement in Republicanism, Proceduralism, and the Mature Dewey: A 'Two Moments of Discourse Ethics' Analysis." *Steve Chilton's Home Page*. Last modified November 5, 2001. http://www.d.umn.edu/~schilton/Articles/Tilburg.html.

Clauzade, Laurent. *L'idéologie ou la révolution de l'analyse*. Paris: Gallimard, 1998.

Cvejić, Bojana, Ana Vujanović, and Marta Popivoda. "Interview with Bruno Latour." In "Art and the Public." Special issue, *TkH* 20 (2012): 72–81.

Ćuruvija, Slavko. *IBEOVAC. Ja, Vlado Dapčević*. Belgrade: Filip Višnjić, 1990.

Deák, František. "Russian Mass Spectacles." In "Political Theatre Issue." Special issue, *The Drama Review* 19 (1975): 7–22.

Deleuze, Gilles, and Félix Guattari. *A Thousand Plateaus: Capitalism and Schizophrenia*. Translated by Brian Massumi. London: Continuum, 1988.

———. *What is Philosophy?* Translated by Hugh Tomlinson and Graham Burchell. New York: Columbia University Press, 1994.

Derrida, Jacques. "Event, Signature, Context." In *Limited INC*, 1–25. Evanston, IL: Northwestern University Press, 1988.

———. *Voice and Phenomenon: Introduction to the Problem of the Sign in Husserl's Phenomenology*. Evanston, IL: Northwestern University Press, 2010.

De Smedt, Christine. "4 Choreographic Portraits." In companion booklet to *4 Choreographic Portraits*, 3–6. Ghent: les ballets C de la B, 2012.

Dewey, John. *The Public and its Problems*. Athens, OH: Ohio University Press, 1927.

Dobričić, Igor, and Sigrid Merx. "Sharp Thoughts, Igor Dobričić vs. Sigrid Merx: The 'Public/Private' and Private-Public: Reactivating the Distinction (response to Dobričić)." In "Art and the Public Good." Special issue, *TkH*, no. 20 (2012): 64–71.

Dolar, Mladen. "Beyond Interpellation." *Qui Parle* 6, no. 2 (1993): 75–96.

———. *A Voice and Nothing More*. Cambridge, MA: MIT Press, 2006.

Driesch, Hans A. E. *The Science and Philosophy of the Organism*. 2 vols. Aberdeen: University of Aberdeen, 1908. http://archive.org/details/scienceandphilo01driegoog.

Duncan, Isadora. "I See America Dancing." In *What is Dance? Readings in Theory and Criticism*, edited by Roger Copeland and Marshall Cohen, 264–65. Oxford: Oxford University Press, 1983.

Eichberg, Henning, and Robert A. Jones. "The Nazi Thingspiel: Theater for the Masses in Fascism and Proletarian Culture." *New German Critique* 11 (1977): 133–50.

Elias, Norbert. *The Civilizing Process: Sociogenetic and Psychogenetic Investigations*. Vol. 1, *The History of Manners*. New York: Urizen Books, 1978. Vol. 2, *Power and Civility*. Oxford: Basil Blackwell, 1982. Originally published as, *Über den Prozeß der Zivilisation. Soziogenetische und psychogenetische Untersuchungen*. Band 1, *Wandlungen des Verhaltens in den weltlichen Oberschichten des Abendlandes*. Band 2: *Wandlungen der Gesellschaft: Entwurf zu einer Theorie der Zivilisation*. Basel: Verlag Haus zum Falken, 1939.

Emerson, Ralph Waldo. *Essays*. New York: Thomas Y. Crowell, 1926. See esp. "Self Reliance," 31–66; "Heroism," 173–87; and "The Over-Soul," 188–211.

———. *The Conduct of Life* (Boston: 1860). http://www.emersoncentral.com/conduct.htm.

Esposito, Roberto. *Communitas: The Origin and Destiny of Community*. Palo Alto, CA: Stanford University Press, 2010.

———. "The Immunization Paradigm." *diacritics* 36, no. 2 (2006): 23–48.

———. *Immunitas: The Protection and Negation of Life*. Hoboken, NJ: John Wiley & Sons, 2011.

Féré, Charles. *Travail et Plaisir*. Paris: Félix Alcan, 1904.

Ferrero, Guillaume. "Les formes primitives du travail." *Revue scientifique*, n.s., 5, no. 11 (1896): 331–34.

Foucault, Michel. "About the Beginnings of the Hermeneutics of the Self: Two Lectures at Dartmouth." *Political Theory* 21, no. 2 (1993): 198–227.

———. *Discourse and Truth: The Problematization of Parrhesia*. *foucault.info*. (online archive). http://foucault.info/documents/parrhesia/.

———. *Essential Works of Foucault 1954–1984*. Edited by Paul Rabinow and Nikolas Rose. London: Penguin, 2000. See esp. Vol.1, "Subjectivity and Truth," 87–92; "The Hermeneutic of the Subject," 93–106; "Sexuality and Solitude," 175–84; "Self Writing," 207–22; "On the Genealogy of Ethics: An Overview of Work in Progress," 253–80; and "The Ethics of the Concern for Self as a Practice of Freedom," 281–302.

———. *The History of Sexuality*. Vol. 3, *The Care of the Self*. Translated by Robert Hurley. New York, NY: Pantheon Books, 1986. Originally published as, *Histoire de la sexualité*. Vol. 3, *Le souci de soi*. Paris: Gallimard, 1984.

———. "Technologies of the Self." In *Technologies of the Self: A Seminar with Michel Foucault*, edited by Huck Gutman, Patrick H. Hutton, and Luther M. Martin, 16–49. London: Tavistock, 1988.

———. "What is an Author?" In *Aesthetics, Method, and Epistemology*, edited by James Faubion, 205–22. London: Penguin, 2000.

Franko, Mark. "Social Choreography: Ideology as Performance in Dance and Everyday Movement." *Dance Research Journal* 38, no. 1–2 (2006): 188–93.

Fraser, Nancy. "Rethinking the Public Sphere: A Contribution to the Critique of Actually Existing Democracy." *Social Text* no. 25–26 (1990): 56–80.

———. "Sex, Lies, and the Public Sphere: Some Reflections on the Confirmation of Clarence Thomas." *Critical Inquiry* 18, no. 3 (1992): 595–612.

Fukuyama, Francis. "The End of History?" *The National Interest*, no. 16 (1989): 3–18. http://www.wesjones.com/eoh.htm.

———. *The End of History and the Last Man*. New York: The Free Press, 1992.

Geertz, Clifford. "Deep Play: Notes on the Balinese Cockfight." In *The Interpretation of Cultures*, 412–55. New York: Basic Books, 1973.

van Gennep, Arnold. *The Rites of Passage*. London: Routledge, 1977.

Gibianskii, Leonid. "The Soviet-Yugoslav Split and the Cominform." In *The Establishment of Communist Regimes in Eastern Europe, 1944–1949*, edited by Leonid Gibianskii and Norman Naimark, 291–313. Boulder, CO: Westwood Press, 1997.

Giri, Saroj. "WikiLeaks Beyond WikiLeaks." *Metamute.org* (the website of *Mute* magazine). http://www.metamute.org/en/articles/WikiLeaks_beyond_WikiLeaks.

Glas Istre. "Tito o fizičkoj kulturi i sportu." Parts 1, 3 & 4. May 4–6, 1978.

Goffman, Erving. *The Presentation of Self in Everyday Life*. New York: Doubleday, 1959.

Habermas, Jürgen. *Between Facts and Norms*. Translated by William Rehg. Cambridge, MA: MIT Press,1996.

———. "The Public Sphere." *New German Critique* 3 (1974).

———. *The Structural Transformation of the Public Sphere: An Inquiry into a Category of Bourgeois Society*. Cambridge, MA: MIT Press, 1991.

Hallward, Peter. "The Politics of Prescription." *The South Atlantic Quarterly* 104, no. 4 (2005): 769–89.

Hannemann, Matthias, "Kalter Kulturkrieg in Norwegen?: Zum Wirken des 'Kongreß für kulturelle Freiheit' in Skandinavien." NORDEUROPA*forum*, no. 2 (1999): 15–41.

Hansard, T. C., ed. *The Parliamentary History of England from the Earliest Period to the Year 1803*. London, 1813. 18:1295.

Hayward, Jack. *After the French Revolution: Six Critics of Democracy and Nationalism*. Hemel Hempstead, UK: Harvester Wheatsheaf, 1991.

Hellebrandt, Frances A., and Jiří Kral. "Scientific Work of the Tenth Sokol Festival." *Science*, n.s., 89, no. 2314 (1939): 413–15.

Hewitt, Andrew. *Social Choreography: Ideology as Performance in Dance and Everyday Movement*. Durham, NC: Duke University Press, 2005.

Hochgeschwender, Michael. *Freiheit in der Offensive? Der Kongreß für kulturelle Freiheit und die Deutschen*. München: Oldenbourg Wissenschaftsverlag, 1998.

Horkheimer, Max. *Critical Theory: Selected Essays*. New York: Continuum, 2002.

Jameson, Fredric. *The Political Unconscious: Narrative as a Socially Symbolic Act*. London: Routledge, 1981.

Kew, Carole. "From Weimar Movement Choir to Nazi Community Dance: The Rise and Fall of Rudolf Laban's 'Festkultur.'" *Dance Research* 17, no. 2 (1999) : 73–96.

Kirn, Gal. "Elementi za analizu jugoslavenskog samoupravljanja: između socijalizma i kapitalizma—interview with Catherine Samary." *Novosti*, no. 669 (2012). http://www.novossti.com/2012/10/elementi-za-analizu-jugoslavenskog-samoupravljanja-izmedu-socijalizma-i-kapitalizma/.

———. "Jugoslavija: od partizanske politike do postfordističke tendencije." *Up&Underground* no. 17–18 (2010). http://www.up-underground.com/wp-content/uploads/2011/04/1718_gal_kirn.pdf.

Kuljić, Todor. *Sociologija generacije*. Belgrade: Čigoja, 2009.

———. *Tito*. Zrenjanin: Gradska biblioteka, 2005.

———. "Titoizam: tri perspektive." http://www.kczr.org/download/tekstovi/todor_kuljic_titoizam_tri_perspektive.pdf.

———. "Yugoslavia's Workers Self-Management." In "alternative economics, alternative societies." Special issue of the online journal *transversal* (August 2005). http://eipcp.net/transversal/0805/kuljic/en.

Kunst, Bojana. "Subversion and the Dancing Body: Autonomy on Display." *Performance Research* 8, no. 2 (2003): 61–8.

Laban, Rudolf, and Frederick C. Lawrence. *Effort: Economy in Body Movement*. London: MacDonald and Evans, 1947.

Lacoue-Labarthe, Philippe, and Peter Hallward. "Stagings of Mimesis: An Interview." *Angelaki* 8, no. 2 (2003): 55–72.

Latour, Bruno. "From Realpolitik to Dingpolitik or How to Make Things Public." In *Making Things Public*, ed. Bruno Latour and Peter Weibel, 4–32. Cambridge, MA: ZKM / MIT Press, 2005.

———. "Why Has Critique Run out of Steam? From Matters of Fact to Matters of Concern." *Critical Inquiry* 30 (Winter 2004): 225–48.

———. "The Year in Climate Controversy." *Artforum* 49, no. 4 (2010): 1–3.

Lazzarato, Maurizio. "Conversation with Maurizio Lazzarato." In *Exhausting Immaterial Labour in Performance*. Joint special issue of *Le Journal des Laboratoires* and *TkH*, no. 17 (2010): 12–16.

———. "Immaterial Labour." In *Radical Thought in Italy*, edited by Paolo Virno and Michael Hardt, 133–47. Minneapolis: Minnesota University Press, 1996. http://www.generation-online.org/c/fcimmateriallabour3. htm.

———. "The Misfortunes of the "Artistic Critique" and of Cultural Employment." In "creativity hypes." Special issue of the online journal *transversal* (February 2007). http://eipcp.net/transversal/0207/lazzarato/en.

Lefort, Claude. *Democracy and Political Theory*. Cambridge: Polity Press, 1991.

Lehmann, Hans-Thies. *Postdramatic Theater*. London: Routledge, 2006. Originally published as *Postdramatisches Theater*. Frankfurt am Main: Verlag der Autoren, 1999.

Lesage, Dieter. "The Portrait of the Artist as Worker." In *Vertoog over verzet. Politiek in tijden van globalisering*. Antwerp: Meulenhoff / Manteau, 2004.

Lilja, Efva. *100 Exercises for a Choreographer and Other Survivors*. Stockholm: Ellerströms, 2012.

Lippmann, Walter. *Public Opinion*. New York: Macmillan, 1922.

Lorey, Isabell. "Becoming Common: Precarization as Political Constituting." *e-flux*, no. 17 (2010). http://www.e-flux.com/journal/becoming-common-precarization-as-political-constituting/.

———. "Governmental Precarization." In "inventions." Special issue of the online journal *transversal* (August 2011). http://eipcp.net/transversal/0811/lorey/en.

———. *Figuren des Immunen: Elemente einer politischen Theorie*. Zurich: diaphanes, 2011.

———. "Identitary Immunity and Strategic Immunization: *Lépra* and Leprosy from Biblical into Medieval Times." In "translating violence." Special issue of the online journal *transversal* (October 2008). http://eipcp.net/transversal/1107/lorey/en.

Lynch, Jack. "Wilkes, Liberty, and Number 45." *CW Journal* (Summer 2003). http://www.history.org/foundation/journal/summer03/wilkes.cfm.

Majstorović, Vojin. "The Rise and Fall of the Yugoslav-Soviet Alliance, 1945–1948." *Past Imperfect*, no. 16 (2010): 132–61.

Martin, John. *Introduction to Modern Dance*. New York: W. W. Norton, 1939.

———. *The Modern Dance*. New York: A. S. Barnes, 1933.

Massumi, Brian. "Fear (The Spectrum Said)." *Positions* 13, no. 1 (2005): 31–48.

———, ed. *The Politics of Everyday Fear*. Minneapolis: University of Minnesota Press, 1993.

Mauss, Marcel. "Techniques of the Body." *Economy and Society* 2, no. 1 (1973): 70–88.

McCarthy, Daniel. "In Praise of John Wilkes: How a filthy, philandering deadbeat helped secure British and American liberty." *Reason* 38, no. 3 (2006). http://reason.com/archives/2006/07/01/in-praise-of-john-wilkes/1.

McCarthy, Thomas. *Ideals and Illusions: On Reconstruction and Deconstruction in Contemporary Critical Theory*. Cambridge, MA: MIT Press, 1991.

McCormack, Derek P. "Politics and Moving Bodies." In *Political Theory* 35, no. 6 (2007): 816–24.

McKenzie, Jon. *Perform or Else: From Discipline to Performance*. New York: Routledge, 2011.

McNay, Lois. *Foucault and Feminism: Power, Gender, and the Self*. Cambridge: Polity, 1992.

Menger, Pierre-Michel. *Les intermittents du spectacle: sociologie d'une exception*. Paris: EHESS, 2005.

———. *Portrait d'artiste en travailleur: métamorphoses du capitalisme*. Paris: La République des Idées / Seuil, 2003.

Merleau-Ponty, Maurice. "'The Intertwining – The Chiasm." In *The Visible and the Invisible*, edited by Claude Lefort, translated by Alphonso Lingis, 130–55. Evanston, IL: Northwestern University Press, 1968.

Milošević, Slobodan. "1989 St. Vitus Day Speech." Translated by the National Technical Information Service of the Department of Commerce of the U.S. *slobodan-milosevic.org*. http://www.slobodan-Milošević.org/spch-kosovo1989.htm.

Morgan, Anna. *An Hour with Delsarte: A Study of Expression*. Boston: Lee and Shepard, 1889.

Mouffe, Chantal. "Artistic Activism and Agonistic Spaces." *Art & Research* 1, no. 2 (2007). http://www.artandresearch.org.uk/v1n2/mouffe.html.

———. *Deliberative Democracy or Agonistic Pluralism*. Vienna: Institute for Advanced Studies, 2000.

———. *On the Political*. London: Routledge, 2005.

Nancy, Jean-Luc. *Being Singular Plural*. Palo Alto, CA: Stanford University Press, 2000.

———. *The Inoperative Community*. Minneapolis: University of Minnesota Press, 1991.

Nussbaum, Martha. "The Professor of Parody." *The New Republic Online* (February 1999). http://www.akad.se/Nussbaum.pdf.

Obrist, Hans Ulrich. "In Conversation with Julian Assange." Parts 1 and 2. *e-flux*, no. 25 (2011). http://www.e-flux.com/journal/in-conversation-with-julian-assange-part-i/; no. 26 (2011), http://www.e-flux.com/journal/in-conversation-with-julian-assange-part-ii/.

Paras, Eric. *Foucault 2.0: Beyond Power and Knowledge*. New York: Other Press, 2006.

Parker, Philip M. *Choreography: Webster's Timeline History 1710–2007*. San Diego, CA: ICON Group International, 2009.

Parkinson, Chrysa. "On Practice." In *6M1L*, edited by Mette Ingvartsen, 24–33. samizdat, 2008.

Patton, Paul. "Foucault's Subject of Power." In *The Later Foucault: Politics and Philosophy*, edited by Jeremy Moss, 64–77. London: Sage, 1998.

Paxton, Steve. "In The Midst Of Standing Still Something Else Is Occurring And The Name For That Is The Small Dance." In *Arts Archives: Theatre Papers, The First Series 1977–78*, edited by Peter Hulton. Exeter: 2004. http://spa.exeter.ac.uk/drama/research/exeterdigitalarchives/theatre_papers/paxton.pdf.

Pickel, Andreas. "The Habitus Process: A Biopsychosocial Conception." Petersborough, ON: Centre for the Critical Study of Global Power and Politics, Trent University, 2005. http://www.trentu.ca/globalpolitics/documents/Pickel051.pdf.

Plato. *Apology*. http://socrates.clarke.edu/aplg0200.htm.

Power, Nina. "The Only Good Public is a Moving Public." *TkH* 20 (2012): 10–15.

Rabinbach, Anson. *The Human Motor: Energy, Fatigue, and the Origins of Modernity*. Berkeley, CA: University of California Press, 1992.

Rancière, Jacques. *The Politics of Aesthetics*. Translated by Gabriel Rockhill. London: Verso, 2004.

Raunig, Gerald. "Inventing Con-dividuality: An Escape Route from the Pitfalls of Community and Collectivity." In "Politicality of Performance." Special issue, *TkH*, no. 19 (2011): 142–48. http://www.tkh-generator.net/en/casopis/tkh-19.

———, Gene Ray, and Ulf Wuggenig, eds. *Critique of Creativity: Precarity, Subjectivity and Resistance in the 'Creative Industries.'* London: MayFly Books, 2011.

Rawls, John. *Political Liberalism*. New York: Columbia University Press, 2005.

Saxonhouse, Arlene W. *Free Speech and Democracy in Ancient Athens*. Cambridge: Cambridge University Press, 2008.

Schechner, Richard. *Performance Studies: An Introduction*. London: Routledge, 2006.

———. *Performance Theory*. London: Routledge, 2003.

Schmitt, Carl. *The Concept of the Political*. Chicago: University of Chicago Press, 1996.

———. *Political Theology: Four Chapters on the Concept of Sovereignty*. Chicago: University of Chicago Press, 2005.

Schnapp, Jeffrey T. "Fascist Mass Spectacle." *Representations* 43, no. 1 (1993): 89–125.

Schneider, Rebecca. "Solo, Solo, Solo." In *After Criticism*, edited by Gavin Butt, 23–47. Oxford: Blackwell, 2004.

Sennet, Richard. *The Fall of Public Man*. New York: W. W. Norton, 1976.

Shapiro, Alan. "Social Choreography: Steve Valk and the Situationists." *choreograph.net*. Edited by Jeffrey Gormly. http://choreograph.net/articles/lead-article-social-choreography-steve-valk-and-the-situationists.

Shaviro, Steven. "Processes and Powers." *The Pinocchio Theory* (blog). *shaviro.com*. August 18, 2011. http://www.shaviro.com/Blog/?p=995.

Sicart, Miguel. "Against Procedurality." *Game Studies* 11, no. 3 (2011). http://gamestudies.org/1103/articles/sicart_ap.

Spencer, Herbert. "Professional Institutions: III. Dancer and Musician." *Contemporary Review* 68 (July 1895): 114–26.

Thoreau, Henry David. *Walden and Civil Disobedience*. Harmondsworth, UK: Penguin, 1983.

Toepfer, Karl. *Empire of Ecstasy: Nudity and Movement in German Body Culture, 1910–1935*. Berkeley, CA: University of California Press, 1997.

Turner, Victor. *The Anthropology of Performance*. New York: PAJ Publications, 1988.

———. *Drama, Fields, and Metaphors: Symbolic Action in Human Society.* Ithaca, NY: Cornell University Press, 1975.

———. *From Ritual to Theater: The Human Seriousness of Play.* New York: PAJ Publications, 1974.

———. *The Ritual Process: Structure and Anti-Structure.* New York: Aldine de Gruyter, 1969.

———. *Schism and Continuity in an African Society: A Study of Ndembu Village Life.* Manchester: Manchester University Press ND, 1972.

Villa, Dana R. "Theatricality and the Public Realm." In *Politics, Philosophy, Terror: Essays on the Thought of Hannah Arendt,* 128–55. Princeton, NJ: Princeton University Press, 1999.

Virno, Paolo. *A Grammar of the Multitude.* Los Angeles: Semiotext(e), 2004.

Welz, Karl Hans. *Autogenic Training: A Practical Guide in Six Easy Steps* (HSTCI, 1991). http://www.autoaura.com/autogenic.html.

Woolf, Virginia. *A Room of One's Own.* New York: Harcourt Brace, 1989.

Žižek, Slavoj. "Good Manners in the Age of WikiLeaks." *London Review of Books* 33, no. 2 (2011). http://www.lrb.co.uk/v33/n02/slavoj-zizek/good-manners-in-the-age-of-wikileaks.

———. *Living in the End Times.* London: Verso, 2010.

———, ed. *Mapping Ideology.* London: Verso, 1995.

———. *The Sublime Object of Ideology.* London: Verso, 1989.

———. "Why are the NSK and Laibach Not Fascists?" *M'ARS* no. 3–4 (1993): 3–4.

VIDEOGRAPHY

"Gazimestan, 600th anniversary of the Kosovo polje battle." From Internet Archive. MPEG video, 71:26. http://archive.org/details/Gazimestan600thAnniversaryOfTheKosovoPoljeBattle. See esp. Slobodan Milošević's "1989 St. Vitus Day Speech" (also in this video).

Authors:
Bojana Cvejić and Ana Vujanović

Publisher:
b_books
luebbener str. 14
10997 berlin
x@bbooks.de
verlag@bbooksz.de
www.bbooks.de

Co-publisher:
Les Laboratoires d'Aubervilliers
41, rue Lécuyer
93300 Aubervilliers
+33(0)1 53 56 15 90
info@leslaboratoires.org

Editor:
TkH (Walking Theory)
theoretical-artistic platform
Kraljevića Marka 4 (Magacin)
11 000 Belgrade, Serbia
tkh@tkh-generator.net
www.tkh-generator.net
On behalf of the editor: Ana Vujanović

Copyediting and proofreading:
William Wheeler

Graphic design and layout:
Katarina Popović

Film stills from the documentary film
Yugoslavia: How Ideology Moved Our Collective Body, by Marta Popivoda

Theoretical comic: *Dull Smart Mobs*, by Siniša Ilić and Ana Vujanović

b_books

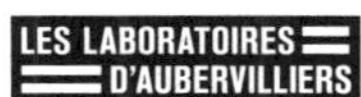

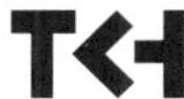

ISBN: 978-3-942214-10-0

Die Deutsche Bibliothek – CIP-Einheitsaufnahme
Ein Titeldatensatz für diese Publikation
ist bei der Deutschen Bibliothek erhältlich.

This book is realized within the project *How to Do Things by Theory* (2010-2012), hosted and produced by Les Laboratoires d'Aubervilliers. It specifically results from the two-year research *Performance and the Public* (2011-2012) by Ana Vujanović, Bojana Cvejić, and Marta Popivoda within the project.

Berlin, 2015.